ANIMAL RIGHTS

Selected Titles in ABC-CLIO's
**CONTEMPORARY
WORLD ISSUES**
Series

For a complete list of titles in this series, please visit
www.abc-clio.com.

Books in the Contemporary World Issues series address vital issues in today's society, such as genetic engineering, pollution, and biodiversity. Written by professional writers, scholars, and nonacademic experts, these books are authoritative, clearly written, up-to-date, and objective. They provide a good starting point for research by high school and college students, scholars, and general readers as well as by legislators, businesspeople, activists, and others.

Each book, carefully organized and easy to use, contains an overview of the subject, a detailed chronology, biographical sketches, facts and data and/or documents and other primary-source material, a directory of organizations and agencies, annotated lists of print and nonprint resources, and an index.

Readers of books in the Contemporary World Issues series will find the information they need to have a better understanding of the social, political, environmental, and economic issues facing the world today.

ANIMAL RIGHTS

A Reference Handbook

Second Edition

Clifford J. Sherry

**CONTEMPORARY
WORLD ISSUES**

A B C 🜨 C L I O

Santa Barbara, California
Denver, Colorado
Oxford, England

Library of Congress Cataloging-in-Publication Data

Sherry, Clifford J.
    Animal rights : a reference handbook / Clifford J. Sherry. — 2nd ed.
        p. cm. — (Contemporary world issues)
    Includes bibliographical references and index.
    ISBN 978-1-59884-191-6 (hardcover : alk. paper) —
    ISBN 978-1-59884-192-3 (ebook)
 1. Animal rights—United States—Handbooks, manuals, etc.
    2. Animal welfare—Law and legislation—United States—
    Handbooks, manuals, etc. I. Title.
    HV4764.S5   2009
    179'.3—dc22   2009031357

 13   12   11   10   9   1   2   3   4   5

This book is also available on the World Wide Web as an eBook.
Visit www.abc-clio.com for details.

ABC-CLIO, LLC
130 Cremona Drive, P.O. Box 1911
Santa Barbara, California 93116-1911

This book is printed on acid-free paper ∞
Manufactured in the United States of America

To my wife, Nancy C. Sherry, who is my partner and best friend and without whom life would not be worth living. This book would not have been possible without her.

Contents

List of Tables

Preface

The controversy surrounding the concept of animal rights is divisive and potentially volatile. It divides society into three unequally sized groups: the animal activists, some of whom believe that all human use of other animals should stop immediately; society in general, which may or may not be aware of the controversy and which may or may not have formed an opinion; and the people who work with animals. The first and last of these groups are discussed in chapter 1. Chapter 2 provides an overview of the problems and controversies involved in these issues, while chapter 3 discusses private and governmental solutions. Chapter 4 provides a timeline of key events and chapter 5 provides biographies of both historical and contemporary individuals involved in the controversy. Chapter 7 presents an annotated list of animal rights/welfare organizations, and chapter 8 contains an annotated list of key books and other media that discuss animal rights/welfare.

In case law, an animal is defined as a nonhuman being that is endowed with the power of voluntary movement (see *Bernardine v City of New York*, 44 N.Y.S.2d 881).

It is important to distinguish between animal welfare and animal rights.

Animals as Property

Many people have strong emotional attachments to companion animals such as dogs and cats. These people often think of and treat their pets as members of the family. However, both common law (court decisions) and state and local statutory law treat these animals, as well as agricultural animals, as property, with no more rights than a sofa or a television set. Owners of animals can sue and be sued in civil court and charged in criminal court because of the actions of the animals they own. Animals cannot be sued or sue in civil court or be tried in criminal court because they appear to lack the ability to know right from wrong and to be able to predict the results of their actions.

The status of animals as property is confirmed by the fact that billions of agricultural animals are commonly bought and sold in numerous transactions within a state, across state lines, and across international borders. Their owners also have the right to slaughter these animals at will. Pets are also bought and sold in thousands of transactions, in some cases, where the animal is purchased directly for a government agency, such as a shelter for abandoned or unwanted animals.

The status of animals as property was also confirmed in a landmark Supreme Court decision in *Diamond v Chakrabarty* (447 U.S. 303, 1980). Chakrabarty genetically engineered a bacterium that was able to break down crude oil. This bacterium could be used to help clean up oil spills. Chakrabarty attempted to patent the bacterium but was denied on the basis of a long-standing informal "rule" that "living things are not patentable." Chakrabarty appealed this decision to the U.S. Supreme Court, which ruled, in a 5–4 vote, in favor of Chakrabarty. Since then, a wide variety of living organisms, including mammals and primates, have been patented. Living organisms have been patented in the European Union and in Japan, but the Supreme Court of Canada decided that living organisms could not be patented.

Animal Welfare

There is less controversy about animal welfare. The first attempt to create laws dealing with animal welfare appears to have occurred in 1800 in Britain when Sir William Pulteney tried to ban the "sport" of bull baiting, in which dogs set upon a restrained bull. The vote in Parliament was close, 43 votes against versus 41 for. In 1822, Richard Martin proposed a bill that would make it an offense to "wantonly" mistreat certain domestic animals. The bill, which became law, was designed to protect the private property of a human, rather than to protect the animal for its own sake. Martin and some of his colleagues went on to form the Royal Society for the Prevention of Cruelty to Animals, which continues its work today.

Traditional animal welfare organizations have a long history in the United States. For example, the American Society for the Prevention of Cruelty to Animals was organized in 1866, and the American Humane Association was organized in 1877. These organizations seek to prevent cruelty to animals and to promote humane care of animals. They are described in more detail in chapter 7.

In the United States, state governments have enacted animal welfare laws to prohibit cruelty to animals. The precise wording varies from state to state. Generally, if a police or animal control officer believes that an animal is being mistreated, he can obtain a warrant to seize the animal and place the animal under the care of an appropriate shelter.

Local governments (e.g., counties, cities, towns) have also enacted anticruelty laws. The precise wording varies, but they generally mandate that animals be provided with access to an adequate supply of food and water, as well as appropriate veterinary care. These laws also require that animals not be beaten, cruelly treated, overloaded, or otherwise abused.

Most local ordinances also provide a humane sanctuary or shelter for abandoned or unwanted animals. Unfortunately, the number of unwanted pets (mostly cats and dogs, but also birds, amphibians, reptiles, and other exotic animals) taken into shelters generally exceeds the number that are adopted out, so the excess is "put to sleep" or "put down," which are euphemisms for euthanasia, or being killed. The precise number of animals killed is controversial, but estimates put it at 6 to 8 million cats and dogs per year. The euthanasia methods vary from place to place. Many of these shelters require pets that are adopted first be spayed or neutered. Local authorities also have licensing laws to help control diseases such as rabies.

Federal, state, and local statutes prohibit animal-fighting venues (e.g., dog fights, cock fights).

The Bounds of Human Responsibility toward Animals

Writers in the 18th century have apparently set the boundaries of discussion of animal rights that continues to today.

Immanuel Kant (1930, 205), writing in *Lectures on Ethics*, observed:

> [So] far as animals are concerned, we have no direct duties. Animals are not self-conscious and are there merely as the means to an end. That end is man. . . . Our duties towards animals are merely indirect duties towards humanity.

At the other extreme is Jeremy Bentham (1935), who is often credited with being the first to discuss animal rights. Bentham wrote, in *Introduction to the Principles of Morals and Legislation*:

> The question is not, Can they reason? Nor can they talk? But, Can they suffer?

Do animals have rights, beyond those dealing with their welfare? Who should decide? It is our responsibility, both individually and collectively, to determine the answers to these complex questions. The answers must be based on reason, not on emotion. The remaining chapters in this book attempt to provide a balanced overview of the issues involved in this controversy and to provide the tools and information that will allow you to form an informed opinion. Once you have formed an informed opinion, it is hoped that you will act on it!

References

Bentham, J. (1935). *An Introduction to the Principles of Morals and Legislation*. New York: Doubleday, Doran.

Kant, I. (1930). *Lectures on Ethics*. Cambridge: Cambridge University Press, 2001.

Acknowledgments

No book is the product of one mind. The subject of animal rights and animal welfare is complex, controversial, and volatile. I have attempted to keep my personal views and beliefs in the background and to provide a balanced view of this controversy.

First and foremost, I would like to thank my wife for her patience, encouragement, and help in editing this book.

I would also like to thank my colleagues, past and present, especially Drs. G. Carroll Brown and W. R. "Bill" Klemm, who have acted as a sounding board for many of the ideas expressed in this book and have often played the role of devil's advocate.

I would also like to thank my editors at ABC-CLIO, especially Holly Heinzer, Lauren Thomas, Kim Kennedy White, and Mildred "Mim" Vason for being patient, kind, and understanding. I would also like to thank Jennifer Boelter at Apex CoVantage.

1

Historical and Philosophical Backgrounds

What Are Humans, Anyway?

Are human beings fundamentally different from other organisms that inhabit Earth? The monotheistic religions (e.g., Judaism, Christianity) believe that humans possess a soul or a spirit but that animals do not. Some Eastern religions (e.g., Hinduism, Buddhism) believe in transmigration of souls and thus believe that some animals have souls.

Those who believe in Darwinian evolution argue that humans are animals and are fundamentally the same as other animals (Darwin 1859). Experts tell us that we humans share much of our DNA with other organisms. Dr. Evan Eichler, a genome specialist from the University of Washington, and his colleagues compared the human and the chimpanzee genomes and reported that humans share 96 percent of their DNA with chimps (Ze et al. 2005).

While it is true that a liver is a liver, a pancreas is a pancreas, and a lung a lung, it seems likely that the major difference between humans and other animals occurs in the brain, especially the cerebral cortex. The cortex is a convoluted layer of nerve cells, comprising nearly 90 percent of all the nerve cells in the brain, which forms the outer surface of the cerebral hemispheres. The major difference in the cortexes of humans and of other organisms occurs in the frontal cortex. This appears to be the site of self-awareness (i.e., individual humans recognize that they are unique individuals separate from other individuals and from their environment and that they have a past and a present). This part of the cerebral cortex also appears to be the site responsible for the ability to think logically, critically, and abstractly. Humans can plan for the future, using memories of the past and reason to make decisions, rather than follow blind impulses.

Generally, most adult humans have a capacity to exercise these functions. Humans at other developmental stages have a basic capacity to engage them that develops over time. But, unfortunately, some humans, because of accidents or developmental disabilities, are never able to fully engage these functions. When do we become persons? Do we become persons at conception, at implantation, at birth, or after adolescence? There is significant division of opinion about the answer to that question, a division that stands at the center of the controversy surrounding abortion and research related to human stem cells and cloning. The discussion of personhood and all that it implies is beyond the scope of this book.

If an animal possesses some or all of these abilities, should the animal be granted limited or full rights? If the animal does not, then should it be granted rights, or should humans be concerned with the animal's welfare rather than its potential rights? This book is an attempt to provide information to allow an interested individual to decide.

How Do We Use Animals?

When thinking about animals and rights, it is convenient to divide animals into seven very unevenly sized groups: (1) agricultural animals; (2) companion animals (pets, especially dogs, cats, and horses); (3) service animals; (4) animals used in the entertainment industry (movies, television, zoos, aquaria, circuses, and rodeos); (5) pests; and (6) hunting, discussed in chapter 2. The seventh group, animals used for basic and applied scientific research, education, and product testing, is discussed in chapter 3.

Agricultural Animals

According to U.S. Department of Agriculture statistics for 2005, the most recent year for which statistics are available, there are more than 33 million cattle, 104 million pigs, 2 million sheep, 9 million dairy cows, and almost 9 billion chickens in the United States (U.S. Department of Agriculture 2005).

Most agricultural animals are now held for some portion of their lives in one of the 250,000 animal feeding operations or one of the 17,000 concentrated animal feeding operations (CAFO). The CAFOs are commonly called factory farms. The majority of broiler and layer chickens, turkeys, and swine are now raised in CAFOs (Centers for Disease Control and Prevention 2009). There are relatively few laws governing the operation of CAFOs and the laws that exist tend to focus on the environmental impact of CAFOs dealing with waste and waste management caused by having a relatively large number of animals in a relatively small space (see chapter 2).

Companion Animals

According to the National Council on Pet Population Study and Control, there are about 61 million dogs and 76 million cats in the United States (NCPPSC 2009). There are no solid numbers on other types of pets. Unfortunately, some people become tired of their pets, whether dogs, cats, or more exotic animals like birds, snakes, and alligators. Some drop these animals at the side of a road and drive off. Some drop the animal at a humane sanctuary or shelter. Because the number of unwanted animals exceeds the holding capacity, more than 6 to 8 million cats and dogs are "put to sleep" or "put down" (a euphemism for being killed) each year (American Humane Society 2009).

Service Animals

Service animals are a diverse group, and it is difficult to collect accurate statistics about the number of these animals. They include seeing-eye dogs that help blind people get around, dogs that help people who are hard of hearing deal with their world, and dogs and primates that help other handicapped people, including paraplegics. They also include dogs that help detect dangerous contraband, such as explosives and drugs, and cadaver-detecting dogs that help locate living and dead humans after natural or man-made disasters. Dogs in the K-9 corps help the military and police guard perimeters, perform search and rescue operations, and detect dangerous people hiding in buildings, caves, and other sites.

Entertainment

Accurate statistics are difficult to obtain about the number of animals used in the entertainment industry. The Performing Animal Welfare Society, in Galt, California, seeks to protect performing animals in traveling shows, animal acts, and animals that appear on television and in the movies. They provide a shelter for abused, abandoned, and retired captive wildlife. This group is discussed in more detail in chapter 7.

In the past few decades, many zoos have abandoned small steel cages used for displaying one or two members of a species in favor of larger, more naturalistic displays that contain multiple members of a species and often members of several species. Zoos also maintain animals that might be endangered or extinct in their natural environments.

The number of cetaceans (whales, porpoises, dolphins) and pinnipeds (seals and related species) that are held in theme parks, such as Sea World, and in aquaria that are owned by cities is difficult to determine, as is the number of fish or invertebrates (e.g., octopus). Some aquaria, like some zoos, maintain species that are endangered or extinct in the natural environments.

Pests

It is estimated that there are one to two rats and two to three mice for every man, woman, and child in large cities. A rat can consume more than 27 pounds of food per year, and rats are omnivores, which mean they will eat anything. They contaminate 5 to 10 times more than they eat with their hair, droppings, and urine. Mice eat about 4 pounds per year and also contaminate 5 to 10 times that much. According to 2001 statistics from the U.S. Department of Agriculture (the latest data available), wildlife caused more than $600 million in damage to field crops, $178 million in damage to livestock and poultry, and $146 million in damage to vegetables, fruits, and nuts in that year. Even using the most advanced techniques available, humans are just barely holding their own when it comes to dealing with these pests (U.S. Department of Agriculture 2009). It is not clear what would happen if these efforts were stopped.

What Is a Right?

Do animals have rights? Do people have rights? What is a right? The Declaration of Independence says:

> We hold these truths to be self-evident, that all men are
> created equal, that they are endowed by their Creator

with certain unalienable Rights, that among these are Life, Liberty, and the pursuit of Happiness. That to secure these rights, Governments are instituted among Men, deriving their just Powers from the consent of the governed.

When Thomas Jefferson penned those stirring and powerful words, he was propounding a radical idea, to liberate humanity from the political oppression and servitude that had been the destiny of most people from time immemorial and that continues to be the fate of most members of our species to this very day. Jefferson and the other Founding Fathers were proposing that people had a right to be free, not because of a ruler's decree or a majority vote but simply because they were men. This concept is at the very foundation of our identity as a nation and gives our moral concerns political force; its philosophical foundations have been used to endorse a variety of political acts, including violence. In order to fully engage these rights, we must liberate ourselves from the ravages of disease and premature death, as well as from ignorance and poverty.

But, at the time that Jefferson penned these words, he apparently owned slaves, as did many of the other Founding Fathers. Many of his male fellow citizens considered women and children to be little more than chattel (property), with few, if any, rights.

To establish a government, the Founding Fathers, in 1787, penned these mighty words:

We the People of the United States, in Order to form a more perfect Union, establish Justice, insure domestic Tranquillity, provide for the common defense, promote the general Welfare, and secure the Blessings of Liberty to ourselves and our Posterity, do ordain and establish this Constitution for the United States of America.

The Constitution is a unique document in the history of humanity, and it has survived the test of time. But, as originally written, it contained flaws. In Article I, Section 2, Subsection 3, for example, it says:

Representatives and direct Taxes shall be apportioned among the several States which may be included within this Union, according to their respective Numbers, which shall be determined by adding to the whole Number of

free Persons, including those bound to service for a Term
of Years, and excluding Indians not taxed, three fifths of
all other persons.

That last phrase, of course, refers to slaves. Clearly, not everyone
living in the United States was considered a "full" human being.
As a charter of freedom, the Constitution left other great gaps in the
protection it afforded individuals from the government and popular majorities. This was corrected in 1791, when the ratification of
the Bill of Rights, the name given to the first 10 amendments to the
Constitution, was completed.

The powerful and potent words of the Bill of Rights, which
protect the rights of individuals, ring down through history.
These rights include, among others, freedom of religion, of
speech, and of assembly and the right to petition the government
(Amendment I); the right to keep and bear arms (Amendment II);
the right to be secure in one's person, house, papers, and effects
against unreasonable seizures (Amendment IV); the right not to
be deprived of life, liberty, or property without due process of
law (Amendment V); the right in criminal prosecutions to have
a speedy and public trial, to be informed of the nature and cause
of accusation, to be confronted with the witnesses against one,
to have compulsory process for obtaining witness in one's favor,
and to have the assistance of counsel for one's defense (Amendment VI); the guarantee that the enumeration in the Constitution
of certain rights shall not be construed to deny or disparage others
retained by the people (Amendment IX); and the provision that
the powers not delegated to the United States by the Constitution nor prohibited by it to the States are reserved to the States,
respectively, or to the people (Amendment X).

A right, in an abstract sense, refers to justice, ethical cor-
rectness, or consonance with the rules of law or the principles of
morals. Law, in the abstract, is considered the foundation for all
rights or the complex of underlying moral principles that impart
the character of justice to all positive law and give it an ethical
content. In a concrete sense, a right is a power, privilege, faculty,
or demand, inherent in one person and incident upon another.
The primal rights pertaining to humans are enjoyed by humans,
grounded in humans purely as such, in the human personality, and existing antecedently to their recognition by positive
law (i.e., a law that was enacted or adopted by a government)
(*Black's Law Dictionary* 1979).

When used as an adjective, the term "right" means morally correct, consonant with ethical principles or rules of positive law. Legal rights confer a theoretical advantage (i.e., the right) of one person over another based on basic and recognized legal rules, while the second person has a corresponding disadvantage. The basic building block of legal rights is liberty, which allows a person to do as he or she pleases without any duty to any other person. One person can limit the liberty of another by making a claim on that individual. That individual then has a "duty" to either act or not act toward the claimant. Claims can exist against specific individuals or groups of individuals, or they can exist against every person in the world (commonly called in rem claims). Immunity "disables" one person from interfering with the liberty of another; that is, it specifies what we cannot do to another. Power provides the ability to sue in a court of law for the violation of a claim or immunity.

Equality means that likes should be treated alike. Unequal treatment must be morally acceptable and rational. Classifications must be reasonable, and unalikes should be treated proportionally to their unlikeliness. If one possesses a quality, such as practical autonomy (discussed later), that justifies a legal right, one should possess that right.

Consciousness, especially self-consciousness, appears to reside in the cerebral cortex, the outer layer of the cerebral hemispheres, which contains the majority of nerve cell bodies. The frontal cerebral cortex, which is located above the eyes, is responsible for our most complex mental activities. Other parts of the cortex are responsible for such complex activities as language, creative thinking, planning, and decision making, as well as the ability to use knowledge acquired by learning and passed on by word of mouth or other sources.

Some, if not all, emotions are felt and expressed by a complex interaction among the frontal cortex, the hypothalamus (an integrating center that controls eating, drinking, and sexual behavior), and the limbic system (a system of brain structures that are involved with the sense of smell and the display of emotions). The frontal cortex is likely the site of working memory, which allows humans to form mental representations of the world and their place in it.

Natural laws exist, can be discovered by human reason, and describe the rights and liberties that human beings are supposed to possess. A right can be defended in a court. Natural rights grow out of and conform to humanity's nature (people's whole mental, moral, and physical constitution) and depend upon a person's mental, behavioral, tempermental, and emotional aspects that characterize a unique individual. Natural rights are distinguished from rights created by positive laws enacted by government to create an orderly civilized society. Natural rights grow from natural law, which are necessary and obligatory rules of human conduct.

Humans have rights. The fact that most humans throughout history and currently throughout the world cannot exercise these rights does not alter the fact that they have them. But how about animals—do they have rights? Are we humans violating these rights when we use animals for our own purposes?

Do Animals Have Rights?

Various individuals and public and private organizations vary in their opinion of whether animals have rights. If animals do have rights, do they have the same rights as human beings? Or is the level of their rights different? The discussion of animal rights is based on religious beliefs, philosophy (especially ethics), and legal issues.

Religious Viewpoint

Buddhists acknowledge the unity of all living beings and believe that humans are not privileged above other living creatures. They believe that the "self" (the atman) passes through many stages, including many potential lives as animals, before reaching the stage of full and perfect enlightenment. In the words of Buddha as recorded in the *Lankavatara Sutra* (2009):

> Whenever there is the evolution of living beings, let people cherish the kinship with them, and that all beings are to be loved as if they were an only child, let them refrain from eating meat.

Animals are also sacred to practitioners of the Hindu religion because they also believe in the transmigration of souls. Earth and the life that exists on it are virtually part of god's body. Cows are considered sacred because they are symbols of the provisions of god and providers of milk, cream, and butter. They are also considered symbols of Krishna, the eighth incarnation of the Hindu god Vishnu. It is illegal to kill cows in India, and they are allowed to wander the streets freely. In the words of Mahatma Gandhi in *The Moral Basis of Vegetarianism* (1959):

> It ill becomes us to invoke in our daily prayers the blessings of God, the compassionate, if we in turn will not practice elementary compassion towards our fellow creatures. . . The greatness of a nation and its moral progress can be judged by the way its animals are treated.

In the *Hadith*, the sayings of the prophet Mohammad, the prophet says:

> One who kills even a sparrow or anything smaller, without justifiable reason, will be answerable to Allah. When asked what would be a justifiable reason, he replied: to slaughter it for food-not to kill and discard it. (*A Manual of Hadith* 2009)

When a Muslim slaughters an animal for food, it must be done in the quickest and most painless way for the animal—by cutting its throat with a sharp object.

The Christian and Jewish view is summarized in the King James Version of the Bible in the first chapter in Genesis, verses 28–30, when God speaks to the first humans:

28 And God blessed them, and God said unto them, Be fruitful, and multiply, and replenish the earth, and subdue it: and have dominion over the fish of the sea, and over the fowl of the air, and over every living thing that moveth upon the earth.

29 And God said, Behold, I have given you every herb bearing seed, which is upon the face of all the earth, and every tree, in the which is the fruit of a tree yielding seed; to you it shall be for meat.

30 And to every beast of the earth, and to every fowl of the air, and to every thing that creepeth upon the earth, wherein there is life, I have given every green herb for meat: and it was so.

In these verses, God places humans in authority (control) over animals and mandates that humans have a vegetarian diet. However, a new Law comes into effect after the flood, when God speaks to Noah (Genesis, chapter 9, verses 1–4):

1   And God blessed Noah and his sons, and said unto them, Be fruitful, and multiply, and replenish the earth.
2   And the fear of you and the dread of you shall be upon every beast of the earth, and upon every fowl of the air, upon all that moveth upon the earth, and upon all the fishes of the sea; into your hand are they delivered.
3   Every moving thing that liveth shall be meat for you; even as the green herb have I given you all things.
4   But flesh with the life thereof, which is the blood thereof, shall ye not eat.

God does not change man's dominion over animals but allows humans to eat animal flesh.

Secular Viewpoint (Philosophical)

Aristotle (384–323 B.C.E.) may have been the first philosopher to construct a theory of moral responsibility. He believed that nature was organized as a ladder, with the gods at the top, humans next, and then other organisms. Aristotle believed that humans could use animals. The Stoics (third century B.C.E.) believed that nonhuman animals were not able to reason and therefore could be used by humans. On the other hand, the Pythagoreans (sixth–third century B.C.E.) believed in the transmigration of souls; they were opposed to any cruelty to animals and supported the idea of a vegetarian diet.

Ethical theory, a branch of philosophy, deals with what moral agents may do, must do, and must not do. Ethicists argue that moral agents must be self conscious (i.e., be aware of themselves as separate and unique entities), have a memory for the past, be rational (i.e., be able to reason), have moral principles (i.e., be able to understand right and wrong, good and bad), evaluate alternatives, and make judgments among the alternatives on the basis of self-interest. These judgments occur when the wants or desires of the moral agent come into conflict with those of another individual or group. Immanuel Kant (1724–1804) argued that since nonhuman animals cannot reason, they cannot be moral agents, but they can be the subject of moral considerations. In other words, a moral agent (e.g., a human being) should consider what impact his actions have on nonmoral agents (e.g., animals) (Kant 1996).

Jeremy Bentham (1748–1832) is often credited with being the first philosopher to discuss animal rights in *Introduction to the Principles of Morals and Legislation* (Bentham 1879). Bentham was one of the founders of Utilitarianism, a school of philosophy that holds that each action is judged by its utility or usefulness. One of the key differences between the laws of England and those of the United States is that the British seek a utilitarian goal, "the greatest good for the greatest number," while U.S. law tends to focus on the greatest good for the individual. Bentham and his followers used suffering as one of the criteria for determining the utility of an action. If an action causes suffering, it is objectionable. This prevention of suffering was extended to animals and serves as the basis for much thinking about animal rights. John Stuart Mill is a consequentialist; he argues that the consequences of an act outweigh other considerations and that the goal of a moral agent should be to spread happiness and relieve suffering, as well as to maximize freedom of choice. Happiness is caused by maximization of pleasure and minimization of pain.

Two influential books, *Animal Liberation: A New Ethics for Our Treatment of Animals,* by Peter Singer, and *The Case for Animal Rights,* by Tom Regan, apparently provide the philosophical basis for the modern animal rights movement.

Singer and Regan are philosophers and use the methods of analytical ethics. They argue that ethics are objective and are rooted in reason and the very logic of our language. Both base their positions on modern secular reasons and eschew arguments based on religious suppositions. A central tenet of analytical ethics is universalizability, which means that any ethical prescription is applicable to everyone in relatively similar circumstances. If a duty can be extended to more people or situations, then analytical ethics demands that it must be extended. Further, if different moral judgments are made in two different cases, analytical ethics demands that one must demonstrate a morally relevant difference between the cases.

Animal Liberation has been called the bible of the animal rights movement. Singer, like Bentham, is a utilitarian and, as such, argues that one should act to bring about the best balance of good and bad consequences for everyone affected by the act. Singer's basic moral postulate is that equal consideration of interests is not arbitrarily limited to members of our own species. Singer argues that avoidance of pain is a characteristic of all sentient creatures, that is, organisms that are responsive to or conscious of sense impressions. He maintains that humans have ruthlessly and cruelly exploited animals and inflicted needless suffering on them and that this must be stopped because all sentient beings should be considered as equals with respect to infliction of pain. According to Singer, a difference in species is no more a morally relevant distinction than other arbitrary characteristics, such as race or sex.

Liberation movements demand an end to prejudice and discrimination based on these arbitrary characteristics. Singer argues that liberation movements force an expansion of moral horizons and cause practices that were previously regarded as natural and inevitable to be seen as the result of unjustifiable prejudice. Further, he argues that, because animals cannot speak for themselves, it is our duty to speak for them. He reasons that the very use of the word "animal" to mean animals other than human beings sets humans apart from other animals and implies that we (humans) are not animals.

Regan, on the other hand, argues that animals have moral rights because of the concept of inherent value, that is, simple nonnatural, unanalyzable properties that are known to us through our moral intuition. He develops a cumulative argument for animal consciousness and the complexity of awareness in animals and maintains that an animal's individual welfare has importance to it, whatever its usefulness to others. Any such creature has inherent value and should be treated as a moral being with moral rights. Regan argues that the benefits of scientific research are real but that they are ill gotten because they violate the rights of the individual (animal), and this is true even if the research produces the best possible aggregate consequences. Thus, Regan uses the principles of justice and equality to develop a theory of moral rights for humans and animals, based on the idea of the inherent value of individuals that are subjects of life.

Despite their differences, as noted, Singer and Regan distinguish between animals and humans and maintain that animals are not equal to humans in all respects. Both Singer and Regan argue that a normal adult human has more value than an animal and maintain that if one must choose between the life of an animal and the life of a human, the death of a human would prima facie be a greater harm. Both argue that these situations arise only when the life of a human being is in direct conflict with the life of an animal.

Secular Viewpoint (Legal)

Hermogenianus, a Roman jurist (fourth century B.C.E.) who was one of the first, if not the first, to collect and organize Roman law, wrote, "Hominem causa omne jus constitum" (All law was established for men's sake), which has been the basis of legal theory since that time.

Steven M. Wise is an attorney specializing in animal rights law. He is the president of the Center for the Expansion of Fundamental Rights (see chapter 7) and the author of *Rattling the Cage: Toward Legal Rights for Animals and Drawing the Line: Science and the Case for Animal Rights* (see chapter 8). Wise would disagree with Hermogenianus and presents a legalistic argument for fundamental animal rights.

Wise proposes to assign humans and nonhuman animals an autonomy value. He assigns humans an autonomy value of 1.0. He also proposes that chimpanzees, bonobos (also known as pygmy chimpanzees), gorillas, orangutans, whales, and dolphins be granted an autonomy value of 0.90 or higher. Wise argues that an animal with an autonomy value of more than 0.90 should be granted the status of a "legal person" and recognized as a potential "bearer of legal rights" under civil law.

Wise argues that an autonomy value of more than 0.90 would guarantee a basic legal right to bodily integrity; that is, no one would legally be allowed to invade another's body. This means that animals with an autonomy score of more than 0.90 would have the right to physical security and should not be used for medical research or any other purpose that might potentially cause pain, harm, or death.

The second basic legal right is bodily freedom; that is, animals with an autonomy value of more than 0.90 should not be confined against their will. In other words, chimpanzees and other animals with similar autonomy values should not be confined in zoos, parks, or research establishments. It is not clear, in Wise's argument, just what should happen to these animals.

How about Dogs?

Outside zoos or aquaria, most people have not had much contact with the great apes or dolphins or whales. Almost everyone has had some experience with dogs, either by owning one as a pet or through interactions with a friend's pet. There are people who think of dogs as little automatons whose life is bounded by instinctual responses to the world. Wise disagrees and suggests that dogs should be granted an autonomy value of about 0.68. Currently, both case and statutory law treat dogs as personal property, whose ownership is recognized under law, in much the same manner as inanimate objects, like a sofa or bed (see *Heiligmann v Rose*, 16 S.W. 931, 1891). But this treatment is slowly evolving. Consider the comments of Judge Eric Andell (Court of Appeals of Texas, First District, Houston) in *Carl Bueckner v Anthony Hamel and Kathy Collins* (886 S.W.2d 368, 1994):

> The intrinsic value of a beloved dog is, or at least should not be strictly determined by the market value of the dog, which may be virtually nil. The intrinsic value of the dog is personal or sentimental. Many people treat dogs as members of the family, in some cases the only family members that they have. The loss of a beloved dog is not the same as the loss of a valuable inanimate object, such as an heirloom. This is because a dog is a living entity that seems to embody traits such as love, trust, courage, loyalty, and playfulness.

Are dogs special? Dogs, apparently descended from wolves, were probably the first animals to be domesticated. Dogs come in a bewildering variety of sizes, shapes, colors, and "personalities," and therefore a human seeking a dog is likely to find one that suits his needs. Many people who own dogs seem to believe that dogs are literally "little people" in fur. Individual dogs can be distinguished from other dogs by their responses to their environment and their unique responses to the wants and needs of their owner. Dogs also appear to experience emotions. On the basis of their demeanor and behavior, they can appear to be happy or sad. Wise would argue that we should grant some limited rights to dogs. However, most experts agree that dogs do not appear to have self-awareness or self-consciousness.

What about Service Animals?

Animal rights activates argue for stopping all use of animals and animal products. But they do not typically discuss service animals. Most service animals are dogs. They help blind and deaf humans deal with their world easily and more effectively. Working dogs help protect policemen and soldiers as they go about their daily activities. Dogs also help detect contraband (especially drugs and explosives) and cadavers. Perhaps most important, during time of crisis, such as after an earthquake, fire, or inclement weather (tornados, hurricanes), these dogs help locate humans in the rubble.

Given the increasing sophistication of computers and small robot-like devices, it is possible that seeing-eye dogs and the dogs that help deaf people will be replaced at some time in the future with nonliving devices that would be as effective as a dog. But it is unlikely that these functions of working dogs will be replaced by nonliving devices anytime soon. Removing the working dogs from their functions would expose police and soldiers to needless and unwarranted danger and make it significantly more difficult to perform their jobs. It is extremely unlikely that any nonliving device will be able to replace the ability of these dogs to find humans, living or dead, in rubble.

What of the Pests?

Secular philosophers, legalists, and other supporters of animal rights do not normally discuss pests. There are a number of widely advertised and popular products that claim that they kill 99.9 percent of "." And that really sounds good. But it leaves alive 0.001 percent of "X." If "X" happens to reproduce quickly, like a bacterium or an insect, then the organisms that are left will rapidly reproduce to refill the niche left by the demise of the 99.9 percent that were killed. But, and this is a big "but," these organisms will have limited or no susceptibility to the product. This is one of the reasons that we have multidrug-resistant tuberculosis and other types of bacteria and insects that are no longer susceptible to the chemicals that were used to control them. This is the dark message of Rachel Carson's *Silent Spring*.

Rats and mice do not reproduce quite as quickly as bacteria or insects, but they do reproduce quickly. Both rats and mice have lived with humans since people first settled into farming and storing products and then started living in towns and cities. Throughout history and up to this very day, human efforts to control these pests have been difficult and have just managed to keep them at bay, without preventing millions, perhaps billions of dollars in lost or damaged property. Trapping rodents is relatively ineffective, as are most poisons. The reason is that rats and mice are neophobic (i.e., they tend to avoid new stimuli in their environment). For example, when presented with a new source of food, they tend to take in a small amount. If that makes them ill, they avoid that food in the future. One of the more successful ways to deal with them is to use anticoagulants (drugs that prevent blood clotting). These drugs do not cause the animal to become sick. Instead, gradually, while the animal moves around in their environment, any small cuts it receives will continue to bleed and bruises will continue to increase in size, ultimately killing it. In 2009, Simone Rost, of the University of Wurzburg, reports that a series of small mutations in rats allows them to survive high doses of these anticoagulants. This means that as these rats reproduce, humans will need to develop a new drug or other procedure to eradicate them.

Key Concepts

It seems likely that a ferocious, man-eating tiger would not engender good feelings and discussion of animal rights, while a cute and cuddly baby tiger might. Many people consider giant pandas, especially baby pandas, to be cute. They are cute and seem familiar, perhaps because many young children have stuffed panda bears. The fact that they appear "cute" makes many people believe that they are harmless. While pandas are not carnivorous (meat eating), they are not harmless and will attack if provoked. Humans tend to empathize with some animals (the baby tiger) and are likely to grant them more rights than animals that are difficult to empathize with (man-eating tigers).

Anthropomorphism

Why would humans grant human-like rights to animals? One reason may be that we humans tend to anthropomorphize (from the Greek *anthropos*, meaning "human," and *morphe*, meaning "shape or form"), that is, to attribute human characteristics to animals and even inanimate objects.

It was vital for our primitive ancestors' survival to be able to instantly recognize an animal or human. This process was unconscious and automatic. Those who lacked this skill did not live to pass on their genes. The human brain has specialized sites that sense and recognize human faces. Jean Piaget, the Swiss developmental psychologist, found that anthropomorphism is common and pervasive in early childhood. It seems to be genetically programmed into our brains and especially our perceptual systems.

We do this in three ways: (1) in creating fables, stories, cartoons, movies, and television programs; (2) in ascribing human characteristics to actual animals, most commonly companion animals, especially dogs but also cats and sometimes horses; and (3) in attributing human or animal characteristics to inanimate objects.

One of the earliest, if not the earliest, fables to give animals human characteristics are those credited to Aesop, a storyteller who lived in Ancient Greece (ca. 620–560 B.C.E.). Many of these fables are still known throughout the world today. Many other authors, such as Lewis Carroll, Roald Dahl, Brian Jacques, C. S. Lewis, Beatrix Potter, and John Lockwood (Rudyard) Kipling, have provided animals with human characteristics. Many of these tales have been made into animated or live-action films, which continue to fascinate young and old alike. Perhaps the most famous anthropomorphic character is Mickey Mouse, a mouse that is familiar to virtually everyone in the world. Mickey began as a cartoon character that was initially relatively mouse-like, but he morphed into a character that walks on two feet, can use his other two feet as hands, wears clothing, speaks, and displays very human-like emotions. Mickey has morphed again and has left the screen and has become a life-size character that roams the streets of Disney theme parks.

The most common inanimate object to be granted human-like characteristics is the computer. The most famous is probably HAL, the "deadly" computer in the film *2001: A Space Odyssey*. While a computer as sophisticated as HAL probably does not exist yet, many people use personal pronouns like "he" or "she" when discussing their computers, as well as attributing to them ethnicity and politeness. Many people also refer to their automobiles using personal pronouns and discuss their actions as if they were living organisms.

These days, when computer chips are increasingly powerful and shrinking in size, there is an increase in the tendency to treat nonliving things as pets and to give them lifelike characteristics. Consider AIBO (Artificial Intelligence roBOt, homonymous with "companion" in Japanese). AIBO is an autonomous robot that resembles a small dog. It can "see" its environment via cameras, can respond to its owner's commands, and appears to learn and mature through stimuli produced by its owner and its environment. Reportedly, a group of AIBOs can play soccer. AIBO was introduced to the world by Sony in 1999; production was discontinued in 2006. AIBO sold for between $850 and $2,000; about 150,000 were sold worldwide.

Tamagotchi, a small handheld toy that is treated like a pet, was released by Bandai in 1996. It is extremely popular with children, and more than 10 million have been sold worldwide. The Tamagotchi is egg shaped and has a small screen and three buttons. Children seem to enjoy feeding the Tamagotchi a piece of food or a snack, playing games with it to help it lose weight, and cleaning up its waste, all accomplished by pressing the buttons. The toys caused a stir shortly after they were released because children were taking them to school so that they could feed them. Apparently, some Tamagotchis could "starve" in less than half a day. The toy was reprogrammed to prevent it from "starving" in less than a day so that children could feed it after school.

Perhaps the most interesting example is the Roomba, which was introduced by iRobot (Boston, Massachusetts) in 2000. Roomba is one of the first consumer robots that can do work in the home. A programmable robotic vacuum cleaner, it is a 13-inch disc that crawls around the home in search of dirt. When the Roomba encounters an obstacle, it backs up and turns in another direction. Its "behavior" seems curiously "animal-like." People have changed their cleaning patterns and the physical arrangements of their home to accommodate their Roombas. Some people have gone as far as naming their Roomba and treating it as a "pseudo" pet.

Speciesism

The term "speciesism" was apparently coined by Richard D. Ryder, a British psychologist, in the 1970s. Like other "isms," such as racism, sexism, and ageism, speciesism separates out a class of individuals that are subjected to some form of ill treatment and denied access to their rights on the basis of their membership in that class.

Humans and animals are obviously different in terms of brain development, behavior, and ability to respond to and modify their environment. Humans learn from other humans, both contemporary and those who have gone before, either through oral traditions or, more commonly today, through books and other media, such as the Internet. But are these differences morally relevant? It can be argued that animals lack the capacity for moral judgment. They cannot exercise or react to moral claims. Animals cannot sue or be sued in civil court or be held to account for their actions in criminal court.

Evolutionists, Darwinian and others, would argue that humans are merely ordinary organisms that are a part of a larger group that includes other living organisms, especially those described as animals. The members of the monotheist religions, Judaism, Christianity, and Islam, believe that humans are separate from animals because humans are made in the image of God and have souls.

Is the lion a speciesist because it hunts, kills, and then eats the antelope? Is the dog a speciesist because it apparently cares little for the squirrel, other than perhaps to chase it?

It has been suggested that speciesism is either bare or indirect. A bare speciesist might claim that we can eat animals because the animals were bred and raised to be eaten. An indirect speciesist might claim that humans have certain characteristics that distinguish them from animals (e.g., the ability to use language, to reason, to plan). Some claim that humans engage in speceisism because of species loyalty, which allows us to favor humans over other organisms.

Sentience

Sentience can be a complex and slippery concept, especially when coupled with the idea that it involves the ability to experience suffering. Most dictionaries define "sentience" as "the readiness to receive sensations." Other dictionaries add that it is "a state of elementary or undifferentiated consciousness." This seems to be a result of the blurring of two concepts: sentience (from the Latin root *sentire*, to feel) and sapience (from the Latin root *sapere*, to know). This goes directly to the distinction between sensation and perception.

Changes in physical events outside the body are brought to the brain via the sense organs. The process begins with a physical stimulus or a change in a physical stimulus out in the world.

Specific physical change activates a set of specific nerve endings. For example, light triggers a response in the sensors in the eye. This causes these nerve endings to generate action potentials (i.e., an electrical impulse that is approximately one-millionth of a second or one millisecond in duration). The action potentials travel down a nerve until they reach a synapse (a gap between a nerve and the next succeeding nerve cell body) located in the thalamus (a switching station made up of individual groups of nerve cell bodies gathered in the same location and that have the same function). If enough action potentials reach the synapse, it activates the nerve cell and causes it to generate an action potential that travels down nerves that synapse on nerve cells in the cerebral cortex. The cortex, which is best developed in humans, is commonly called the gray matter and contains the majority of nerve cell bodies in the nervous system. The cortex overlies the white matter (made up of nerve fibers) and nuclei (e.g., the thalamus).

Visual stimuli activate the sensors in the eye, which activates visual cells in the thalamus, and end in the visual cortex that is located in the back of the cerebral hemispheres. It is unlikely that any interpretation occurs at the level of the thalamus; that is, no perception takes place there. It is likely that a limited amount of interpretation takes place at this level of the visual cortex. The majority of interpretation, comparing these current sensory inputs to ones that happened in the past and determining how to respond to the current input, occurs in the frontal cortex, the likely site where perception occurs.

Pain and Suffering

There has been a good deal of research into the physiology of pain in both humans, who can tell researchers how they feel, and animals, which generally cannot. As described in detail later, it is likely that humans and animals, especially those that do not have a well-developed cerebral cortex, process the perception of pain and its consequences differently. These differences are central to the question of animal rights. That is, if an animal's perception of pain is similar to that of humans, then the animal's welfare should include methods to minimize pain. There is far less research on suffering, which centers on perception. The level of suffering people experience varies widely and does not seem to correlate with the level of pain experienced.

Pain

Background

All living organisms attempt to avoid certain classes of stimuli. It is not clear if this means that these stimuli are painful. For example, a paramecium is a single-cell organism. As it swims around in its environment, if it encounters a concentrated salt solution, it will back away and move in another direction. Clearly, paramecia find a concentrated salt solution to be noxious and respond to it. Does the paramecium experience pain? Probably not, since it lacks a nervous system. Other primitive organisms, like hydra, which is a simple multicell organism that possesses different tissues, respond in much the same manner as a paramecium when it encounters a noxious stimulus. They contract and move away. Do they feel pain? Probably not; they are making a relatively simple response to a relatively simple stimulus. Flat worms and round worms respond in much the same manner. It is unlikely that mollusks (e.g., snails, clams, squids) and crustaceans (e.g., lobsters, shrimps, crabs, wood lice, water fleas, and barnacles) experience pain.

Changes in the environment of an organism are sensed (detected) by specialized nerve cells. For example, rods and cones in the eye sense changes in the amount and quality of light. A nociceptor (Latin, *nocere*, to injure) is relatively unspecialized and consists of free nerve endings. Most of these free nerve endings are located in the skin, where they sense noxious stimuli.

The difference between activating a nociceptor and experiencing pain is complex and poorly understood. It is not clear where in the nervous system nociception activation becomes perceived as pain. Reflex action takes place in the spinal cord, but it is unlikely that this activity is perceived as pain. It is also unlikely that this occurs in the thalamus (a switching center) or in the somatosensory cortex, where other sensory inputs to the skin, such as hot, cold, and touch, seem to be "sensed." The activity of nociceptors is likely perceived as pain when the signal reaches the frontal cortex. It is unlikely that animals that do not possess a well-developed frontal cortex experience pain in the same manner as humans. It is not clear if nonhuman primates, which have a frontal cortex, experience the result of noceptive activation as pain in the same manner as humans, how the "pain" is perceived, and if it has the same "meaning" for these animals as it does for humans.

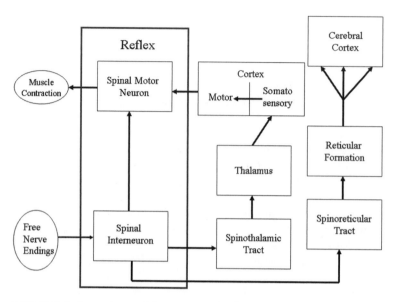

FIGURE 1.1 A schematic drawing of the connections within the spinal cord and brain involved with pain and responses to it.

How would you define pain? Virtually everyone has experienced it at one time or another, sometimes rather intensely. The responses to noxious stimuli are summarized in Figure 1.1.

Briefly, the activation of the nociceptors leads to (1) stereotyped reactions, which are called reflexes; (2) conscious perception of the pain stimulus; and (3) a response to the conscious perception of the painful stimulus. Oversimplifying, when a hand is placed on a hotplate, a reflex is triggered by increased activity in nociceptors in the hand. These fibers synapse (connect to) interneurons located in the spinal cord, which increase their activity, in turn causing an increase in motor neuron activity in the same segment of the spinal cord. This causes the muscles in the hand and arm to contract and the hand to be withdrawn. This is a rather crude movement and typically occurs before the subject is aware of any pain and can take any conscious action. The interneurons synapse with long fibers that cross the spinal cord and ascend to higher centers located in the cerebral hemispheres. These long fibers are a part of the spinothalamic tract, which carries the information to the thalamus and from there to the somatosensory cerebral cortex, ultimately ending in the frontal cortex. Once the pain is perceived, it triggers a conscious response, which involves inputs from the motor cortex (responsible for precise movement of the muscles), the cerebellum, and the basal ganglia (which are involved in movements that are more automatic, such as walking). These neurons synapse with motor neurons in the spinal cord and tend to smooth the withdrawal response and possibly elicit an expletive, like "ouch!" or something more colorful. This does not mean that the subject must think "I need to move my arm." This response is probably more automatic, much like walking.

Like humans, animals respond to noxious stimuli with reflex movements, but it is not clear if they experience the activation of nociceptors as pain. It is likely that their responses are more reflex-like. This is especially true of animals that lack a well-developed cerebral cortex, especially a well-developed frontal cortex.

It is likely that the first reflex response is essentially independent of motivational level, but that the conscious response can probably be moderated by differences in motivational level.

Nociception and pain are not normally covered in any detail in sensation and perception classes in the psychology curriculum or in anatomy/physiology or physiology classes in the biology curriculum. These topics are normally covered in clinical curricula (medicine, dentistry, veterinary medicine), but generally the focus is on pain management, rather than the study of nociception and pain. There are hundreds of books, designed for both lay and professional readers, that deal with pain and pain management. Selected books are highlighted in chapter 8.

Studying Pain

Max Von Frey, in the late 1890s, identified specific sites on the skin that, when stimulated, caused pain. These spots were more numerous than those responding to hot, cold, and pressure. Each of these spots was associated with specific receptors—in the case of pain, free nerve endings, which are called nociceptors. The activation of the nociceptors is a protective mechanism for the body. It occurs whenever something biologically harmful is happening, as when tissue is being damaged. But it is not clear what the fundamental nature of the painful (algesic) stimulus is. However, the evidence suggests that the algesic stimulus is one of several small molecules that are released when tissue is damaged. Examples are bradykinin, prostaglandin, histamine, and serotonin.

Human skin varies in thickness from 0.5 to 2.5 millimeters, while the epidermis is never more than one millimeter thick. The free nerve endings appear to lie 150 to 200 microns (about the thickness of a sheet of paper) below the surface, probably at the point where the epidermis and dermis meet. The skin (epidermis and dermis) typically lies on top of (subcutaneous) fat that varies in thickness from a few millimeters to several centimeters. This, in turn, typically lies over muscle and perhaps a bone.

These nociceptive fibers are bipolar, that is, the free endings are located in the skin and the cell bodies are in the dorsal root ganglion of the spinal cord. The other end of the fiber enters the dorsal root and synapses (connects to) secondary fibers.

There are two types of bipolar neurons that respond to stimuli that are noxious. Type A-delta, when activated, causes a relatively sharp pain, like a toothache, as well as a prickling pain that occurs when the skin is struck with a needle or when a widespread area of the skin is strongly but diffusely irritated.

The other type of free nerve endings, Type C, causes a more diffuse, aching sort of pain that is typically not felt on the surface of the body; it is felt deep inside the body, in and around the viscera (the "guts"). Ischemia (decrease or lack of blood flow to an organ) can cause pain in organs, as can a muscle spasm. These fibers may also be responsible for the burning pain that occurs when the skin is burned.

The spinothalamic tracts carry prickling pain sensation to the thalamus and from there to the cerebral cortex. The spinoreticular fibers, which carry aching or burning sensations, form connections with the reticular activating system, which transmits the sensation to virtually all parts of the brain, especially to the thalamus (a switching center located near the center of the brain), the hypothalamus (a center for emotions), and the cerebral cortex. These sensations are able to arouse someone who is asleep, to create a state of excitement and a sense of urgency, and to cause defense reactions. There is a third tract, the spinomesencephalic, that synapses with neurons in the brain stem that send nerves back down the spinal cord that regulate pain transmission. (discussed later). The brain itself is insensitive; that is, it does not contain any free nerve endings.

In contrast to the other senses, nociceptive sensations do not normally diminish unless the stimulus is removed. That is, they do not adapt. A classical example of adaptation occurs when one enters a room that contains fresh flowers; one ceases to smell the scent of the flowers after a few minutes, even though the scent is actually still present. The physical stimulus (the scent of the flowers) is still present, but the sensation gradually decreases and then disappears.

Hardy and his colleagues used radiant heat (i.e., infrared) stimuli for eliciting pain responses (see chapter 8). They discovered that pain thresholds are fairly similar for all humans and likely for animals, as well. For example, most people feel pain when a small area of their skin is heated to 45°C, and virtually everyone perceives pain before the temperature reaches 47°C. Psychophysics is a technique that allows scientists to develop a mathematical relationship between the intensity of a physical stimulus (radiant heat) and a subjective psychological response (verbal report of the intensity of pain). Using this technique, Hardy was able to determine the intensity of a radiant heat stimulus (which can be precisely measured) that will cause a detectable difference in the degree of pain. This is called a just noticeable difference (JND). Most humans can detect approximately 22 JNDs between the level where no pain can be perceived and the most intense pain a person can distinguish. So, contrary to popular belief, the sensory experience of pain is probably similar for most people, but their perception of the pain may vary widely.

Using a technique called microneurography, a scientist can place an electrode in a nerve, such as the peroneal nerve. This nerve lies near the surface of the thigh and its position with respect to bony and other landmarks is fairly well known, as is the innervation territory of this nerve and its branches. This nerve contains both afferent (toward the body, i.e., sensory) and efferent (away from the body, i.e., motor) fibers. By stimulating the skin with thermal or other painful stimuli and moving the electrode, it is possible to identify nerve fibers that carry pain information. By noting the transmission speed, it is possible to determine if the fibers are type C or A-delta. This allows scientists to determine the rate and pattern of action potentials that are generated by a specific noxious stimulus and also to determine how this correlates with the intensity of the physical stimulus and the reported level of pain. This allows scientists to compare the effects of a painful physical stimulus on the rate and pattern of action potentials in animals and in humans and thereby determine the approximate level of pain the animal might be experiencing.

In the 1990s, a remarkable new technique, Blood Oxygen Level Dependent functional Magnetic Resonant Imaging, commonly called BOLD fMRI, was developed. This technique is noninvasive and allows images of the brain with a temporal resolution of about 100 milliseconds and a special resolution of one to two millimeters. This means that parts of the brain that are involved with specific events, such as pain, can potentially be identified and studied.

The BOLD system works because deoxygenated hemoglobin is magnetic, whereas oxygenated hemoglobin is not. Therefore, areas of the brain with more oxygenated blood generate more intense images. A basic assumption of this technique is that when an area of the brain is active, it contains more oxygenated blood than when it is not active. It is important to note that there is a three- to six-second time lag between when a brain area is activated and when the blood-flow increases to it can be detected.

The BOLD system allows scientists to identify areas of the brain that are involved with pain and to compare and contrast these areas for different humans. For example, using the BOLD system, Coghill et al. (2003) found that humans with high and low sensitivity to a painful thermal stimulus showed differences in their response in the anterior cingular cortex (a primitive part of the cortex involved with affective [emotional] sensations and with the orienting response [directing attention to the painful stimulus with emotions]). There were differences in the primary somatosensory cortex and in the prefrontal cortex. These differences were not seen in the thalamus. This suggests that these differences are due to subjective psychic responses, rather than to direct responses to the physical stimulus. Kurata et al. (2002) reported that the secondary somatosensory cortex is also activated, as is the anterior cingular cortex, the prefrontal cortex, the motor cortex, and the lenticular nucleus (located near the center of the cerebral hemispheres and involved with the control of the muscles). Activation of these centers is involved with evaluation of and judgment about the stimulus and planning for movement that will minimize injury.

It is possible to use psychophysics and microneurography to determine the relationship between the intensity of a physical stimulus (e.g., infrared) and the rate and pattern of firing of nociceptors in humans and then to compare the results to the findings of experiments in animals that use the same levels of physical stimuli. One can thereby determine if the rate and pattern of firing is similar in animals. If they are similar, then the BOLD system could be used to determine if the same brain structures are involved in animals and in humans. These experiments would further our understanding of the way animals perceive noxious stimuli.

Theories of Pain

There are three different theories of pain perception. Supporters of the *specificity* theory, which originated with the 17th-century philosopher Rene Descartes, argue that when specific pain receptors are stimulated the free nerve endings transmit information directly into a pain center in the brain. When these receptors are stimulated, we feel pain and only pain. This theory fails to account for the many psychological variables that influence the amount of pain different individuals experience. Perception of pain depends on the level of anxiety and attention. There are numerous examples of soldiers who fail to notice severe wounds until the heat of battle has subsided. In one study conducted in the emergency room of a hospital, more than a third of the patients who had suffered substantial damage to their bodies did not report feeling pain. This theory also cannot account for phantom-limb pain. This occurs when someone perceives pain in a limb even though that limb has been amputated. The pain may be quite intense. But, how can someone experience pain when the pain receptors are no longer present?

Proponents of the *pattern* theory of pain perception, which originated in the second half of the 19th century, claim that particular patterns of stimulation must be produced and that this stimulation must reach a threshold before pain is experienced. They argue that there are no specific pain receptors. On the basis of our earlier discussion, we can conclude that this theory is probably incorrect.

The third theory was developed, in 1965, by Drs. Ronald Melzack and Patrick Wall (1989) and combines the specificity and pattern theory, with an attempt to include psychological factors. This theory is commonly called the *gate control* theory. Melzack argues that there are two sets of fibers, one large and the other small, involved in pain sensations that form connections with two centers in the spinal cord. One of these centers is called the substantia gelatinosa (located in the posterior part of the spinal cord and made up of nerve cell bodies and very short nerve fibers). The large fibers stimulate the cells in the substantia geletinosa, while the small fibers inhibit them. Both the large and small fibers and the output of the substantia gelatinosa project onto a second set of cells in the spinal cord, the transmission cells, which transmit pain sensations to higher centers in the brain. The substantia gelatinosa acts as a gate. When substantial large-fiber activity is present, the perception of pain is decreased. When substantial small-fiber activity is present, pain perception is increased. Signals from the higher centers, that is, the brain, also feed into the gate control system (that is, the transmission and substantia gelatinosa cells) and modulate the control of pain sensations. Therefore, it is clear that pain perception is more than the simple stimulation of free nerve endings!

But, the story of pain perception is still more complicated. It has been known for centuries that opium and its derivatives are analgesics; that is, they decrease or eliminate the effects of pain. More specifically, opiates, like morphine, do not block the physical sensation of pain but they do minimize the suffering that arises in our response to pain.

Scientists studying the mechanisms of action of opiates discovered that certain parts of the brain are especially sensitive to the effects of opiates. Brain cells in these areas have opiate receptors. These receptors work like a lock and key; that is, they respond to chemicals that have the chemical structure of an opiate and not to any other chemicals. But, opiates are derived from a plant; they do not occur in the body. Or do they? These questions sent scientists on a quest to find endogenous opiates, that is, substances that resemble the opiates and that are produced inside the body. Biochemists and neurobiologists discovered that there are at least two classes of molecules that have significant opium-like analgesic effects. They are the enkephalins and the endorphins.

A variety of exogenous drugs in addition to the opiates are available to help control pain. They include local anesthetics, like Novocain, that deaden nerves by apparently increasing their firing threshold. Another is aspirin, which blocks the production and release of endogenous chemicals, the prostaglandins. These chemicals are released when tissue is damaged and may be one of the chemicals that stimulate the free nerve endings.

Suffering

The precise relationship among nociception, pain, and suffering is complicated and controversial. There have been relatively few scientific studies on suffering. Most of the thinking about suffering is based on religious or legal viewpoints.

Religious Viewpoint

The Christian and Jewish view of the origin of suffering is summarized in the New King James version of the Bible in the third chapter in Genesis in verses 1–3, where God forbids Adam and Eve to eat from the tree of life:

1 Now the serpent was more crafty than any of the wild animals the LORD God had made. He said to the woman, "Did God really say, 'You must not eat from any tree in the garden'?"

2 The woman said to the serpent, "We may eat fruit from the trees in the garden,

3 but God did say, 'You must not eat fruit from the tree that is in the middle of the garden, and you must not touch it, or you will die.'"

When God appeared in the Garden, He discovered that Adam and Eve had eaten the fruit of the tree of life. In verses 15–19 of Genesis 3, God says that man's punishment for eating this fruit would be to suffer:

15 "And I will put enmity between you and the woman, and between your seed and her Seed; he shall bruise your head, and you shall bruise His heel."

16 To the woman He said: "I will greatly multiply your sorrow and your conception; in pain you shall bring forth children; your desire shall be for your husband, and he shall rule over you."

17 Then to Adam He said, "Because you have heeded the voice of your wife, and have eaten from the tree of which I commanded you, saying, 'You shall not eat of it': Cursed is the ground for your sake; in toil you shall eat of it all the days of your life.

18 Both thorns and thistles it shall bring forth for you, and you shall eat the herb of the field.

19 In the sweat of your face you shall eat bread till you return to the ground, for out of it you were taken; for dust you are, and to dust you shall return."

For Christians, perhaps the most important discussion of suffering occurs in the New Testament, especially the Gospels, which describe the birth, life, ministry, suffering, crucifixion, and resurrection of Jesus Christ. The reason for the suffering of Jesus is described in the New International Version of the Bible, Matthew, chapter 16, verses 15–16, 20–21, and chapter 26, verses 36–39:

Matthew Chapter 16

15 But what about you?" he asked. "Who do you say I am?"
16 Simon Peter answered, "You are the Christ, the Son of the living God."
20 Then he warned his disciples not to tell anyone that he was the Christ.
21 From that time on Jesus began to explain to his disciples that he must go to Jerusalem and suffer many things at the hands of the elders, chief priests and teachers of the law, and that he must be killed and on the third day be raised to life.

Matthew 26

36 Then Jesus went with his disciples to a place called Gethsemane, and he said to them, "Sit here while I go over there and pray."
37 He took Peter and the two sons of Zebedee along with him, and he began to be sorrowful and troubled.
38 Then he said to them, "My soul is overwhelmed with sorrow to the point of death. Stay here and keep watch with me."
39 Going a little farther, he fell with his face to the ground and prayed, "My Father, if it is possible, may this cup be taken from me. Yet not as I will, but as you will."

How the suffering of Jesus affects those who believe in Him is shown in 1 Peter, chapter 2, verses 20–24, and in Hebrews, chapter 2, verses 7–10:

1 Peter, Chapter 2

20 But how is it to your credit if you receive a beating for doing wrong and endure it? But if you suffer for doing good and you endure it, this is commendable before God.

21 To this you were called, because Christ suffered for you, leaving you an example, that you should follow in his steps.

22 "He committed no sin, and no deceit was found in his mouth."

23 When they hurled their insults at him, he did not retaliate; when he suffered, he made no threats. Instead, he entrusted himself to him who judges justly.

24 He himself bore our sins in his body on the tree, so that we might die to sins and live for righteousness; by his wounds you have been healed.

Hebrews, Chapter 2

7 You made him a little lower than the angels; you crowned him with glory and honor

8 "and put everything under his feet." In putting everything under him, God left nothing that is not subject to him. Yet at present we do not see everything subject to him.

9 But we see Jesus, who was made a little lower than the angels, now crowned with glory and honor because he suffered death, so that by the grace of God he might taste death for everyone.

10 In bringing many sons to glory, it was fitting that God, for whom and through whom everything exists, should make the author of their salvation perfect through suffering.

Moslems have similar beliefs. In the Koran, chapter 4, verses 116–120, the Prophet Mohammad says that followers of Satan will suffer:

116 And whoso opposes the Messenger after guidance has become manifest to him, and follows a way other than that of the believers, We shall let him pursue the way he is pursuing and shall cast him into Hell, and an evil destination it is.

117 Allah shall not forgive that anything be associated with Him as partner, but He will forgive what is short of that to whomsoever He pleases. And whoso associates anything with Allah has indeed strayed far away.

118 They invoke besides Him none but lifeless objects, and they invoke none but Satan the rebellious,

119 Whom Allah has cursed. He said, "I will assuredly take a fixed portion from Thy servants;

120 And assuredly I will lead them astray and assuredly I will arouse in them vain desires, and assuredly I will incite them and they will cut the ears of cattle; and assuredly I will incite them and they will alter Allah's creation." And whoever takes Satan for a friend instead of Allah, he certainly suffers a manifest loss.

Secular Viewpoint

The concept of "pain and suffering" in legal terms is divisive and controversial and has been and continues to be a source of debate in civil litigation involving torts (a wrongful act that does not involve a contract). This category includes personal injury, product liability, professional malpractice, and wrongful death. The courts have attempted to define suffering and to determine the amount of monetary damages associated with various degrees of suffering.

One compelling aspect of this debate occurs when curative measures are unavailable or ineffective, such as with patients with terminal cancer. These patients often have considerable pain and suffer because they are aware that, if untreated, the pain will continue and potentially increase. Recently, institutions (see *Estate of Henry James v Hillhaven Corporation*, North Carolina Superior Court, 1991) and individual physicians (see *Bergman v Chin*, California Superior Court, 2001) have been successfully sued in civil courts for failure to provide adequate pain medication.

According to the Merriam-Webster Dictionary, the word "suffer" comes from Latin (*sufferre* where *sub* means "up" and *ferre* means "to bear"). "To suffer" has a number of different definitions, including "to feel pain or great discomfort in body or mind"; "to undergo something unpleasant"; "to endure something"; "to have an illness or weakness"; or "to be adversely affected."

The philosophical, clinical, and psychological literature dealing with suffering is not as systematic or thorough as that dealing with pain. The psychological study of hedonics (pleasure) is relatively new. It is possible to think of suffering as one end of a hedonic continuum where one extreme is happiness (subjective well-being) and the other is pain and suffering (see Figure 1.2).

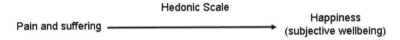

FIGURE 1.2 Most humans strive to avoid pain and achieve happiness.

Suffering is an unpleasant and disagreeable experience that virtually everyone attempts to avoid. Suffering is an individual phenomenon. What causes one person to suffer might not cause another to suffer at all. Suffering is not purely physical, although it is often associated with physical pain.

Suffering is synonymous with awareness. Without awareness there can be nociception but not suffering. Suffering does not appear to depend totally on the magnitude of the pain but rather is related to uncertainty about how long the pain will last.

A response to pain has at least three dimensions. The first is the sensory discriminative dimension, which provides the basic sensory information about the pain, such as its location in the body and its sensory quality, that is, whether it is piercing, burning, or aching. This system helps us to locate where we hurt and what the hurt feels like. The second dimension is the motivational affective system. This system is primarily responsible for the unpleasant feelings that are almost invariably associated with the experience of pain. The third dimension is the cognitive evaluative system, which is involved in determining the meaning of the sensory experience of pain. It processes sensory information, compares it to past experiences, and determines the probable outcome of the various methods that can be used to respond to the pain. This psychic reaction to pain varies rather dramatically among individuals and is determined in part by past experience with pain and, in humans, at least, on cultural background. Reactions to pain vary from essentially no reaction at all to anguish, anxiety, crying, depression, nausea, and excess muscular excitability. It is this last component that is most closely associated with suffering.

Animals that lack higher brain sites such as the cerebral cortex (i.e., invertebrates, fish, amphibians, and reptiles) probably experience pain at the level of sensory motor integration; that is, they sense something and respond to it. For animals with more complex brains, that is, those that have a primitive or well-developed cerebral cortex (birds and mammals), the experience of pain is more complex.

But, it is unlikely that we share the second and third dimensions with other animals other than possibly the great apes and possibly whales and dolphins, which are the only organisms whose brain/body ratio approaches (and in some cases exceeds) humans. These two dimensions require a well-developed cerebral cortex, significant cognitive ability, and self-consciousness. Animals other than the great apes and cetaceans do not possess these characteristics, and therefore it seems unlikely that they experience pain and suffering the same way as humans. This means that humans should be concerned with these animals' welfare and try and minimize their exposure to noxious stimuli and pain but also that these animals do not have rights.

It seems clear that strong advocates of animal rights believe that animals perceive and respond to noxious stimuli in the same manner as humans. If this is true, as it might be for the great apes and cetaceans, then they should possibly be granted some, potentially limited rights.

For the first time in history, on June 25, 2008, the Spanish Parliament's environmental committee approved a resolution that would grant chimpanzees, bonobos, gorillas, and orangutans the right to life and protection from exploitation, either for scientific research or entertainment. Backers of this resolution believe that it will be signed into law. The resolution also calls for the Spanish government to promote similar declarations throughout the European Community. If this resolution does become law in Spain and is adopted by other members of the European Community, it will have far-reaching effects and undoubtedly lead to considerable litigation. It is not clear what would happen to great apes that are held by research facilities, zoos, and elsewhere in Spain.

Dr. Martin Balluch, of the Verein Gegen Tierfbriken (Association against Animal Factories, in Vienna, Austria), brought suit on February 6, 2007, to have the legal status of a chimpanzee named Matthias Hiasl Pan determined in the district court in Modling, Lower Austria, and asked that he be appointed the legal guardian of the chimpanzee. The court held several hearings and decided not to consider holding a more formal proceeding. The decision was appealed to the Austrian Supreme Court for Civil and Criminal Matters on September 26, 2007, where the judges refused to decide the issue. The matter appears to currently be on appeal to the European Court of Human Rights in Strasbourg, France. If this effort is successful, it will potentially have far-reaching effects.

Summary

This chapter provides an overview of the concept of rights and how they apply to animals and humans and presents philosophical, religious, and scientific viewpoints. It also discusses differences in viewpoints about animal rights, why some observers think that animals have rights and others believe that animals have no more rights than an inanimate object, such as a sofa or television.

It seems that the controversy and divisiveness of this issue will not abate and that, despite recent moral and scientific insights, the controversy will continue for the foreseeable future. This seems especially true for discussions involving the great apes and likely for those concerning cetaceans, as well.

If we humans do come to some resolution of this complex issue, it is not clear if it will be based on science and logic, on an emotional response, on a system of religious beliefs, or on some combination of the three.

References

American Humane Society. 2009. *Animal Shelter Euthanasia.* http://www.americanhumane.org/about-us/newsroom/fact-sheets/animal-shelter-euthanasia.html. Accessed April 15, 2009.

Bentham, Jeremy. 1879. *Introduction to the Principles of Morals and Legislation.* http://books.google.com/books?id=EfQJAAAAIAAJ&dq=Jeremy+Bentham. Accessed April 15, 2009.

Black's Law Dictionary. 1979. St. Paul, MN: West Broughton.

Broughton, Janet, and J. P. Carriero, (eds.). 2007. *A Companion to Descartes.* New York: John Wiley.

Centers for Disease Control and Preventions. *CAFO.* http://www.cdc.gov/cafos/about.htm#bg. Accessed April 15, 2009.

Coghill, R. C., J. G. McHaffie, and Y. F. Yen. 2003. "Neural Correlates of Interindividual Differences in the Subjective Experience of Pain." *Proceedings of the National Academy of Science* 100 (14): 8538–42.

Darwin, Charles. 1859. *On the Origin of Species.* http://www.gutenberg.org/etext/1228. Accessed April 15, 2009.

Fitzgerald, P. A. "Hermogenianus." *Encyclopædia Britannica Online.* http://www.britannica.com/EBchecked/topic/1271629/Fitzgerald-P-A. Accessed April 15, 2009.

Gandhi, R. K. P. 1959. *The Moral Basis of Vegetarianism.* Ahmedabad, India: Navajivan.

Hardy, J. D., H. G. Wolff, and Helen Goodell. 1952. *Pain Sensations and Reactions.* Baltimore: Williams & Wilkins.

Kandel, E. R., J. H. Schwartz, and T. M. Jessell. 1991. *Principles of Neuroscience.* New York: Appleton & Lange.

Kant, Immanuel. 1996. *The Metaphysics of Morals,* ed. Mary Gregor. Cambridge: Cambridge University Press.

Krieger, Dorothy T. 1982. *Endorphins and Enkephalins.* Chicago: Year Book Medical Publishers.

Kurata, J., K. R. Thulborn, F. E. Gyulai, and L. L. Firestone. 2002. "Early Decay of Pain-Related Cerebral Activation in Functional Magnetic Resonance Imaging: Comparison with Visual and Motor Tasks." *Anesthesiology* 96 (1): 35–44.

Lankavatara Sutra. fourth century. http://www.darkzen.com/downloads/The%20Lankavatara%20Sutra.pdf. Accessed April 15, 2009.

Manual of Hadith. eighth century. http://www.aaiil.org/text/had/manhad/manhad.shtml. Accessed April 15, 2009.

Melzack, R., and P. Wall. 1989. *The Challenge of Pain.* New York: Penguin.

National Council on Pet Population Study & Control. (2009). Available at: http://www.petpopulation.org/. Accessed April 15, 2009.

Regan, Tom. 2004. *The Case for Animal Rights.* 2nd ed. Berkeley: University of California Press.

Ryder, Richard. 2000. *Animal Revolution: Changing Attitudes towards Speciesism.* New York: Berg.

Singer, Peter. 1983. *Animal Liberation: Towards an End to Man's Inhumanity to Animals.* Wellingborough, Northamptonshire: Thorsons.

U.S. Department of Agriculture. 2005. *Animal Inventory.* http://www.ers.usda.gov/news/BSECoverage.htm. Accessed April 15, 2009.

U.S. Department of Agriculture. *Wildlife Damage Management.* http://www.aphis.usda.gov/wildlife_damage/. Accessed April 15, 2009.

Ze, Cheng, Mario Ventura, Xinwei She, Philipp Khaitovich, Tina Graves, Kazutoyo Osoegawa, Deanna Church, Pieter DeJong, Richard K. Wilson, Svante Pääbo, Mariano Rocchi, & Evan E. Eichler. 2005. "A Genome-wide Comparison of Recent Chimpanzee and Human Segmental Duplications." *Nature* 205 (437): 88–93.

2

Problems and Controversies

> No man shall exercise any tyranny or cruelty toward any brute
> creature which are usually kept for man's use.
>
> —"The Body of Liberties," Massachusetts Bay Colony, 1641

Drs. Charles S. Nicoll and Sharon M. Russell analyzed 20 important books on animal rights as selected by Charles R. Magel. Dr. Magel is the author of *Keyguide to Information Sources in Animal Rights* (see chapter 8). These books contained 4,562 pages. Nicoll and Russell found that 2,598 of these pages were concerned with ethical and moral questions regarding the use of animals by humans; 1,680 pages were critical of the various ways in which humans exploit animals; 216 pages considered the history of the animal rights movement and its current status; and 68 pages focused on the plight of wild animals.

Of the 1,680 pages that covered the various ways humans use animals, 63.3 percent dealt with the use of animals in biomedical research and education; 30.6 percent with the use of animals for food; and 6 percent with all other uses of animals (2.3% for pets and pound animals; 2.3% for hunting; 0.8% for fur garments; and no figures are given for entertainment). Nicoll and Russell point out that more than 6 billion animals (includes only mammals and birds, not fish, amphibians, or reptiles) are used in some way in the United States each year, with about 96.5 percent being used for food and 0.3 percent for research and teaching. The concern/use ratio, that is the ratio of the number of pages in animal rights publications devoted to a form of animal use to the number of animals used for that purpose, is disproportionate. The concern/use ratio for animals used for food (30.6% pages/96.5% use) is 0.32, while the concern/use ratio for research and teaching (63.3%/0.3%) is 211.00. It is not clear why there is so much focus on the use of animals in research and teaching.

Agriculture

As indicated in the introduction, by far the largest group of animals that people deal with at some level or other is agricultural animals: cattle, dairy cows, swine, chickens, turkeys, ducks, goats, and sheep. Since the end of World War II, the number of farms and ranches in the United States has steadily decreased, and the size of the existing operations has steadily increased. For example, according to the Department of Agriculture, in 1950 there were approximately 3 million pig farms in the United States, housing about 19 pigs each. By 2005, the number of pig farms had dropped to about 67,000, but they housed about 60 million pigs. Similarly, in 1950 there were about 50,000 chicken farms (raising broilers), each averaging about 12,000 birds. In 2005, there were fewer than 20,000 farms, but they averaged more than 300,000 birds per farm. Similar trends are seen in cattle and dairy operations, as well as in turkey farming.

At one extreme, it is estimated that about 0.7 percent of the U.S. population are full-time farmers who earn their living by being actively involved with dealing with animals on a daily basis. About 2 percent of the population is involved in the slaughter and processing of agricultural animal products. These people have a vested interest in the use of animals in agriculture.

At the other extreme are people who reject some or all uses of animal products (e.g., meat, milk, eggs, hides, and, in some cases, even silk or honey). Many of these people identify themselves as vegetarians and vegans. A lacto-ovo vegetarian does not eat meat, fish, or birds but does eat dairy products and eggs. An ovo-vegetarian does not eat meat, fish, birds, or dairy products but does eat eggs. A lacto vegetarian does not eat meat, fish, birds, or eggs, but does eat other dairy products. Vegans do not eat any animal products, whether meat, fish, birds, eggs, dairy, or honey. They also do not use animal products such as leather, wool, or silk. The Vegetarian Resource Group (2009) reports that in 2006, approximately 2.3 percent of the population considered themselves vegetarians and 1.4 percent considered themselves vegans. For health reasons, many people limit their intake of meat and increase their intake of fruits and vegetables, but these people do not consider themselves vegetarians.

Between these two extremes, seemingly the majority of people want to have meat and other animal products easily available, providing a wide variety of choices, and want them to be inexpensive.

In order to take advantage of the economics of scale, as indicated earlier, the size of individual animal operations has significantly increased in size. The discovery of vitamin supplements that could increase the utility of the feed that is supplied the animals, as well as the use of antibiotics and vaccines to control disease, has allowed this rapid increase in size. Pesticides have allowed control of insects and other pests that are drawn to the waste products that are produced and concentrated. There are approximately 450,000 animal feeding operations (AFO) and 6,600 concentrated animal feeding operations (CAFO) in the U.S. No federal legislation or rules govern the conditions on small farms and ranches, AFOs, or CAFOs. A handful of mega-companies control a significant percent of the market. They include Tyson, ConAgra, and Cargill. For example, approximately 80 percent of cattle processing is controlled by IMP, Monfort (owned by ConAgra), Excel (owned by Cargill), and Farmland National.

Agricultural Animal Welfare Issues

Cattle are fed grass and hay. Most cattle are raised on ranches, which range in size from a few hundred acres in the Midwest to tens of thousands of acres in the West. Many cattle are grazed on public land owned by the federal government. Breeding is generally by "natural presentation," where a bull mates with a cow that is receptive. Cows that fail to conceive are generally culled and sent to the feedlot. Most cattle are brought to the feedlot from cow and calf operations scattered across the country and treated for internal and external parasites. Cattle feedlots were probably the first CAFOs. Most feedlots have thousands of animals on location at any one time, kept in pens that contain several hundred animals. They are fed concentrates (corn, soy beans, or other grain), with little or no roughage (hay). This means their manure is very "loose." As many as 1 percent of the animals confined in this way become "bullers," or steers that are ridden by other steers ("riders"). Unless the bullers are removed from the pen, they will be ridden to the point of injury or death.

Dairies have increased in size and complexity. Many of these operations have thousands of cows in a constant cycle of pregnancy and milk production. Virtually all of the dairy cows are bred by artificial insemination. Calves are removed shortly after birth. Cows are retained to replenish the herd, and bulls are typically castrated and sent to feed lots or are used for veal production.

Male calves are taken from their mothers within a few days of birth. Smaller calves are fed milk substitutes and small amounts of grain. They are slaughtered before they reach 150 pounds, often within days of birth. About one-third of the calves fall into this category and are called baby veal (or "bob veal"). The remaining calves are typically confined to a "veal crate," a box that is 22 inches wide and 54 inches long, not enough room for the calf to turn around or even lie down. This prevents the calf from moving around and causes the calves' muscles to atrophy. The calves are fed a milk substitute that lacks iron and other essential nutrients. The calves are slaughtered at about 14 weeks of age. The lack of exercise makes the veal "tender," and the lack of iron makes the veal pale pink or white. The United Kingdom and other members of the European Union banned the use of crates in 2007, and the American Veal Association began phasing out crates in 2007. The current trend is to house these calves in small groups.

Some cattle, generally those in smaller operations, are not sent to the feedlot but continue to be fed grass and hay. The meat tends to be leaner and have a different flavor from that of animals fed concentrates. Small dairy operations allow cows to graze on grass, and the milk from dairy cows tends to have a different flavor.

Most male chickens are killed at one day of age because they are not suitable for meat production (their meat has a "gamey" flavor that most consumers do not like) and because they are more aggressive than hens, which increases housing problems. Broilers, which are raised for meat, are generally housed in buildings with concrete floors covered with sawdust or chopped straw. Each building contains thousands to tens of thousands of chickens. Because of the large number of chickens, normal social groups typically do not form (i.e., no pecking order is created). Therefore, the lighting in these buildings is kept low to discourage the hens from pecking each other. Some operators "de-beak" (remove part of the upper beak) to also discourage pecking and cannibalism. When the chickens reach about five pounds, generally at about six weeks of age, they are sent for slaughter. The houses are cleaned after the chickens are removed. Toward the middle of this cycle, the level of ammonia can be very unpleasant, and by the end of the cycle it is really unpleasant.

Laying hens (egg producers) are typically raised in battery cages, approximately 18 by 20 inches (about the size of a file drawer), which can contain as many as 11 chickens. Food is brought to the chickens via conveyers, and manure drops out of the bottom of the cage. These chickens are almost always de-beaked. These cages are housed in sheds that contain thousands of cages. The lighting in these sheds is constantly varied to maximize egg production. These chickens typically produce about 300 eggs per year. When their egg production falls off, they are sent to slaughter.

Because of animal rights activists' complaints about high-intensity growing practices, some producers are raising "free range" broilers and layers. This means that the animals are not confined in large number in buildings or in cages. According to rules in both the European Union and the United States, these chickens must have access to the outdoors and typically are allowed to graze on natural vegetation, supplemented with grain.

In contrast to chickens, both male and female turkeys are used for food. They are hatched in incubators, and at about three weeks of age they are transferred to growing sheds similar to those used in chicken rearing. The turkeys are typically de-beaked, and the wattle (a fleshy lobe hanging down from the chin or neck) is removed from male turkeys. Turkeys reach market weight at about six months of age, when they are sent to slaughter.

Ducks and geese are also hatched in incubators and raised in sheds similar to chickens. About 28 million ducks were slaughtered in 2006 when they were about seven weeks old. Geese are typically slaughtered when they reach 8 to 14 pounds. When ducks or geese are slaughtered, the small fine pin feathers (down) are removed. The down is used in manufacturing coats and quilts. Some geese and ducks are raised for pâté de foie gras (literally pie of fatty liver) production. France is the biggest producer, with 18,450 tons in 2005, while Hungary and Bulgaria produced 1,920 and 1,500 tons, respectively and the United States produced about 400 tons, mostly in New York and California. These ducks and geese are force-fed grain several times per day, far more than they would normally eat. The force-feeding continues twice a day for two weeks for ducks and three or four times per day for up to 28 days for geese. This causes the liver to be 5 to 10 times larger than the liver of a normal bird. In 2004, Governor Arnold Schwarzenegger of California banned the force-feeding of ducks and geese and prohibited the sale of foie gras. Some cooks substitute chicken livers, liverwurst, or monkfish livers for duck and geese liver.

More than 90 percent of the pigs raised in the United States are raised in CAFOs. Virtually all of the pigs are bred by artificial insemination. The pregnant and nursing sow is generally kept in a metal crate that measures about two feet wide and that is too small for her to be able to turn around. Virtually all piglets are removed from the mothers when they are about one month old. Hundreds of individuals are raised in barns and are fed concentrate (grain) so that they will rapidly gain weight.

Smithfield Foods is the largest pork producer in the world. In response to concerns expressed by several supermarket chains and McDonalds, in 2007 Smithfield announced that it would phase out the use of these crates over the next decade.

Sheep and lambs are typically not raised in CAFOs. Most lambs that are slaughtered for food are raised in small flocks in the East or Midwest or on larger operations in the West. Sheep raised for wool are generally raised in large flocks that are grazed on public land in the West.

Enter the 21st Century

Even before humans stopped being mainly hunters and gatherers and settled down to become farmers, they began the domestication of animals (e.g., dogs). Humans selected traits in animals that were beneficial or useful and bred animals to type (i.e., certain traits were selected and animals that had these traits were bred to each other). This process might require many generations before a trait settled and animals bred true to type. These techniques have been used for hundreds of years and have stood the test of time. Gregor Mendel discovered that he could breed different strains of a pea and that he could predict the traits of the offspring. Farmers began experiments with corn in the 1930s. They found that they could cross two pure strains of corn to produce a hybrid that resulted in stronger plants with higher yields, which is called "hybrid vigor." In the past, a farmer would save some of his crop to use as seed for the next season. Seeds from hybrids do not yield hybrids, so each crop is grown from seed obtained from large seed companies. When there were thousands of family farms, each farmer might plant a different strain or hybrid. But, as the number of farms decreased and the average size of existing farms increased, there was an increasing tendency for many farmers to plant the same hybrid. This allows farmers to take advantage of economies of scale (thousands of acres of crop can be treated in the same manner, saving time and money). The major problem with planting thousands of acres of the same strain is that if a new disease or parasite should appear, it could cause a devastating loss.

Genetic engineering has allowed humans to shorten dramatically the process of selecting for desirable traits, often to a single generation. For example, plant geneticists isolate the gene for a specific trait in one plant of one species and insert that gene into another, unrelated plant of another species. These traits might include pest and disease resistance, as well as tolerance for herbicides, cold, and drought. Geneticists can also insert genes that increase the food value of a plant. For example, the Institute for Plant Sciences at the Swiss Federal Institute of Technology has developed a strain of "golden" rice that contains significant amounts of beta carotene or Vitamin A.

It is also possible to insert genes from nonplant organisms into plants. The best-known example is the insertion of genes from a bacterium, *Bacillus thuringiensis* (Bt), into corn. This provides the corn with its own "internal" pesticide. The Bt bacterium produces crystal proteins that are fatal to insect larva.

About 54 percent of the soybeans and 25 percent of all of the corn grown in 2000 were genetically modified. Soybean derivatives are very commonly added to food products, so it is likely that most Americans have been exposed to genetically modified food.

In the United States, three regulatory organizations promulgate rules dealing with genetically modified foods. The Environmental Protection Agency determines if genetically modified plants will cause environmental problems; the Department of Agriculture determines if it is safe to grow such plants; and the Food and Drug Administration (FDA) determines if they are safe to eat.

Current FDA rules (developed in 1992) require companies that wish to create new genetically modified foods to consult with the FDA. This consultation is voluntary, and the company does not have to follow the FDA's recommendations.

There are two ways that humans can be exposed to genetically modified plants: (1) directly, by eating the plants; and (2) by eating products (e.g., meat, milk, eggs) of animals that have been fed genetically modified plants. Current FDA rules and regulations do not require genetically modified foods to be labeled as such. It is not clear what effects eating genetically modified plant food may have on humans and other animals.

A variety of organizations, both academic institutions and private companies, have begun to experiment with inserting "foreign" genes into animals. For example, researchers at the University of Illinois inserted the cow genes that control milk production into pig genes to increase the milk production of sows. The FDA has not promulgated rules dealing with genetically altered food animals, but it seems likely that the FDA will treat "foreign" genes under the same rules it applies to new drugs for animals. It is not clear what labeling will be required when the genetically modified animals reach the marketplace.

The FDA has apparently approved the sale of cloned animals. There are at least two private companies that are actively cloning food animals: Trans Ova (Sioux Center, Iowa) and ViaGen (Austin, Texas). Cloned animals are essentially identical twins of the donor animal, which passes on its genes directly to the clone. Samples of the donor's cells, obtained by an ear punch or biopsy, are required. The cells are grown in culture and the nucleus (containing the DNA) is injected into an egg that has had its genetic material removed. These eggs are implanted in receptive females using standard embryo transfer techniques. After a normal gestation period, a clone is delivered. Clones, which cost more than $10,000, are used primarily for breeding purposes and have yet to reach the consumer marketplace.

There are even plans to eliminate the animal almost entirely. There is at least one organization, New Harvest, that is attempting to grow meat in vitro, literally, in glass. They plan to take a small sample of cells from an animal, place them in culture with a nutrient-rich medium, and allow the cells to reproduce and grow. Jon Vein, of Los Angeles, California, has received U.S. patent number 6,835,390, titled "Method for Producing Tissue Engineered Meat for Consumption." It is not clear if this method can produce enough meat products to be economically viable, how long it will take for the cultured meats to reach the marketplace, or how such products will be treated by government regulators. People for the Ethical Treatment of Animals has offered a $1 million prize to "the first person to come up with a method to produce commercially viable quantities of in vitro meat at competitive prices by 2012."

Since genetic engineering is a relatively new phenomenon, equally creditable scientists have been arguing on both sides of safety issue. Safety testing has generally been conducted on rats and other small organisms. Most of this work has been conducted by scientists involved with biotech companies, with relatively little work done by independent scientists. The Grocery Manufacturers of America has estimated that more than 70 percent of prepared products (e.g., breads, cereals, frozen pizza, hot dogs) may contain genetically engineered ingredients. The number of controlled human studies related to genetically modified food is very limited, and there are no long-term human studies, so, while it appears that genetically engineered food may be safe, there are no guarantees that problems will not arise in the future. Keep in mind the number of drugs that were tested under controlled conditions, including in extensive human trials, and then marketed but that then had to be recalled.

These new methods (genetic modification, cloning, in vitro meats) have been available for less than a generation, and it is not clear what risk or benefit they will provide for humans in the long term. There are no easy answers to these questions, and the answers may not be clearly known for generations.

Science

The second largest use of animals by humans is for scientific endeavors, such as basic and applied scientific research and product testing, and for education. Animals are also used in the training of clinical professionals, medical doctors, dentists, veterinarians, and others in allied medical fields, as well as in high school and college biology classes (such as dissections of frogs, fetal pigs, or cats).

The National Science Board was formed by Congress in 1950, as a part of the National Science Foundation. The Board provides advice to the president and Congress about science and technology. Among its other tasks, the Board performs systematic polling and other procedures to determine how Americans view science and technology. It published its findings in *Science and Engineering Indicators* (National Science Board Science and Engineering Indicators 2008). Among its findings were that Americans get most of their information about science from television and that some people have difficulty distinguishing between reality and fantasy.

The Internet is the favorite source of information when people are seeking information about specific scientific issues. Both Americans and Europeans do not appear to have a solid knowledge of science, and as many as 60 percent believe in pseudosciences, such as astrology. Most Americans do not clearly understand scientific progress and how new ideas are generated, investigated, or analyzed. Many Americans do not believe that scientific research pays enough attention to the moral values of society.

How Do Scientists Do Science?

The main motivation for basic research is to expand humanity's knowledge without regard to any possible commercial value of the results of the research. Applied research, on the other hand, attempts to answer a specific question for a specific purpose. Typically, applied research seeks results that have some commercial value. For example, a scientist might test a new drug or chemical to determine what it does and if it is safe so that officials can decide whether it can be marketed. Separate experiments might attempt to determine the major effect of the drug, the optimum dose of the drug, the best route of administration, the dose at which side effects occur, what these side effects are, and whether the drug causes cancer, mutations, or birth defects, and, if so, at what dose level, as well as the drug's potential interactions with other drugs, foods, and environmental agents.

The first step in the process of performing an experiment that involves animals, whether it is a basic or applied research project, is to determine what is already known about the topic. This is important, and current regulations require (see later discussion) the scientist to determine what has been published in primary sources like hard-copy or online journals, as well as in secondary sources such as books, monographs, treatises, theses, and dissertations. These sources are located by doing computerized literature searches and searching the Internet (especially Google Books and Google Scholar). The next step is to find, obtain, and read the pertinent papers that have been identified by these searches. The scientist focuses on the methods and procedures that were used in this earlier research; the drug, dose, and route; the animal species used, including the number of animals, their strain, age, and sex; and the statistical procedures that were used, as well as the results obtained. When the important papers have been identified, the scientist does a computerized Science Citation Index search (http://thomsonreuters.com/products_services/scientific/ Science_Citation_Index), which yields a list of all papers that have cited each author's work. This allows a scientist to follow the impact of a particular idea or technique forward in time. If no one cites a particular paper, it may mean that the ideas or techniques described in the paper have had minimum or no impact. In contrast, if many people cite that paper, it means that the ideas or techniques are having an impact.

The U.S. Department of Agriculture regulations to implement the 1985 amendments to the Animal Welfare Act of 1966 (see chapter 3) require that scientists demonstrate that the proposed work does not duplicate studies that have already been performed and that they have refined their experimental techniques to minimize the number of animals required to obtain the needed data, as well as to minimize the amount of stress and pain the animals are exposed to. They must also demonstrate that the animals cannot be replaced with an in vitro, computer, or statistical model or with an alternate (lower) species, such as fish or invertebrates.

In addition to the searches the scientist performs on a specific topic, she also searches AGRICOLA (http://agricola.nal. usda.gov/), which provides worldwide coverage of the literature dealing with the welfare aspects of animals used in exhibition, education, and research, and BIOETHICSLINE (http:// wings.buffalo.edu/faculty/research/bioethics/bio-line.html), which provides citations related to the ethics of human and animal experimentation.

The scientist is now ready to design the experiment and write the experimental protocol. The specific format of the protocol varies from institution to institution, but in general it contains at least four main sections: introduction/rationale; methods and procedures; staffing; and literature searches/rationale for animal use. In the introduction, the scientist provides the background for the proposed project based on his own thinking and his reading of the papers uncovered by the literature searches. The scientist also discusses why he thinks it is important to do the experiment and how he thinks the experiment will add to our knowledge of our world and how it works. The methods and procedures section describes how the experiment will be conducted. This includes what species of animals will be used, how many animals will be used in each experiment, what experimental procedures will be used, what variables will be observed, and how these variables will be quantified and evaluated. It also discusses what statistical techniques will be used to evaluate the data.

In the next section, the experimenter describes what literature searches he did and provides a rationale for why he selected the animals he selected and why his data could not be collected in an in vitro preparation, in a lower animal, such as an invertebrate, or through the use of a computer model. In the last section, he describes the people who will work on the project and provides information about their background and training.

Once the protocol is written, it is likely that the scientist will ask some of his colleagues to play devil's advocates and to read the protocol over carefully, looking for any potential problems in the rationale, in the design of the study, or in the statistical analysis. In some institutions, this local evaluation may be a formal requirement.

Once he has completed this informational (or formal) review, the researcher is ready to submit his protocol to the Institutional Animal Care and Use Committee (IACUC) (see chapter 3). This body represents the general community's interests in the proper care and treatment of animals. During the meeting with the IACUC, the experimenter defends his protocol; that is, he must be prepared to answer any substantive questions posed by the members of the IACUC. One question that usually arises is whether the experimenter has considered alternatives to any procedures that are likely to cause pain or distress. In any practice that is likely to cause pain, the experimenter will be directed to consult with a doctor of veterinary medicine to plan the procedure and also to help to plan for the use of tranquilizers, analgesics, and anesthetics. He will also be questioned about the number of animals that he is proposing to use to determine if the number is adequate for the purpose but not excessive. He will also be asked about the sensitivity of his experimental techniques and his statistical procedures. At the conclusion of the meeting, the IACUC either signs off on the protocol or requests revisions. Once the protocol is approved, the experimenter is responsible for following it in all experiments. During the course of the experiments, if any significant changes in methods/statistics are required, the protocol must be amended to reflect these changes, and the amendments must be approved by the IACUC.

Now the scientist is ready to seek funds to do the actual work. Research is funded by three different mechanisms. Private companies fund applied research and sometimes basic research.

The purpose of this research is to develop new products, to improve existing products, or to test new products to determine if they are toxic and, if they are, at what level and how the toxicity is manifested. For example, a drug company might have its chemists synthesize a new chemical compound. Then they will try to determine what the new compound does, and so on, as described.

The other two funding mechanisms are contracts and grants. There are several major differences between contracts and grants. A contract typically defines a specific task or program that the government or some private agency wants performed. The agencies of the federal government, for example, advertise their wants and needs on the Internet in "Commerce and Business Daily" (http://cbdnet.gpo.gov/). A contract generally starts with a Request for Proposals (RFP), which appears as an advertisement in "Commerce and Business Daily" and describes the task or program in varying amounts of detail. An individual responds to the RFP by describing her experience and capabilities, as well as why she thinks she can perform the task (the responder may, of course, also be a company). This initial response can contain a description of the applicant's approach to the task. The professional staff of the federal agency then determines who is qualified to do the work and provides those applicants with a more detailed description of the task. The applicants take this information, design the experiment(s), and determine what staff and materials will be needed to perform the work. They then develop two proposals. One proposal describes how the experiments will be conducted and evaluated, as well as what staff, material, and facilities will be required to perform the work. A second proposal defines the costs of doing the work. These are submitted to the agency, which evaluates the two proposals separately. First, the professional staff of the agency determines if the methods, procedures, and staffing are appropriate to the task. Some applicants are eliminated at this stage. Second, the agency determines if the costs are realistic. Again, some applicants are eliminated. In the final stage, the contract is awarded (in general) to the group with the best design and the best price. Private companies, such as drug companies, also perform needed work by contracting out the research. Unfortunately, there is no central clearinghouse that describes the needs and wants of these companies.

Grants are the major mechanism for supporting basic research. Grants are usually generated by applicants. That is, the applicant comes up with an idea, does the work described for contract applicants (i.e., develops a protocol, has it approved, and so on), and then writes a proposal. The proposal can be submitted to a federal agency, such as the National Science Foundation; one of the branches of the National Institutes of Health; the Environmental Protection Agency; one of the research offices that serve the Department of Defense, such as the Office of Naval Research; or any of a variety of other federal departments and agencies. Or the researcher can send the proposal to a private agency that supports research, such as the American Heart Association, or to a private foundation, such as the Morris Animal Foundation.

The deadlines for submission and the form that the proposal must take vary from agency to agency. The methods for judging the proposal also vary from agency to agency, but they contain the major sections mentioned earlier. For example, all applications or proposals submitted to the Public Health Service that involve the care and use of animals must contain the following information: identification of the species and approximate number of animals to be used; the rationale for involving animals and for the appropriateness of the species and numbers to be used; a complete description of the proposed use of the animals; a description of procedures designed to ensure both that discomfort and injury to animals will be limited to that which is unavoidable in the conduct of scientifically valuable research and that analgesic, anesthetic, and tranquilizing drugs will be used where indicated and appropriate to minimize discomfort and pain to animals; and a description of any euthanasia method to be used. Most other granting agencies have similar requirements with respect to animal use. The proposals are subjected to some form of peer review; that is, the grant proposal, with or without its budget, is sent to several impartial experts in the area covered by the grant proposal. These experts are asked to evaluate the proposal and to determine if the work proposed is new and unique, if the amount of work that is proposed is appropriate for the staffing and budget, and if the methods and procedures are appropriate. These experts are also asked to provide written comments and to indicate whether they recommend funding the project. Some agencies also request these experts to assign the proposal a numerical score that represents their overall evaluation of the proposal.

If the grant or contract is funded, the scientist is ready to actually perform the work. It is important to note that this process, from the inception of the idea to the start of the work, can take as long as a year, sometimes even longer. While the contract application or grant application is being reviewed by a funding agency, there is often little or no feedback. If the researcher does not win the contract sought, she has essentially no recourse but to apply when another RFP appears. If the grant is not funded, the researcher again has little recourse but to reapply, trying to take into account the comments made by the reviewers.

After the experiment is completed, the experimenter is generally expected to present her methods, data, and conclusions at a scientific meeting and/or publish them in a refereed scientific journal. This is an important step. First, it tells other scientists what experiment was performed and the results obtained. This helps minimize needless repetitions of experiments. Publication provides another tier of quality control for science. When a paper is submitted to a refereed scientific journal, the editor sends the paper to two or more referees, who are (theoretically) impartial experts in the area. The experts review the paper in much the same way that the IACUC reviews the protocol. If these experts find some flaw in the paper, they return it to the author with their comments. She has an opportunity to correct the flaws and resubmit the paper. If the referees do not find any problems with the paper, it is published in the journal. Once it is published, it is open for review by the entire scientific community. If anyone finds a flaw with the paper, that criticism will very likely be pointed out in a future publication in an article by the scientist who found the flaw. If a scientist cannot publish her work, it is unlikely that she will succeed in obtaining new funding.

It is important to note that there is intense competition for funds and journal space. There are several tiers of quality control (i.e., local evaluation of a protocol; evaluation by the IACUC; evaluation by a funding agency; evaluation by the referees prior to publication; and evaluation by the entire scientific community after publication). Also, not all repetitions of an experiment are meaningless or wasteful. One way that scientists (and, in fact, society at large) come to trust experimental results is to have the experiment replicated by another laboratory and to obtain the same results.

Testing! Testing! Who Do We Test? Why Do We Test?

Background

With the exception of nutrients, such as carbohydrates, fats, and proteins, that provide our bodies with the energy required to carry on the basic processes of life, and the nutrients, such as protein, minerals, and water, that are necessary for building and maintaining our bodies, many of the chemicals in our environment are potentially toxic.

No one, not the Environmental Protection Agency, the Food and Drug Administration, nor the bureaucrats who administer the Occupational Safety and Health Act, know precisely how many new chemicals or chemical compounds are added to our environment each year. Best estimates suggest that 2,000 to 3,000 new chemicals are created by industry each year. Many of these chemicals are produced in small amounts (a kilogram or less), and few people are exposed to them. Others are produced in multi-ton quantities, and thousands or millions of people are exposed to them. The vast majority of these new chemicals, especially if they do not have anything to do with food or drugs, have not been screened, on even the most basic level, to determine their potential health risks.

This category includes chemicals that are obviously poisonous, such as pesticides and herbicides. It also includes solvents and chemical intermediates, the building blocks of many of our modern wonders, such as plastics and synthetic fibers. But, it also includes less obvious things, such as chemicals that are naturally present in our food (e.g., alkaloids, glycosides, and tannins), as well as chemicals that are intentionally (e.g., food colors, artificial flavors, antioxidants) or unintentionally (e.g., antibiotic residues) added to our food. It also includes antibiotics and other drugs that are used to treat the maladies and ailments that plague humans and animals.

The Ethics of Testing

One of the more shameful episodes of scientific investigation began in 1932 in Macon County, Alabama. The U S. Public Health Service set up an experiment involving some 412 persons with syphilis, 204 undiseased controls, and 275 individuals who had been cured of syphilis with treatments then in use, that is, heavy metals such as bismuth, mercury, and arsenic. These subjects were poor black farmers. It is unlikely that they understood the experiment; they therefore could not give informed consent to be a subject in the experiment. This trial was not secret; the data was reported in the medical literature from time to time, as was acquired. Shockingly, the men with syphilis were not systematically treated, even after penicillin became readily available in the

1940s. This led Dr. Edmund C. Casey, the incoming president of the National Medical Association, an association of black physicians, to reportedly say at the time the story of the Tuskegee experiment became widely known, "First you try it in mice, then in rats, and then in blacks—because chimpanzees are too expensive." We can only hope that there will never be a similar episode.

In order to prevent such outrages, scientists or clinicians who use human subjects for biomedical research are generally required to acknowledge that they are aware of, understand, and ascribe to the two international ethical codes that guide biomedical research with human subjects.

One is the Nuremberg Code of Ethics in Medical Research, which was developed in 1948 by the Allies during the war crimes trials that followed World War II. It was used as a standard against which the practices of the Nazis involved in horrific (and generally worthless) experimentation on humans were judged. The Code sets forth what criteria must be met before any experiment using human beings as subjects can be judged morally acceptable. Point (3) of the Code says:

> The experiments should be so designed and based on the results of animal experiments and a knowledge of the natural history of the disease or other problem under study that the anticipated results (will) justify the performance of the experiment. (Grodin 1990)

The second standard is the Declaration of Helsinki, which was adopted by the 18th World Medical Assembly in 1964 and was revised at the 29th World Medical Assembly in 1975. The revised Declaration of Helsinki, in the section titled Basic Principles, point (1), says:

> Biomedical research involving human subjects must conform to generally-accepted scientific principles and should be based on adequately performed laboratory and animal experimentation and on a thorough knowledge of the scientific literature.

In the year 1025, Avicenna wrote *The Canon of Medicine*, in which he described the process of drug discovery and testing. His words sound strikingly like those we use in the 21st century:

The drug must be free from any extraneous accidental quality.

It must be used on a simple, not a composite, disease.

The drug must be tested with two contrary types of diseases, because sometimes a drug cures one disease by its essential qualities and another by its accidental ones.

The quality of the drug must correspond to the strength of the disease. For example, there are some drugs whose heat is less than the coldness of certain diseases, so that they would have no effect on them.

The time of action must be observed, so that essence and accident are not confused. The effect of the drug must be seen to occur constantly or in many cases, for if this did not happen, it was an accidental effect.

The experimentation must be done with the human body, for testing a drug on a lion or a horse might not prove anything about its effect on man. (Avicenna 1999)

The Risks of Not Testing

Testing helps researchers avoid potential medical catastrophes, a few of which are discussed here. Some candidate drugs are acute poisons. Exposure to a high enough dose of some of these (in some cases, such as organophosphates, as little as a few milligrams) will kill on the spot. The effects of exposure to chronic poisons are cumulative, and repeated exposure over a long time period will cause serious, potentially life-threatening problems.

Mutagens cause permanent alterations in the molecular structure of the genes (i.e., changes in the structure of the DNA). Many of these changes cause severe problems, and many are life-threatening.

Teratogens cause birth defects. At least 1 out of every 12 live births has a birth defect. Clinicians do not know the cause of the majority of these birth defects; some, perhaps the majority, are caused by exogenous (environmental) agents.

Carcinogens cause cancer, which has been and continues to be a leading cause of death. There are at least 100 different forms of cancer. Normal healthy cells grow, divide, and replace themselves in an orderly manner. Cancer cells lose this ability for controlled growth and divide and grow rapidly. They invade and destroy nearby tissues. And they metastasize, that is, they spread to distant parts of the body and form new tumors.

How Do We Test?

Today, the U.S. Food and Drug Administration requires a specific protocol for drug testing. During preclinical drug development, a sponsor evaluates the drug's toxic and pharmacologic effects through in vitro and in vivo laboratory animal testing. Genotoxicity screening is performed, as well as investigations of drug absorption and metabolism, the toxicity of the drug's metabolites, and the speed with which the drug and its metabolites are excreted from the body. At the preclinical stage, the FDA generally asks, at a minimum, that sponsors (1) develop a pharmacological profile of the drug; (2) determine the acute toxicity of the drug in at least two species of animals, and (3) conduct short-term toxicity studies lasting from two weeks to three months, depending on the proposed duration of use of the substance in the proposed clinical studies.

Traditionally, the first step is to test in mice and rats, then to test in other species, such as dogs, mini-pigs, or nonhuman primates. These tests are expensive and time consuming, and some scientists and clinicians claim that they can be replaced by in vitro tests, which would minimize the number of animals used.

A variety of methods, most using innovative cell cultures of individual tissues, are being tested and validated (i.e., the results obtained are being compared with those obtained in whole-animal studies). For example, MatTek's patented EpiDerm System uses normal, human-derived epidermal keratinocytes (NHEK) that have been cultured to form a multilayered, highly differentiated model of the human epidermis. These "ready-to-use" tissues, which are cultured on specially prepared cell culture inserts using a serum-free medium, attain levels of differentiation on the cutting edge of in vitro skin technology. Ultrastructurally, the EpiDerm Skin Model closely parallels human skin, thus providing a useful in vitro means to assess dermal irritancy and toxicology. The European Union has endorsed EpiDerm to replace the Draize Skin Irritation Test, which was developed by Dr. John H. Draize of the FDA to test cosmetic products. In Dr. Draize's method, the test substance is applied to the animal's eye or skin and the animals are observed for 14 days to detect changes in the skin or eye.

Education

Approximately 5.7 million animals are killed to be used in classroom dissections. These include mice and rats, but more typically frogs, fetal pigs, and cats. Virtually everyone would agree that science literacy is vital to our nation's ability to remain a leader in science and medicine. However, it is unclear what value added is obtained from having junior high, high school, and college students who are nonscience majors perform dissections of animals as part of an introductory or comparative anatomy biology class. Advocates claim that this is a unique opportunity to have students learn about anatomy and the relative size and placement of internal organs. It helps them see, feel, and observe the natural variations of these organs. Opponents claim that some students object to actual dissections for moral or other reasons. They claim that virtual simulations such as those available on the Internet (e.g., http://www.digitalfrog.com or http://www.froguts.com) are less expensive than dissections involving real animals and provide a similar learning experience. Anatomical models like the Giant American Bullfrog (http://www.sciencelab.com) can also be used. The Human Society of the United States provides a list of CD-ROMS, videos, and anatomical models at its Web site, http://www.hsus.org/.

On the other hand, it is unlikely that simulations would provide students in preprofessional and professional curriculums (e.g., medicine, dentistry, veterinary, chiropractic, physical therapy) with the same knowledge and experience they gain in actual dissections. For them, dissections provide a background for other courses, such as physiology.

Live animals are commonly used in physiology and pharmacology classes in professional schools. Animal activists argue that computer programs and other forms of simulation can be used in place of live animals. Most experts, however, agree that experiments with live animals provide the students with knowledge and experience about dealing with living organisms.

This is especially true of surgeons. If you were about to have surgery, would you like your surgeon to pick up his scalpel and step to the table, where you are the first living organism he has cut into? Probably not! Surgery is still an art, and the only way to learn it is by practice, initially in animals, typically dogs or mini-pigs, and then, under the guidance of a skilled surgeon, in humans.

Animal Fighting

While there are aspects of animal rights and animal welfare that are the source of disagreement, there is one area where there is general agreement: animal fighting. One of the reasons that the Royal Society for the Prevention of Cruelty to Animals and its American counterpart were organized in the 19th century was to prevent animal fighting, and these groups continue their efforts to this day. The enforcement branch of the U.S. Society helps law enforcement officials enforce local and federal laws against animal fighting. The Humane Society of the United States, which was established in 1954, is a strong advocate for anti-animal-fighting efforts. The Humane Society is backed by 10 million Americans.

In the past, there were a variety of forms of animal fighting. In the 19th century, bear and bull baiting were apparently the most popular types of animal fighting. In these fights, one or more dogs was turned on a bear or a bull in a ring. These fights were to the death. These types of animal fighting are no longer popular. But another form of animal fighting was popular then and continues to be popular to this very day in some circles—dog fighting.

Dog Fighting

Dog fighting is a "contest," typically between two dogs that are placed in a pit (a small arena) where the dogs fight, often to the death. The pit is typically 14 to 20 feet square with walls that are 3 to 4 feet tall. These fights can last several hours and end when one of the dogs either cannot or will not continue to fight. While any large dog can be used, the American pit bull terrier (also known as the American Staffordshire terrier, Staffordshire bull terrier, or bull terrier) is the most common "combatant." Pit bulls have extremely strong jaws and are predisposed to inflict severe wounds and broken bones. These dogs are bred for generations to be aggressive toward other animals, and this aggressiveness can generalize to humans, especially children. The crossing of pit bulls with bullmastiffs and presa canarios may create larger and more vicious fighters.

These dogs are typically mistreated (beaten), and they are often deprived of food and water to make them more vicious. They are exercised on treadmills and catmills (where the dog is chained to a pole attached to a central beam and a small dog or cat is chained to another pole; the pit bull chases the other animal, never catching it). The trainer may also use a jump-pole, which has bait attached to it; the dog is trained to jump and hang onto the bait. This helps strengthen the jaws and the pit bull's tendency to clamp its jaws on an opponent and not release the hold. The dogs typically have chains wrapped around their necks, often with added weights, to strengthen their neck and upper-body muscu- lature. The dogs are "trained" to fight and kill by "practicing" on small dogs and other small animals (e.g., cats, rabbits).

Dog fighting is not a spur-of-the-moment activity; it takes time and effort to set up a pit. Since these events are illegal, they do not usually have a permanent location but must move from place to place. Dog fights are often attended by dozens of people, includ- ing children. These people often wager hundreds or thousands of dollars on the outcome of the fight. Dogs that do not die as a re- sult of the "contest" often sustain serious injuries. Some losers are killed by their owner. Because of the type of injuries, it is unlikely that owners would seek legitimate veterinary care for their animals because the veterinarian would likely report them. Therefore, the dogs are provided with inexpert care and often suffer for days to weeks before succumbing. If they survive, they are often returned to the pit, even more vicious because of their experience.

Michael Vick was a National Football League (NFL) quar- terback playing for the Atlanta Falcons. Vick, one of the highest paid players in the NFL, was suspended in August 2007 because, in April 2007, an elaborate dog-fighting arena was discovered on property he owned on Moonlight Road in Surry County, Vir- ginia. Vick and several co-defendants were convicted of criminal conspiracy in U.S. federal district court. Vick lost his NFL salary ($130 million), as well as his promotional agreements with Nike and other sportswear companies. Thanks to plea agreements with state and federal authorities, he was released to a federal halfway house program in May 2009 and while there was required to work at an "approved job."

Dog fighting is not a secret activity. It is popularized in a num- ber of magazines, such as *The Sporting Dog Journal*, which claims a circulation of more than 10,000 worldwide. Other magazines that promote dog fighting include *The American Warrior* and *The Pit Bull Chronicle*. "Dogmen" also have a presence on the Internet.

Recently, a new form of dog fighting has appeared in urban areas. There is no pit. The dogs are just turned on each other and fight. Street fighters can buy a fighting dog for a few hundred dollars.

Cock Fighting

Cock fighting is an ancient blood sport said to have been intro- duced by Julius Caesar. Gamecocks are specially bred roosters that have been selected for their fighting abilities for generations. Currently, cock fighting is a felony in 33 states and the District of Columbia and is a misdemeanor in the remaining states. It is legal and very popular in Puerto Rico.

A cock fight typically occurs in a ring when two gamecocks are released into the ring. They fight until one bird dies; sometimes both birds die. Some birds are fitted with a "naked spur," but, in most cases, they wear a cockspur (a leather bracelet attached to the bird's leg) with a curved, sharpened spike. This spike significantly increases the ability of the bird to do significant damage to its opponent.

Although it is illegal in all 50 states, cock fighting, like dog fighting, is not a secret activity. The United Gamefowl Breeders Association's mission statement states:

> The purpose of this Association is to bind breeders and fanciers of gamefowl into an organization for their mutual benefit and for the exchange of better methods and ideas tending toward perpetuation and improvement of the various breeds of gamefowl and also to improve marketing methods and to cooperate with Universities, State, Federal and any other public or private agency which seek to control poultry diseases. (United Gamefowl Breeders Association 2009)

This sport supports at least two magazines, the oldest and best known of which is *The Gamecock*; the other *The Feathered Warrior.*

Bullfighting

Bullfighting is a traditional spectacle in Spain, Portugal, southern France, Mexico, and several Latin American countries. Bullfighting traces its origins back to ancient Rome. Currently, about 250,000 bulls, many specially bred on ranches that specialize in raising bulls for the ring, are killed each year. These bulls are selected for a combination of aggressiveness, strength, vigor, and intelligence. Bulls must be more than four years old and must weigh more than 900 pounds to be used in the ring.

There are a number of different styles of bull fighting. The Spanish style is most common. The matador is dressed in a "suit of lights." The actual fight is divided into three stages. The first stage begins when the bull enters the ring and is tested by the matador. The picador, mounted on horseback, enters the ring and stabs a mound of muscle in the bull's back. The bull loses blood from this wound (which weakens the bull) and typically holds its head and horns lower for the rest of the fight. In the next stage, three banderillas attempt to place two sharp sticks near the initial wound. This causes more loss of blood and weakens the bull's neck muscles. In the third stage, the matador enters the ring with a red cape and performs a series of stylized passes with the cape, demonstrating the matador's bravery and his control over the bull. The fight ends when the matador makes a series of passes with the cape and stabs the bull between its shoulder blades, piercing the aorta or heart. When this is successful, the bull generally dies within seconds or minutes. If the strike is not accurate, the bull may linger for hours before it dies.

Support for bullfighting may be waning. A Gallup poll conducted in Spain in 2002 found that about 70 percent of the respondents expressed "no interest" in bull fighting; among the 30 percent who expressed "some" or "a lot" of interest, more than half were 65 years of age or older.

Hunting

Considering the advent of the iPod and the cell phone and that we have robotic explorers on Mars, it is sometimes easy to forget that we are fewer than 500 generations from when most of our ancestors were hunter-gatherers. Subsistence hunting, a system in which animals provide the only or main source of meat (protein), continued well into the 19th century and in some areas into the 21st century. Early hunters had to have considerable skill to find, track, stalk, and get close enough to ultimately kill an animal, often with a spear or bow and arrow. If the animal was merely wounded, the hunter would have to track it until it died.

These hunters used every part of the animal. Consider the words of Red Cloud, a former chief of the Sioux, talking about the uses of the buffalo (*Bison bison*):

His meat sustained life; it was cut into strips and dried,
it was chopped up and packed into skins, its tallow and

> grease were preserved—all for winter use; its bones af-
> forded material for implements and weapons; its skull
> was preserved as great medicine, its hide furnished
> blankets, garments, boats, ropes, and a warm and por-
> table house; its hoofs produced glue, its sinews were
> used for bowstrings and a most excellent substitute for
> twine. (Dary 1974)

When the first Europeans set foot on North America, it is estimated that there were between 30 and 60 million buffalo on the
continent, but the animals were hunted to near extinction and
reduced to a few hundred individuals by the later part of the
19th century, located mainly in the region near and around Yellowstone National Park. In contrast to hunters like Red Cloud,
commercial hunters, like Buffalo Bill Cody, killed hundreds to
thousands of buffalo in a day; they would take the hide, which
was used in industrial belts or made into clothing, or the tongues,
which were considered a delicacy in Northern cities, leaving car-
casses weighing 900 to 2,000 pounds to rot. In the late 1880s, buffalo bones were collected and shipped to the East, where they
were ground up to be used as fertilizer.

Some estimates suggest that there were more than 5 billion
passenger pigeons (*Ectopistes migratorius*) in the United States
when the first Europeans arrived. At this time, they formed the
second biggest migrating flocks, often containing millions of birds
(the largest flocks were formed by desert locusts). Commercial
hunters on a massive scale reduced that number in the late 1800s,
and the world's last passenger pigeon died in a Cincinnati zoo in
1914.

White-tail deer (*Odocoileus virginianus*), also called Virginia
deer, are native to much of North and Central America and to
northern portions of South America. By the mid 1930s, the total
population of white tails was reduced to about 300,000 animals, because of commercial and unregulated hunting and loss of habitat
due to poor land practices and deforestation. Conservation practices have proved so successful that the deer is now considered a
nuisance in many parts of its range.

An avid big-game hunter, Theodore Roosevelt saw wildlife
habitats shrinking as the United States steadily became more
urban and the number of privately held farms and ranches steadily
decreased. In order to help conserve the nation's natural wildlife
resources, Roosevelt founded the Boone and Crockett Club in

Missoula, Montana, in 1887. One of the Club's key precepts is the concept of the fair chase:

> Fair chase as defined by the Boone and Crockett is the ethical, sportsmanlike, and lawful pursuit and taking of any free-ranging wild, native North American big game animal in a manner that does not give the hunter an improper advantage over such animals. (Boone and Crockett Club 2009)

The U.S. Fish and Wildlife Service (2009) reported in 2001 that about 13 million Americans age 16 and over engaged in hunting. Of these, 11 million sought big game, such as deer and elk. Approximately 40 percent hunted on public land. In 2005, the service permitted hunting in 319 of the nation's 545 wildlife reserves in order to manage wildlife populations.

The Fund for Animals reported in 2004 that 91 percent of all hunters were male, 97 percent were white, and about 50 percent were between the ages of 35 and 54. They collectively spent more than $6 million for licenses, tags, and other fees required by state wildlife agencies. Total expenditures associated with hunting were more than $20 billion about half of which was spent on hunting equipment.

Each state has its own rules and regulations that control the hunting season for native species; specify when hunters are allowed to hunt for specific species; state the fees charged for hunting specific animals (approximately $100 or less); and impose limits on the number of animals that a hunter can kill in a day and in a season. For some animals, such as feral pigs (*Sus scrofa*), domestic pigs that have returned to the wild, there is no season or limit.

The opportunities for sport hunting, where animals are hunted for the enjoyment of the hunt, as well as for meat or trophies, are limited. In response, some farmers and ranchers lease their land to hunters in order to supplement their income. A lease can sell for several hundred to several thousand dollars. In exchange for the fee, the property owner limits the number of hunters on his land. The size of the leases range from tens to thousands of acres, usually fenced with four- to five-foot-tall fencing. The mammalian prey is generally white tail deer or elk (*Cervus Canadensis*), which is one of the largest species of deer. These animals are usually active around dawn and dusk and hide during daylight hours. Most sport hunters are employed and have a limited amount of time available to hunt; because of these limits on their free time, limits on the hunting season, and the fact that animals typically hide during the day and can generally escape by jumping the fence, often hunters are frustrated and fail to get their quarry. In the 1960s, landowners began to supplement forage with shelled corn or cottonseed meal (a high-protein byproduct left after cottonseed oil has been removed) that is dispensed by an automatic feeder at specific times during the day in order to attract the animals to particular areas and thus make it easier for hunters to locate them. Laws dealing with feeders vary from state to state. Some landowners feed year round, some from the beginning of September to mid-March. This provides two benefits: (1) it leads to bigger, healthier animals, and (2) perhaps more important, it lets hunters know where animals are likely to be found. Hunters can build a blind nearby, either on the ground or, more commonly, in a tree. When the animal comes to feed, the hunter shoots.

In the Western states (e.g., Arizona, Colorado, New Mexico, Montana, Oregon), much of the land is owned by the federal or the state government. Hunting permits are granted on some of these lands. Generally, in order to be successful, a hunter must employ an experienced local guide to help him locate animals.

Wallace Byron Grange, who wrote a book about hunting (Grange 1949), was one of the pioneers in the development of game farming and game management during the 1940s. He was a pioneer in the use of eight-foot deer-tight fencing.

Since then, more than 2,000 game ranches or hunting preserves scattered over 25 states have appeared. They range in size from less than 100 acres to several thousand acres, all surrounded by game-tight fencing, which prevents the exotic animals from escaping and keeps native domestic and wild animals from entering. Most of the exotic animals are hoofed stock from around the world (e.g., various species of antelope, cattle, deer, goats, and sheep). But they also include "surplus" animals, like lions, rhinoceros purchased from zoos, and "retired" circus animals, including elephants. Animals in these facilities do not roam freely (except within the boundaries of the preserve) and are dependent on humans for food and shelter. These game preserves are privately owned, and therefore hunters are not required to have state hunting licenses and do not face a bag limit other then the size of the hunters wallet. Most of these operations charge a daily fee for the use of the facilities and a kill fee that varies according to which animal is killed; fees can vary from a few hundred dollars to thousands of dollars. Sometimes called "canned hunts," these hunts offer guaranteed trophies, with relatively little actual hunting involved. Many game ranches advertise a "No Kill, No Pay" policy. Most of these hunters are after trophies, such as antlers, heads, skins, or displays prepared by a taxidermist. Some take some or all of the meat from the animal. It is not clear what happens to the remains of the animals if only a trophy is taken.

Hunting preserves are a big business. Hunters spend more than $250 million at these facilities. In 2007, the Agricultural and Food Policy Center at Texas A & M University reported that nationwide the exotic wildlife industry has a direct economic impact of $679 million annually and supports more than 14,000 jobs, mostly in rural America.

Many state wildlife agencies are opposed to these facilities because they funnel revenue away from the agency. Most game wardens are deeply committed to the "fair chase" concept, and many are concerned about transmission of diseases such as tuberculosis, brucellosis, and chronic wasting disease. On the other hand, some state agriculture departments support these facilities as a way for farmers and ranchers to increase their profits.

There is relatively little federal and state regulation of these operations. On the federal level, the Animal Welfare Act does not appear to apply to private game preserves. The Endangered Species Act does not prohibit ownership of threatened or endangered species and potentially allows hunting of these privately owned animals. The Humane Slaughter Act has not been interpreted to include exotic captive wild animals. A variety of federal legislation such as the Captive Exotic Protection Act has been proposed, but none has been enacted into law.

Oregon was apparently the first state to ban hunting of exotic or game mammals held or obtained by private parties. Hunting of captive mammals is completely banned in Arizona, California, Connecticut, Hawaii, Maryland, Massachusetts, Minnesota, Montana, Nevada, Washington, and Wyoming, and partial bans are in place in Delaware, Georgia, Mississippi, North Carolina, Utah, Virginia, and Wisconsin. Five states—Iowa, New Hampshire, New Mexico, Oklahoma, and Texas—include wild animals in their anticruelty statutes.

The ultimate "canned hunt" was developed by John Lockwood. He calls the activity Live-Shot. It allows a hunter to take part in a real hunt without leaving the comfort of his living room by using the Internet. The first hunt was scheduled for April 9, 2005. Reportedly for a $14.95 membership fee and a $1,000 deposit toward the cost of the animal, along with a valid Texas hunting license, a member can use an Internet connection to control the actions of a Remington 30–06 rifle that is attached to a small motor. A video camera is embedded in the rifle's scope, allowing the hunter to aim the rifle at an animal, which is enticed into range by a feeding station, and to pull the trigger using an automobile car-lock activator attached to the rifle. The actual location for the hunt is a privately owned ranch near San Antonio, Texas. Theoretically, the hunter could be located anywhere in the world where Internet access is available. Mr. Lockwood reportedly claimed that his main purpose for designing the system was to allow people who were unable to get into the field for physical or other reasons to be able to hunt.

This concept caused a firestorm of controversy. Organizations that are typically opponents of hunting, such as the Humane Society of the United States and the Safari Club International, are opposed to computer-based hunting. Buckmasters, a hunter advocacy group, sponsors hunts for disabled people, and proponents of hunting such as the Safari Club International are opposed to computer-based hunting.

Virginia was the first to ban Internet hunting. The Texas Parks and Wildlife Department has banned Internet hunting of native animals. However, Texas does not have control over nonnative species. At least 30 other states have some type of ban on Internet hunting. Representative Brad Sherman (D-CA) introduced a bill, "Computer-Assisted Remote Hunting," in the House of Representatives on June 14, 2007, and Senator Sheldon Whitehouse (D-RI) introduced a similar bill in the Senate on December 6, 2007. These bills would amend the federal criminal code to ban computer-assisted remote hunting and establish penalties for engaging in such activity. As of December 21, 2008, these bills had not been voted on.

Fox Hunting

Fox hunting involves tracking, chasing, and generally killing a fox, most commonly a red fox. Fox hunting originated in England in the 16th century, when the king owned all of the land and everything on it. Fox hunting is an expensive sport centered on the hunt club. Each club has a Master of the Fox Hounds, who maintains the kennels and provides training for the hounds, typically dogs of a specialized breed, foxhounds, which are trained to follow a scent. The Master is responsible for running the hunt in the field. Each hunter has one or more specially trained horses, typically called field hunters or, more simply, hunters. Fox hunting may be the origin of the steeplechase (in which the horse and the rider race over a course that contains obstacles over which the horse must jump) and "point to point" horse racing (traditional horse racing where horses compete on a race track).

The hunt is the setting for a variety of social activities, including the hunt itself. Hunters typically wear traditional hunting gear. The Master generally wears a scarlet coat, riding pants, and English dress boots.

The hunt begins when the hounds are "cast" into the rough brushy areas where red foxes typically hide during daylight hours. When the hounds pick up the scent of a fox, they trail it for as long as they are able. When the hunters hear the hounds, they follow in the most direct route possible, which may mean crossing fence lines and other obstacles and trekking across private property (i.e., trespassing). The hunt continues until the fox evades the hounds, goes to ground, or is overtaken and killed by the hounds. The main hunting season runs from November to May.

Cub hunting occurs in the autumn and is used to train the hounds to restrict their trailing to foxes. This allows young hounds to find, attack, and kill young foxes. A hound can enter the pack when he successfully joins in a hunt like this. Hunters claim that this culls weaker foxes.

Opponents, mostly animal welfare activists, claim that fox hunting is cruel to the fox, because the hunt causes fear and distress and ultimately death. Hounds are often euthanized when they come to the end of their working life.

Hunters claim that fox hunting helps keep down the number of foxes, which farmers consider vermin. They claim that the fox is generally killed quickly.

The British Parliament passed the Hunting Act of 2004, essentially outlawed hunting with dogs (especially fox hunting and cub hunting), and the ban took effect in October 2005. The Act was challenged in the British courts and in the House of Lords, but the challenge was rejected. The Act does not prohibit "drag hunting," where an object is dragged over the ground for the hounds to follow. This activity does not involve any animals.

Fox hunting or, more correctly, fox chasing is popular in the United States. Both Thomas Jefferson and George Washington reportedly kept fox hounds before and after the Revolutionary War. There were 171 registered fox hunter packs in the United States and Canada in 2007. In addition to sponsoring fox hunts, they provide stewardship of the land and attempt to protect fox habitat.

One of the first official acts of the Nazis when they first came to power was to ban hunting with hounds; the ban was ordered by Hermann Goering on July 3, 1934, and was extended to Austria when Germany annexed it. Considering their treatment of fellow humans, the Nazis had among the most stringent animal welfare laws (see chapter 3).

Coon Hunting

A raccoon is a medium-size omnivorous (i.e., plant- and animal-eating) mammal that is native to North America. It has a characteristic black face mask and a ringed tail. Most raccoons are active during the evening and night. In populated areas, some humans consider them pests. Hunting and road kill are the leading cause of death.

Raccoon or, more commonly, coon hunting is a popular sport in the United States, especially in the South. Coons are excellent tree climbers and swimmers. The hunt begins when the coon hound, especially a Bluetick hound, comes across a coon scent. The dogs follow the scent and the coon. Hounds on the trail make a particular howling bellow when they find a scent and begin following it. They continue to follow the raccoon until they lose the scent or the raccoon runs up a tree. The quality of their howling changes when the coon is treed. The hunters follow the sound to the tree and kill the coon. Hunters claim that raccoon tastes good.

Entertainment

It is not clear how many animals are used by the various components of the entertainment industry and it is not clear how much oversight is provided either by public or private agencies.

Circus

The circus can trace its ancestry back to the Roman Empire. After the fall of Rome, there were no large circuses, except for itinerant showmen who traveled from town to town performing at fairs. The modern circus, with one or more circular rings surrounded by ranks of seating, emerged in the 18th century in England. Circuses consist of a variety of acts, including animal acts featuring big cats, elephants, horses, birds, sea lions, and a variety of domestic animals. Circuses typically travel from place to place, stay for a few days, and then move on. Animals are shipped in trucks or by train, often without heat or air conditioning. Circus animals, especially the big cats, spend most of their time in small cages. Animal trainers generally claim that they use positive reinforcement and rewards to motivate the animals to perform. Animal rights activists claim that animals are often abused, even when performing in public. Circuses and other traveling shows are covered by the Animal Welfare Act (see chapter 3), but it is not clear how well these standards are enforced. In 2007, Ringling Brothers and Barnum & Bailey Circus, the largest circus in the United States, was sued by the Fund for Animals, the American Society for the Prevention of Cruelty to Animals, and the Animal Welfare Institute, which alleged that it mistreated its elephants, including using abusive training methods, chaining the elephants by one front foot and one back foot, preventing normal movement, and separating baby elephants from their mothers. This suit began in the district court of the District of Columbia in 2003 and had not been decided as of the end of 2008.

Films and Television

It is not clear how many animals are used in films or television or how the number changes from year to year. Some animals, like Benji, Flipper, Lassie, Rin Tin Tin, Flicka, and Francis the Talking Mule, are stars, while other wild and domestic animals have supporting roles (e.g., horses and cattle in westerns on television or in motion pictures). The Hollywood Office of the Human Society of the United States and the Performing Animal Welfare Society (see chapter 7) provide some oversight. Since 1986, the Humane Society has presented the Genesis Award annually to major news and entertainment media that raise public awareness of animal issues. The Humane Society also publishes its annual Foe Paw, which lists television shows, magazines, and advertisements that it feels carry an anti-animal message. One example is the Happy Cows advertisement from the California Milk Advisory Board. The Humane Society maintains that most dairy cows are essentially "milking machines."

Rodeo

Rodeos began as ranch-to-ranch contests featuring competition in traditional cattle handling. In 1882, Buffalo Bill (Wild Bill) Cody created perhaps the first, if not the first, rodeo performed for an audience. A rodeo typically consists of a series of timed events. These include steer wrestling (bulldogging), in which the cowboy jumps off a horse and "wrestles" the steer to the ground. In calf roping or tie down roping, a cowboy ropes a calf with a lariat, and the horse steps back to keep the lariat taut. The cowboy dismounts, throws the calf to the ground, and ties three of its legs together. Team roping consists of two riders (cowboys or cowgirls) who capture and restrain a steer. One of the cowboys, the "header," lassos a running steer around its horns. The second rider, the "heeler," ropes the steer's two hind legs. Once they have control of the animal, the riders face each other and gently pull back until the steer falls on its side. Bronc riding takes two forms, both of which are timed. In bareback bronc riding, a cowboy hangs onto a surcingle (a strap), commonly called "rigging," that circles the horse's girth (just behind the front legs) while the horse tries to buck him off. Saddle bronc riding allows the rider to have a saddle bronc saddle, which is a specialized saddle that does not have a horn. A heavy lead rope, commonly called a bronc rein, is fastened to the halter on the horse. In bronc riding, if the cowboy remains on the animal for eight seconds, he is removed by a rider on a trained horse. In another rodeo act, cowboys try to ride a full-grown bull. Generally the bull has a strap around its girth that the cowboy hangs onto while the bull tries to buck him off. Bulls are unpredictable and may attack a rider when he is on the ground, either because he was bucked off or because he dismounted after eight seconds. Rodeo clowns try to attract the attention of the bull and keep it from attacking the rider. Cowgirls take part in barrel racing, in which a horse and rider gallop around a cloverleaf pattern of barrels and try not to knock over any of the barrels.

Individual competitors, both professional and amateur, and rodeo sanctioning organizations, such as the Professional Rodeo Cowboys Association, claim that rodeos are humane and do not harm the animals involved. Sanctioned events have a veterinarian present and facilities to deal with injured animals.

Animal rights organizations object to some relatively common rodeo practices. These include bucking or flank straps that are designed to cause the horse to buck. During competition, the flank strap is loosely fitted around the flank area. When the contestant is ready, the chute is opened and the flank strap is pulled tight, causing the animal to buck, trying to escape the buck strap.

If the contestant remains on the animal for eight seconds, he is removed by two riders, one of whom picks up the rider and the other of whom releases the flank strap; generally, the animal stops bucking immediately. Opponents of rodeos also object to metal or electric cattle prods that are used to start the animal bucking.

Zoos

Zoos have evolved from privately held menageries. The first public zoo in America was the Zoological Society of Philadelphia, which was incorporated in 1859. In March 1889, Congress created the National Zoological Park, which was put under the direction of the Smithsonian Institution's Board of Regents. Most of the top 50 cities (by population) in the United States have a least one and sometimes several zoological gardens. Many smaller cities and towns also have zoos. Zoos have changed over the past few decades; whereas animals used to be displayed in small cages made of concrete and iron, usually with one or two members of a species to a cage, today many zoos have slowly replaced these cages with large enclosures that contain multiple members of the same species and often representatives of several different species. These areas are often viewed from trams or monorails. Often these enclosures have a specific theme, such as a representation of an African savanna that contains animals associated with that locale. Zoos are essentially tourist attractions, where the public can view different animals, but, in addition, they engage in education, research, and conservation, including captive breeding programs.

In addition to traditional zoos, drive-through safari parks are becoming increasingly common. One of the first, if not the first, safari park was the Africa U.S.A. in Boca Raton, Florida. In these parks, humans are allowed to drive out among the animals and feed and pet them through the windows of their car. These parks typically have a variety of hoofed stock, both native and exotic, as well as ostriches or emus.

Lion Country Safari was started in 1967 by a group of South African and British entrepreneurs in Loxatatchee, Florida. Six additional parks were opened near big cities, but they ultimately closed, leaving only the park in Loxatatchee. Visitors were allowed to drive through the park, which contained giraffes, rhinos, and zebras that roamed freely. Lions were segregated behind fences or water barriers.

In 2004, there were more than 2,400 animal exhibits registered with the U.S. Department of Agriculture (USDA). Many of these were roadside attractions that varied dramatically in size and in the quality of care provided the animals.

The Association of Zoos and Aquariums (see chapter 7) is a nonprofit, voluntary accrediting agency for zoos and aquariums. In order to be accredited, an organization must adhere to rigorous standards of animal care, provide educational exhibits, and be actively involved with conservation efforts. Fewer than 10 percent of the organizations registered with the USDA are accredited.

Marine Mammal Theme Parks

There are a number of marine parks scattered across the United States. The main purpose of these parks is entertainment. Sea Lion Park at Coney Island, New York, founded in 1985, was probably the first park of its type. It provided a show featuring sea lions performing various tricks. Sea Lion Park closed in 1902. In 1938, Marine Studios in Florida set up a large marine tank to film underwater shots of dolphins. This became a tourist attraction, and the dolphins were trained to perform simple tricks. During the 1970s, a variety of aquaria with captive dolphins opened across the United States, Europe, Japan, and in various locations in Southeast Asia. During this time, Sea World USA opened parks in Orlando, Florida; San Diego, California; and San Antonio, Texas. These parks feature shows in which orcas (commonly called killer whales, the largest species of dolphins), dolphins, beluga whales, seals, sea lions, and other marine mammals perform tricks. These tricks include "kissing" their trainer, fetching balls, jumping through hoops, performing somersaults, and making synchronized leaps. Trainers also ride the back of the animal or balance on its nose as it comes up and leaps out of the water. The tricks are based on natural behaviors or behaviors that have been modified by training. The animal is trained to perform these tricks on command, generally for a food reward. Very few cetaceans breed in captivity, so most of the animals in these facilities are captured in the wild. It is not clear when or even if wild caught cetaceans adapt to captive life. Indications of lack of adaptation include stereotyped behavior (e.g., swimming endlessly around in circles), becoming aggressive, or inflicting injury on themselves or others.

Fashion

It is not clear how many animals are used to make clothing and other accessories. Typically, mammals are used to make coats and, in times past, hats (most notably the beaver hat). Birds are used for their plumage. Leather is used to make shoes, boots, and coats.

Fur

Fur coats have been popular for centuries. Proponents argue that fur coats provide warmth, while animal activists claim that there are synthetic materials that are as warm as fur. Large cats (e.g., tiger, leopard), among the most sought-after skins for coats, are endangered species; therefore, it is illegal to possess their skins or to make coats or other clothing from their skins. Furriers have two sources for other fur-bearing animals: those trapped in the wild and those raised on fur farms.

European beavers were hunted to virtual extinction for their skins and castoreum, a secretion of their scent glands that was thought to have medicinal properties and that was used in making perfume. Beavers were extinct in England by the 16th century and were endangered in most parts of continental Europe. The discovery of the American beaver led to the formation of one of the oldest corporations in North America, the Hudson's Bay Company (French Compagnie de la Baie d'Hudson), incorporated by a British royal charter in 1670. The company's primary business was the fur trade, and it provided most of the fur pelts that were used for making felt hats, fur coats, and fur trim for garments. The company controlled much of this activity in what became Canada and in the northern and western parts of the United States well into the 19th century. Its traders and trappers (sometimes called mountain men) ranged far and wide and were often the first Europeans to explore distant territories. It is estimated that when the Europeans arrived in North America, there were more than 200 million beavers living there. By 1988, that number had been reduced to approximately 10 million.

It is estimated that there are about 20,000 people who trap nonpest fur-bearing animals. Of this number, about 4,000 are considered serious trappers, who earn part or all of their income from trapping. These trappers typically live in a rural or small community and are usually men in their mid-40s. The rules and regulations covering trapping vary from state to state; each state regulates the types of animals that can be trapped, the season they can be trapped, and the number of animals that can be trapped.

Steel-jawed (typically leg-hold) traps were invented in the late 16th century. These traps consist of two jaws, with or without teeth, a spring, and a trigger in the middle. The trap is placed along animal trails or is scented with pheromones (smelly chemicals that attract the animal). A trapper typically sets his traps on the banks of a lake, river, or pond if he is after beaver, mink, river otter, or muskrats. He then returns several days later to determine if he has caught any animals; if he has, he kills them.

Although many individuals and organizations object to leg-hold traps and at least six states have prohibited their use, they continue to be used. Numerous attempts have been made to redesign these traps to make them more humane, but it is not clear if these redesigned traps are being used.

More than 30 million animals are raised in cages and killed for their fur. Minks are the animal most commonly raised this way, but so are large numbers of foxes, sables, chinchillas, and ferrets. Sixty to seventy-five percent of the fur coats sold in the United States are made from cage-reared animals. This industry is typically regulated by state departments of agriculture, and the rules and regulations vary from state to state. Mink farming tends to be concentrated in the northern states. The animals are typically raised in small wire mesh cages. A typical mink cage is about 2.5 feet long, 1 foot wide, and 1 foot high. The cages are adjacent to each other, which is stressful for minks, which are solitary animals that generally come together to mate, usually in March; the young (commonly called kits) are born in May. Litters vary from 3 to 13 kits. These animals molt in the late summer and are harvested when their winter fur is in its prime, in late November and in December. They are typically fed agricultural byproducts, such as damaged eggs, expired cheeses, or offal (the entrails and internal organs of butchered animals, basically everything except the bones and muscles) from meat- or poultry-processing plants. Minks are euthanized by bottled gas that contains pure carbon dioxide and carbon monoxide. It takes approximately 50 mink skins to make a mink coat.

Feathers

Two sorts of feathers are typically used in clothing: down and plumage. Down is the small feathers that grow closest to the bird's body. These feathers do not have a quill, which is found primarily in the feathers on the chest of the bird. In most cases, the down is removed when the bird is euthanized. But some down is plucked from live birds, especially from geese and ducks. Geese in breeding flocks are plucked every 5 weeks from the time they are 10 weeks old until they are four years old. About five ounces are collected each time. Down is used to fill coats, quilts, sleeping bags, pillows, and comforters.

It is not clear who started using feathers in fashion. Marie Antoinette is often credited with using feathers as an accessory, often inserted into piled up hair styles. Later, plumage was used to decorate dresses and especially hats. The use of feathers reached a peak in the 19th century, when fashion designers employed the plumage of a wide variety of birds, including the ostrich, egret, heron, pheasant, peacock, lark, starling, blackbird, oriole, grebe, kingfisher, and bird of paradise, as well as various species of parrots and parakeets. Reportedly, between 1890 and 1930, more than 50,000 tons of feathers were imported into France for use in the fashion industry.

Feathers were a lucrative business; an ounce of the best-quality feathers could sell for $40 at the beginning of the 20th century. Imports of feathers were taxed, and, later, the quantity of feathers that could be imported was restricted; ultimately importation was completely halted in many countries. Smuggling then became a significant part of the industry. In the United States, two federal laws were passed. The first was the Lacey Act of 1900 (31 Stat 188), which made the secretary of agriculture responsible for the preservation, distribution, introduction, and restoration of game birds and other wild birds and required him to report on the propagation, uses, and preservation of birds covered under the act. The act also prohibited the transport of living or dead foreign birds or animals. The Migratory Bird Treaty Act (40 Stat 775; 16 U.S. Code 702) made it unlawful to pursue, hunt, take, capture, or kill, as well as to possess or to offer to sell, migratory birds. Fashion changes, and the uses of feathers have declined significantly.

Leather

Leather is created by tanning (a chemical treatment that changes the structure of the skin) the hides or skins of various animals, including reptiles, birds, and mammals. Cattle hide is by far the most common; the hide is generally a byproduct of the meat industry.

Lamb and deer skins are used because their leather tends to be soft and pliable. Other animals whose hides are used for leather include ostriches and reptiles (large snakes and crocodiles), which are often used to make boots.

Cetacea: Whales, Porpoises, and Dolphins

In the King James Version of the Bible, Genesis 1:19–22 says:

19 And the evening and the morning were the fourth day.
20 And God said, Let the waters bring forth abundantly the moving creature that hath life, and fowl that may fly above the earth in the open firmament of heaven.
21 And God created great whales, and every living creature that moveth, which the waters brought forth abundantly, after their kind, and every winged fowl after his kind: and God saw that it was good.
22 And God blessed them, saying, Be fruitful, and multiply, and fill the waters in the seas, and let fowl multiply in the earth.

Chimpanzees (and the other great apes) are members of the same genus as humans and share more than 95 percent of their genetic material with humans. The Cetacea, comprising whales, porpoises, and dolphins, are the only organisms whose brain/body ratio approaches (and in some cases exceeds) that of humans. Given this brain size, there is significant controversy about just how intelligent these creatures are. Since they lack appendages, it is unlikely that they have a material culture (e.g., produce tools), but many exhibit complex social behavior. Cetaceans produce a wide variety of sounds. Some of these sounds are used for echolocation, for orientation, and for locating food, in much the same manner that people use sonar to locate objects in the water. But, scientists believe that some of these sounds are used for communications between individuals. These *songs* are quite complex and hauntingly beautiful.

John Lilly (see chapter 5) attempted to develop species-to-species communication with captive dolphins, as well as to understand dolphin-to-dolphin communications. This intriguing work is described in *Man and Dolphin* and *The Mind of the Dolphin* (see chapter 8).

Cetaceans are wholly aquatic mammals that are found in all the world's oceans and seas, as well as in certain rivers and lakes. Living cetaceans are divided into 38 genera and consist of approximately 90 species. Dolphins and porpoises are members of the family Delphinidae, which contains 18 genera and approximately 62 species. The word "dolphin" is usually applied to small cetaceans that have a beaklike snout and a slender, streamlined body. "Porpoise," on the other hand, typically refers to small cetaceans with a blunt snout and a short, rather stocky body. They typically range in length from 4 to 14 feet (1.2 to 4.3 meters) and weigh between 50 and 500 pounds (23 and 225 kilograms). The genus *Orcinus* contains only one species, *O. orca,* commonly called the killer whale. Typically black and white in color, these whales are approximately 20 feet (6 meters) in length and weigh about 386 pounds (850 kilograms).

The scientific name for the beluga whale is *Delphinapterus leucas.* Belugas are typically white; they are about 13 feet (4 meters) long and weigh about 227 pounds (500 kilograms). The name "beluga" causes some confusion, because it is also applied to the great white sturgeon (a fish, not a mammal), which is one of the principal sources of caviar.

These are the species that are commonly encountered in marine aquaria, such as the marine parks discussed earlier. For those who wish to see these animals live, an alternative to these parks is to observe cetaceans in their natural habitat. Whale watching from the shore or from small boats is a popular activity, and commercial whale-watching trips on large crafts are becoming increasingly popular. Organizations that offer such excursions can be found on both coasts and often specialize in sightings of specific whales.

The blue whale measures more than 90 feet in length, four times the length of a common city bus, and weighs more than 286,000 pounds (129,727 kilograms). It is the largest living organism, and its tongue alone weighs more than an elephant! Blue whales can be observed from the shores of Big Sur or from boat trips into Monterey Bay, both in California. Since this activity is very popular, some activists argue that is it important to protect whales from intrusion, harassment, or exploitation. However, most agree that quietly watching them in their own habitat engaging in their natural behaviors is an amazing experience.

Cetaceans can be distinguished from fish by the position of the tail fluke; in cetaceans it is set in a horizontal position, while the tail fin of a fish is set in a vertical position.

Whaling

The Basques, in northern Spain, were apparently the first whalers; they began whaling from the shore in the 12th century. Three genera have been pursued by commercial whalers: the right whale (*Balana*), the humpback whale (*Megaptera*), and the rorquals or finners (*Balanoptera*). The sperm whale (*Physeter macrocephalus*) and the bottlenose whale have also been hunted.

By the middle of the 19th century, whaling appeared to be dying out, because the pursued species had been hunted to near extinction. In 1860, a Norwegian sailor, Svend Foyn, invented the harpoon gun (this did not come into common use until the 1880s). The harpoon gun allowed whalers to profitably focus on the capture of smaller, more active whales. What these whales lacked in the amount of oil each one yielded they made up in quantity.

Since 1900, more than 800,000 cetaceans have been killed. They were hunted for meat and for blubber, which was rendered to make whale oil, which in turn was used for making fuel for oil lamps and in the manufacture of soap and candles. Whale oil was also used as a fine lubricant. Other parts of the whale were used, as well. The whale's bones and teeth were carved and decorated (the finished product is called scrimshaw) and were also used to make buttons, chessmen, cufflinks, and brooches; its skin was used to make shoe leather and coverings for a variety of products; its tendons were used to string tennis racquets. Manufacturers use spermacerti (sometimes called cetaceum), a pearly white, waxy, translucent solid obtained from oil in the head of a sperm whale, to make candles; in the production of cosmetics, especially emollients (lotions or salves to soothe and soften the skin); as a lubricant, especially for delicate instruments; and in polishes, soaps, crayons, and various food coatings. In addition, although it is very expensive, Ambergris, a wax-like, brown colored material that is produced in the digestive system of sperm whales and that is found floating on the ocean or washed ashore, is commonly used as a fixative for high-quality perfumes or soaps.

Whales were also killed to obtain whale bone, or baleen. Baleen is an elastic, horny substance that grows in place of teeth in some whales (suborder *Mysticeti*) and that takes the form of thin parallel plates on each side of the palate. Baleen was used to stiffen corsets.

In 1946, the short-lived League of Nations drew up the International Convention for the Regulation of Whaling. Few countries followed its mandates. The International Whaling Commission (see chapter 7) was formed in 1949 to control whaling and to guarantee a supply of whales for future use. The organization has no powers of enforcement, however, and during its first 30 years of existence, more than 2 million whales were killed. The member nations of the Commission voted a moratorium on all commercial whaling beginning in 1985, and this remains in effect today. Two nations, Norway and Japan, continue to engage in commercial whaling despite this moratorium. The Commission does not bar indigenous or subsistence whaling in various parts of the world. The number of whales taken by indigenous people is relatively small.

Activists claim that whaling is inherently cruel and that whales sometimes take hours or days to die. In addition, they assert that modern sonar interferes with whales' normal communications. Whalers, on the other hand, claim that, with modern harpoons, whales that are taken die quickly.

Chapter 3 discusses potential solutions to these problems and controversies.

References

Avicenna. 1999. *Canon of Medicine*. Chicago: KAZI Publications.

Boone and Crockett Club. 2009. Fair Chase Statement. http://www.boone-crockett.org/huntingEthics/ethics_fairchase.asp?area=huntingEthics. Accessed April 26, 2009.

Dary, David A. 1974. *The Buffalo Book: The Sage of an American Symbol*, Avon Publishing, p 55.

Declaration of Helsinki. http://www.cirp.org/library/ethics/helsinki/. Accessed April 16, 2009.

Food and Drug Administration. Code of Federal Regulations Title 21 Food and Drugs Chapter 1, Subchapter A General, Part 56 Institutional Review Boards. http://www.accessdata.fda.gov/scripts/cdrh/cfdocs/cfCFR/CFRSearch.cfm?CFRPart=56. Accessed August 17, 2009.

Food and Drug Administration. Investigational New Drug. http://www.fda.gov/cder/Regulatory/applications/ind_page_1.htm. Accessed April 16, 2009.

Grange, W. B. 1949. *The Way to Game Abundance.* New York: Scribner.

Grodin, M. A. 1990. The Nuremberg Code and Medical Research: The Hastings Center Report. http://www.questia.com/googleScholar. qst?docId=5002154468. Accessed April 16, 2009.

National Science Board Science and Engineering Indicators. 2008. Chapter 7: Science and Technology: Public Attitudes and Understanding. Available at: http://www.nsf.gov/statistics/seind08/ pdf/c07.pdf. Accessed April 16, 2009.

Nicoll, C. S., and S. M. Russell. 1990. "Analysis of Animal Rights Literature Reveals the Underlying Motives of the Movement: Ammunition for Counter Offensive By Scientists." *Endocrinology* 127 (5): 985–89.

United Gamefowl Breeders Association. 2009. Mission Statement. http://www.ugba.info/. Accessed April 16, 2009.

U.S. Fish and Wildlife Service. 2009. Available at: http://www.fws. gov/. Accessed August 20, 2009.

Vegetarian Resource Group. 2009. Available at: www.vrg.org. Accessed April 16, 2009.

3

Possible Solutions

Research, Research, Research!

Although curiosity about the structure and function of the body probably predates written history, prior to the 19th century there was relatively little animal research except for dissections. Aristotle (384–322 B.C.E.) and one of his students, Erasistratus (304–250 B.C.E.), wrote descriptions of animals that were probably based on dissection.

Galen (about 129–216 C.E.) was not allowed to dissect human bodies. He did dissect a variety of animals, including a Barbary ape and other mammals, including but not limited to dogs, cats, weasels, and camels, as well as fish, reptiles, and birds. Galen also performed surgery on living animals, including oxen, horses, sheep, swine, and nonhuman primates. This was before anesthetics were available, so these animals were awake. Galen was the first to point out that the brain was the seat of our highest functions. If the brain was damaged, it also affected the mind.

Claude Bernard, who is often called the father of physiology, was born in 1813 in Saint-Julien, France. When Bernard entered medical school in 1834, bloodletting was still a common treatment for a variety of diseases. Germ theory (that is, the idea that disease could be caused by microorganisms) was not yet established, and the drugs in common use could be, in the words of Dr. Oliver Wendell Holmes, "sunk to the bottom of the sea, it would be all the better for mankind—and all the worse for the fishes." Leading physicians of the day believed that chemistry and physics could advance in the laboratory, but biology and medicine could not.

Bernard worked in the laboratory of Francois Magendie (1783–1855). Magendie was one of the first of the modern animal experimenters. In 1822, Bernard cut the anterior and posterior roots of the spinal cord of living animals and discovered loss of sensation followed section of the posterior roots and loss of movement followed section of the anterior roots.

Bernard believed that medical knowledge, like other forms of scientific knowledge, could be won by systematic experiments. He was the first to state the principle of scientific determinism, that is, the principle that identical experiments should yield identical results. Bernard published his *Introduction à la médecine expérimentale* (An Introduction to Experimental Medicine) in 1865; the work was translated into English by Henry Copley Green in 1927.

Drs. Charles S. Nicoll and Sharon M. Russell (1991) note that two notable men, Wolfgang Amadeus Mozart, who died in 1791, and Alexander the Great, who died in 323 B.C.E, both died in their mid-30s. In the centuries between the deaths of these men, the art and science of medicine had not significantly changed. In contrast, 80 percent of our current biomedical knowledge has been acquired since the 19th century, and 50 percent of it was learned in the 20th century. The rapid growth of medical knowledge is at least partially the result of animal research in the 19th century (and continuing today) as part of an effort to determine how normal living systems work and to use this information to determine the effects of disease. Modern animal rights activists use the same argument they used in the 19th century—that we know all we need to know. We do know a good deal about how to control infectious diseases and parasites, and we are just beginning to understand our own impact on the world. Unfortunately, new diseases, like AIDS, seem to crop up without warning. An ancient disease, such as tuberculosis, which was almost wiped out, has once again become a serious threat because the bacteria that cause TB have become resistant to most of the antibiotics and combinations of antibiotics that were formerly used to control it.

One of the major breakthroughs in the 20th century is the development of transgenic mice, both knock-ins and knock-outs that hold the promise of being able to test new therapies prior to human trials. Knock-out mice are genetically engineered to turn off one or more genes to determine their function based on a comparison of the changes in function or behavior between the normal and knock-out mouse. A knock-in mouse is genetically altered by inserting a foreign gene to replace an endogenous gene.

Interest in basic and applied research continued to grow in the 20th century but especially around the time of World War II. The National Institute of Health was created by the Ransdell Act in 1938, the National Institutes of Health in 1948, and the National Research Foundation in 1950. The National Institutes of Health and the National Research Foundation have been and continue to be the major supports for basic applied research. (Perhaps the biggest impetus for increased support for science was the launching of Sputnik 1 by the Soviet Union on October 4, 1957.)

Private (Nongovernmental) Solutions

Although animal rights (in Europe, more frequently animal liberation) and animal protective organizations seem to have overlapping goals, they have different historical roots and pursue different goals today. Both trace their lineage to organizations that arose in the 19th century in Great Britain. These organizations and their more recent descendants are private, nongovernmental agencies. They generally have relatively small paid professional staff and a larger number of unpaid volunteers and are supported by members and by the general public through donations of money, goods (sometimes called gifts in kind), or volunteer services. Some of these organizations were founded in the 19th century, but most of the newer ones were founded in the late 1970s and 1980s (see later discussion and chapter 7).

Animal Welfare

A number of groups exist in England and in the United States that are dedicated to promoting animal welfare. The following discussion focuses on a few of them.

England

Bull baiting was a popular "blood sport" in England for several centuries. Most towns in England, including London, had a bull-baiting ring. The bull was chained to an iron stake, which allowed it some freedom of movement. Often pepper was blown up the bull's nose to enrage it. Then dogs were set upon the bull in an attempt to immobilize it. In a variant of this "sport" commonly called "pinning the bull," dogs were set upon the bull one at a time, and the goal was for the dog to fasten his teeth on the bull's snout.

Sir William Pulteney proposed a bill to ban bull baiting in the House of Commons in April 1800. This was apparently the first attempt to pass a law dealing with animal welfare. Two cabinet members, William Windham and George Canning, were opposed to the bill. They argued that bull baiting, which was enjoyed by working-class people, was no crueler than fox hunting, which was a sport of the upper classes. The bill was defeated on April 18, 1800, by a vote of 43 to 41.

The first successful animal welfare legislation was the Act to Prevent Cruel and Improper Treatment of Cattle (sometimes called Martin's Act), sponsored by Richard "Humanity Dick" Martin and passed by Parliament on July 22, 1822. This act protected horses, mares, geldings, mules, asses, oxen, cows, heifers, steer, sheep, and other cattle. The act stated that if any person or persons were to wantonly and cruelly beat, abuse, or ill treat any of these animals and if a complaint was made to a Justice of the Peace or Magistrate within 10 days of the offense, a trial was to be held. If the person was convicted, he would be fined no more than 5 pounds and no less than 10 shillings. If the person would not or could not pay the fine, he was to be committed to the House of Correction, without bail, for three months or less.

Martin was also one of the founders, along with more than 20 other reformers, in 1824, of the Society for the Prevention of Cruelty to Animals. The stated purpose of the Society was to provide enforcement of Martin's Act. At the time the organization was formed, there was little or no compassion for animals, which were commonly viewed as commodities supplying food, transport, or sport. The Society was granted royal status by Princess Victoria and changed its name to the Royal Society for the Prevention of Cruelty to Animals (RSPCA) in 1840. Today the RSPCA is a charity in England and Wales that promotes animal welfare and that is funded by voluntary donations. The RSPCA lobbied Parliament throughout the 19th century for the passage of animal legislation (discussed later). While the Association has no statutory powers, its inspectors try to identify individuals or organizations that mistreat animals. Its representatives cannot enter anyone's premises without permission but generally seek help from local government officials to obtain search warrants. The Society has no power to prosecute offenders other than by private prosecution. The Society today sponsors more than 100 animal clinics and welfare centers, including wildlife centers and several sites that can hold lost, neglected, or homeless animals. Its current budget is more than 82 million pounds. In 2007, the Society investigated more than 100,000 complaints of cruelty, which resulted in the conviction of more than 1,000 defendants and in 861 orders barring individuals from keeping animals.

United States

The American Society for the Prevention of Cruelty to Animals was founded, in New York City, by Henry Bergh in 1866. It was the first humane society in North America, and most of its activities are centered in New York City and New York state. The major goal of the Society is to work toward a day when animals can live without unnecessary fear or pain. In the 19th and early 20th centuries, the Society focused its efforts on horses and livestock. Today the focus is on companion animals. The Society supports a variety of animal shelters and has fostered programs for pet adoption; it also actively promotes spay/neuter programs for adopted animals to reduce the number of unwanted pets and to minimize unnecessary euthanasia. The Society has the legal authority to investigate and make arrests for crimes against animals. Its Humane Law Enforcement (HLE) Division investigates 400 to 500 cruelty complaints each month, resulting in approximately 100 arrests a year. This aspect of the ASPCA has been featured on the television show *Animal Planet*.

The Massachusetts Society for the Prevention of Cruelty to Animals was founded by George Thorndike Angell in 1868 (the organization was renamed MSPCA-Angell in 2003). The Society published a periodical, called "Our Dumb Animals," whose mission was "to speak for those who cannot speak for themselves." Angell also launched a nationwide network of human education clubs called "Bands of Mercy" in 1881 and ultimately recruited more than 250,000 boys and girls.

Yet another group, the American Human Education Society, was founded, in 1880, to provide instruction about kindness, compassion, and respect for all living things.

The American Humane Association was founded in 1877 by representatives of 27 humane organizations from 10 states. The Association, working through a network of individuals and organizations. Its Mission statement states that their mission is to create a more humane and compassionate world by ending abuse and neglect of children and animals. The Association publishes *The Link*, which promotes awareness of the relationship between animal abuse and other forms of violence and highlights the importance of the benefits from the human-animal bond. The regional Los Angeles office of the Association is responsible for monitoring the use of animals in the entertainment industry, especially television and film. If no animals are hurt or killed in the making of a movie or television show, its producers are allowed to use the No Animals Were Harmed end credit disclaimer.

Animal Rights

England

One of the first organizations, if not the first, to seek animal rights (liberation) was the Society for the Protection of Animals Liable to Vivisection, which was founded, in 1875, by Frances Power Cobbe (1822–1904), a feminist, social reformer, and animal rights activist, to protest the use of animal experimentation. Cobbe also founded the British Union for the Abolition of Vivisection, in 1898, to protest the use of dogs in vivisection. The Union does undercover investigations of scientific laboratories, engages in political lobbying, and promotes cruelty-free cosmetics (i.e., those not tested on animals). It also works to eliminate toxicity testing of chemicals on animals and supports effective nonanimal substitutes. The organization's ultimate goal is to eliminate all animal experimentation, and it publishes a list of health-related charities that do not support animal research. The Union was one of the founding members, in 1990, of the European Coalition to End Animal Experiments, which claims to be the leading organization in the attempt to ban animal research in Europe. The Union was also a founding member of the International Council for Animal Protection, which is developing international guidelines for animal testing.

United States

The American Anti-Vivisection Society was founded in Jenkintown, Pennsylvania, by Caroline Earle White and Mary Frances Lovell, in 1883. Early on, the Society was also actively involved in developing laws for the treatment of cattle in transit and for enforcing the 28-hour law, which requires that cattle be watered, fed, and allowed to rest at least once every 28 hours during transport.

The Society has continued to propose and support both federal and local legislation to end pound seizure laws and to add birds, mice, and rats to the Animal Welfare Act.

The National Antivivisectionists Society was founded in 1929 in Chicago, Illinois, by Clarence E. Richards. Early support came from a British actor, George Arliss. The Society strives to ban all animal research. The Society notes: "The word vivisection literally means cutting apart living animals. At the turn of the 20th century, the meaning of the term was widely known. Over time, the definition of vivisection has commonly come to mean any animal experimentation or animal research. Now, vivisection can refer to any experimentation on animals including non-invasive psychology research, product testing, or dissection."

Between the end of the 19th century and the middle of the 20th century, relatively few animal rights organizations were founded in England and in the United States. At least in part, because of the increase in research utilizing animals that followed the end of the World War II, Peter Singer, an Australian ethicist, published the book *Animal Liberation*. Singer is a utilitarian, which means that he believes that actions should do the most good and cause the least harm for as many individuals as possible. Most other utilitarian philosophers focused on human-human interactions, but Singer added what some people consider a novel interpretation—the idea that humans must give equal consideration to animals in human-animal interactions. Singer apparently does not believe in animal rights but rather focuses on the moral claims of animals—the belief that both humans and animals can suffer.

No one would argue that minimizing pain is a worthwhile objective. But animals inflict pain on other animals to survive. Consider the domestic cat, the most common household pet in the United States. It generally lives a relatively pampered and well-fed existence and does not have to hunt for food. But cats are instinctive hunters, and, even if they are not hungry, they are ruthless in handling the small animals and birds that fall victim to them. The cat is acting out of instinct and does not have any knowledge of moral considerations. Humans are different from all other species in that we are the only species that is concerned about the welfare of other species. Humane medical research furthers humans' ability to survive by providing a way to develop methods to treat diseases that have plagued humans from ancient times and to recognize and treat new diseases when they occur. Our first duty as humans in the constant struggle to survive is to our own species.

Not all philosophers agree with Singer and Regan. Dr. Carl Cohen, a professor of philosophy at the University of Michigan at Ann Arbor, is a strong advocate of humane animal research, which he believes serves humans and animals alike. He argues that to refrain from using animals in research on utilitarian grounds is morally wrong.

One of the first of the modern animal rights organizations was the People for the Ethical Treatment of Animals (http://www.peta.org), which was founded in Norfolk, Virginia, in 1980, by Ingrid Newkirk and Alex Pacheco. The early history of PETA is intimately tied to the work of Dr. Edward Taub.

In 1981, Dr. Taub, a scientist at the Institute of Behavioral Research in Silver Springs, Maryland, was conducting research on the effects of somatosensory deafferentation (the elimination of sensation by cutting sensory nerves or interrupting sensor nerve impulses) in monkeys in which all sensation had been surgically eliminated from one or both forelimbs. According to Dr. Taub, in the middle of May 1981, Alex Pacheco approached Taub and asked for a job in his laboratory. Since Taub could not afford to pay him, Pacheco agreed to work as a volunteer. Pacheco worked in Taub's laboratory for five months. During this time period, Taub asserts that Pacheco never pointed out any deficiencies in the facilities or questioned any of the procedures used in the laboratory. Without Taub's permission, during the night, Pacheco allegedly took photographs of the conditions in Taub's laboratory and admitted five observers to the laboratory. Each of the five observers ultimately filed an affidavit that was highly critical of the conditions in the laboratory. Pacheco, who failed to mention to Taub that he was the president and one of the co-founders of PETA, an antivivisectionist organization, took his photographs and affidavits to the Montgomery County police. The police raided Taub's laboratory and seized Taub's research subjects (17 monkeys) and some of his research records.

The search and seizure received major local and national media coverage, which he believes was organized by PETA. The monkeys were placed in the care of PETA. When Taub petitioned for the return of his monkeys, they disappeared. They were reportedly transported to Gainesville and then back to the Washington area. During this unauthorized transportation, the monkeys were subjected to considerable stress. Taub filed charges that alleged that the animals had been treated cruelly, but he claims that the charges were never investigated.

Dr. Taub was charged with 119 counts of violating the Maryland anticruelty statutes (Maryland Code 1957, 1976 Repl. Vol., Article 27 § 59). His first trial resulted in the complete dismissal of 113 of the 119 counts; he was found guilty of failing to provide adequate veterinary care by an outside veterinarian to six monkeys (*Taub v State*, 296 MD. 439, 441, 463 A.2d 819, 820, 1983). Taub maintained that it was extremely rare for a veterinarian to have experience with animals with the condition he was studying and that he was a recognized expert in its treatment, with more than 25 years' experience. In his second trial, Taub was cleared of five of the remaining six charges. The conviction related to a monkey whose arm was amputated seven weeks after the animal was removed from Taub's laboratory because of a supposed infection of the bone (osteomyelitis), which was said to have been caused by the inadequate care received in Taub's laboratory. A pathology report based on an examination of the arm reported that the animal did not have osteomyelitis. On appeal, the Court of Appeals of Maryland overturned this final conviction (see 445–5, 463 A2d at 822) on the grounds that the statute did not apply to federally funded research, which is covered by the federal Animal Welfare Act. (This Act provides for the protection of animals used in research facilities, while at the same time recognizing and preserving the validity of use of animals in research.) Since Taub was the recipient of a grant from the National Institutes of Health (NIH), the court found that he was also subject to the pertinent NIH regulations governing the care and treatment of animals used in the research that was the subject of the grant.

During the media uproar surrounding the incident in Taub's laboratory, NIH decided to suspend and then terminate his grant. Taub appealed the decision to the Department of Health and Human Service Departmental Grant Appeals Board. While the Board did not reinstate Taub's grant, it did report that it found no evidence of inadequate veterinary care. It did find that Taub was well qualified to treat problems associated with deafferentiation. The Ethics Committee of the American Psychological Association, the Animal Care Committee of the Society for Neuroscience, and an ad hoc committee of the American Physiological Society all agreed, reportedly by unanimous vote, that Taub was not guilty of any wrongdoing. Taub, who moved to the Psychology Department of the University of Alabama at Birmingham, maintains that his research at Silver Springs and at Birmingham has led to improved treatment of some patients who have suffered a stroke and that the disruption of his work delayed the application of this treatment to patients by about eight years.

PETA is one of the largest and most active of the animal rights organizations. According to PETA's Web site, it has about 2 million members and supporters and has affiliates in the United Kingdom, Germany, the Netherlands, India, and the Asia-Pacific region that it helps support. It conducts rallies and demonstrations to focus attention on the exploitation and abuse of animals in experimentation, on the manufacturing of fur apparel, and on the slaughter of animals for human consumption; it also hosts special events involving celebrities, who use their fame to speak out on animal rights issues. PETA also lobbies for, sponsors, and supports animal rights legislation and serves as the media contact for some of the more radical animal rights organizations (see later discussion).

Consider this statement of Ingrid Newkirk, one of the founders of PETA, which has become the battle cry for animal activists:

> Animal liberationists do not separate out the human animal, so there is no rational basis for saying that a human being has special rights. A rat is a pig is a boy. They are all mammals. (Vogue, September 1989)

Other comments by Newkirk include:

> Even if animal research resulted in a cure for AIDS, we'd be against it.
> Even painless research is fascism, supremacism, because the act of confinement is traumatizing in itself. (*Washingtonian*, August 1986)

Alex Pacheco, one of the other founders of PETA, has said: We feel that animals have the same rights as a retarded human child (*New York Times*, January 14, 1989).

According to PETA's IRS Form 990 for 2006 (PETA 2009), the group obtained direct public support of more than $28 million. In that year, PETA paid its employees more than $5 million and spent more than $6 million for consultants, more than $2 million for legal fees, and almost $500,000 for professional fundraiser fees. PETA supported its overseas affiliates and other animal rights organizations through grants that exceeded $3 million.

The Animal Welfare Institute was founded in New York in 1951 by Christine Stevens, a prominent socialite and the widow of Roger Lacey Stevens, a New York real estate magnate. Stevens was the president of the Institute until her death, in 2002. The Institute has actively worked to improve the welfare of animals used in experimentation, tighten the regulation of concentrated animal feeding operations, and regulate the trapping and farming of fur-bearing animals. The Institute also originated the Save-the-Whales Campaign in 1971. Stevens formed the Society for Animal Protective Legislation as the Institute's lobbying arm in 1955. The Society has helped write more than a dozen laws on behalf of wild and domestic animals, including the Humane Slaughter Act and the Laboratory Animal Welfare Act, especially the 1985 amendments to the Act (see chapter 6).

According to its IRS Form 990 filing for 2006 (Animal Welfare Institute 2009), the Institute received more than $3 million in direct public support; it pays its staff a total of more than $600,000. It pays approximately $200,000 in legal fees and allocated about the same amount of money for its lobbying efforts.

There are a number of more radical groups that are opposed to medical and other forms of animal research. These organizations are more shadowy and do not present any information about their leadership or membership. It is not clear how many members these organization have, how they are supported, or whether they meet together. One such organization, the Animal Liberation Front, first appeared in England in 1979. Its credo states:

> The Animal Liberation Front (ALF) carries out direct action against animal abuse in the form of rescuing animals and causing financial loss to animal exploiters, usually through the damage and destruction of property. (http://www.animalliberationfront.com)

Tim Daley, reportedly a member of ALF, said: "In a war, you have to take up arms and people will get killed."

Because the activities of ALF are against the law, its activists work anonymously, either as individuals or in small groups, without any central organization or coordination. ALF provides guidelines for individuals or small groups that want to consider themselves part of ALF. The purpose is to liberate animals from places of abuse, find them good homes, and allow them to live out their lives free of abuse. ALF seeks to inflict economic damage to those who profit from animal exploitation and to reveal the actions of individuals who exploit animals by performing nonviolent direct actions and liberations.

The Animal Rights Militia and the Justice Department, both started in England in the 1990s, are shadowy organizations, more accurately nonorganizations, of individuals and small groups that engage in direct action, including inflicting harm on human beings, in pursuit of their goals. The Animal Defense Militia, another group, calls itself an underground movement of covert operatives dedicated to the autonomy of nonhuman vertebrates through "any means necessary." According to its Web site, it has declared war on PETA, because PETA is not radical enough.

Organization and Support

Before the advent of the World Wide Web, it was relatively difficult to obtain information about animal welfare or rights groups unless you happened to be on their mailing list. Most of these organizations now have Web sites that offer varying amounts of detail about their activities. Most provide a relatively detailed description of their programs and little else. Others may provide additional information, such as a list of officers and perhaps a list of the board of directors, as well as the number of members, some financial data, and, relatively rarely, an annual report.

It is not clear if any of these organizations were started with an endowment. An endowment is a transfer of money or property to an institution. Generally, an endowment (the principal) is meant to be invested and whatever earnings accrue are used to forward the mission of the organization. It is likely that most of these organizations are supported by membership fees, money or gifts in kind from the general public, or bequests (of money, property, or real estate) left to the organization in a donor's will.

Donations to many of these organizations are tax deductible (i.e., the donor can deduct the amount of money or the fair market value of the gifts from his federal and, in some cases, his state income taxes). In order for this to occur, the organization must apply to the Internal Revenue Service for tax-free status, generally as a 501(c)3 entity (the number refers to a specific part of the IRS code). The organization must obtain an Employee Identification Number and prepare bylaws and articles of incorporation. These documents must describe the purpose of the organization and explain how it expects to achieve its purpose; it must also specify how the officers and board of directors will be selected and their terms of office. The group must also supply a budget for the first two years. To maintain its status as a 501(c)3 entity, the organization must submit a Form 990 (Return of Organization for Income Tax) to the IRS, which discloses its financial status. It is possible to obtain copies of Form 990 for specific organizations from Web sites like GuideStar.

Organizations with 501(c)3 status are limited in the amount of lobbying (i.e., attempts to influence actions by Congress or state or local governing bodies) they may do. They also are required to limit their contact (and their suggestions regarding such contact to the general public) with members or employees of legislative bodies to propose, support, or oppose specific legislation. They can, however, involve themselves with issues of public policy by conducting educational meetings or preparing or distributing educational materials. These organizations are also not allowed to directly or indirectly participate in any political campaign.

Demographics

Most of the organizations discussed in this chapter and in chapter 6 may or may not provide data about their total membership, but none provide any demographic data. Drs. Wesley V. Jamison and William M. Lunch (Jamison and Lunch 1992) were able to collect demographic data from some of the participants in a march on Washington on June 10, 1990, that was sponsored by animal activists, including the American Society for the Prevention of Cruelty to Animals, the Doris Day Animal League, the Humane Society of America, the New England Antivivisectionist Society, and the People for the Ethical Treatment of Animals. There were approximately 24,000 marchers representing animal rights groups for 25 states, as well as Israel, Canada, and Australia. One of the coordinators was Peter Singer, also of the National Alliance for Animal Legislation, and the co-chair was the philosopher Tom Regan.

The researchers collected data from a random sample of the marchers (n = 412) using an eight-page survey. These marchers were likely more committed and had stronger views than the average animal rights activist because they had spent time and money to travel to participate in the march. Wesley and Jamison found that 79 percent of the sample had some college or university education; 22 percent had undergraduate degrees, and 19 percent had graduate or professional degrees. Whites made up 93 percent of the responders, blacks 2 percent, and American Indians, Hispanic Americans, and Asians 1 percent each, which closely mirrors the composition of other social movements. The mean annual income of participants was $37,400, and the median income was $33,000. Approximately 8 percent had incomes of $80,000 a year or more. Sixty-eight percent of those interviewed were female, and 32 percent were male; the mean age was 29, and almost a third were under 30. Forty-four percent were professionals (e.g., doctors, lawyers), while 69 percent listed their current job as "working for pay" and 14 percent were full-time students. Sixty-six percent of the respondents lived in metropolitan areas, suburbs, or cities with a population of more than 50,000. Information sources included newspapers (22%), television (22%), magazines (19%), and direct mail (15%).

Movement activists rejected the domination of humans over animals. The activists objected to research that used animals regardless of the level of harm to the animal or the benefit to humans. Fifty-six percent of the responders were opposed to animal research that does not harm the animals, while 26 percent approved of such use. More than 84 percent were opposed to research that would harm the animal. Only 4 percent were opposed to having pets in the home. More than 52 percent of the activists believe that science does more harm than good. The activists tended to be moderately liberal or liberal; 37 percent described themselves as independent, 35 percent as Democrats, and 14 percent as Republicans. Parade participants were more politically active and had the time and the resources to be involved with social movements and politics. Ninety-eight percent approved of contributing money to animal rights causes, and 90 percent had already done so, while 98 percent believed in campaigning for candidates who favor animal rights and 38 percent had already done so. Most of the respondents were very skeptical of science and scientists.

Science Activists

Most scientists belong to one or more professional organizations, such as the American Society for the Advancement of Science, which was founded in 1848 and is the world's largest scientific organization. It serves more than 262 affiliated societies and academies, which covers most of the biological and physical sciences worldwide. Its major publication, *Science*, is the largest peer-reviewed scientific journal in the world. Many scientists also are members of specialized organizations that represent their scientific interests, such as the Society for Neuroscience, whose members are involved in basic, applied, and clinical research on the nervous system.

These organizations have one or more national and/or regional meetings where scientists present their most recent findings. Many of these organizations provide proceedings of these meetings (either in print, online, or both), administer one or more professional refereed scientific journals, hold symposia that cover a variety of topics, such as instructions for using newly developed techniques, and publish specialized monographs. Most meetings include exhibits by companies that specialize in scientific equipment and other items that might be of interest to the attendees, and a jobs bank, where potential employers and employees can meet. The majority of the societies that deal with biological, biomedical, or psychological research have a protocol or statement that defines their views on animal research and how animals that are used in research by members should be treated. These organizations are generally funded by membership fees and journal subscriptions.

Scientists tend to be more interested in doing research than in public relations. Therefore, they have been slow to respond to the comments and criticisms raised by the animal rights movement. The opponents of animal research, especially those that are politically astute, tend to focus on restricting the supply of animals and increasing the regulatory encumbrances that make doing research more expensive, potentially raising costs to an unacceptable level. Most of the organizations that promote science and the use of animals in basic and applied research, in education, and in product testing have only recently been organized.

There are a number of organizations of scientists that take positions on animal research. The National Association for Biomedical Research, founded in 1979 by Francine Trull in Washington, DC, has a membership of about 300 "public and private universities, medical and veterinary schools, teaching hospitals, voluntary health agencies, professional societies, pharmaceutical companies and other animal research-related firms." The Association represents the views of its members before Congress and provides information to its members about legislative and regulatory issues. According to the organization's 2006 Form 990, it received about $1 million dollars from membership dues and spent about $117,000 in legal fees in that year.

The Foundation for Biomedical Research was founded in 1985 by Francine Trull in Washington, DC. The Foundation is dedicated to improving human and animal health by promoting and supporting humane and responsible animal research. It is supported by membership fees.

There are several other groups, as well. The Incurably Ill for Animal Research was founded in 1985 by a group of multiple sclerosis patients who support humane and responsible use of animals in research. Americans for Medical Progress was founded in 1991 by a committee of concerned physicians and scientists. Through publications and outreach efforts, it tries to provide a forum for scientists and those who are touched by the results of humane, necessary, and valuable use of animals in research. A third group, States United for Biomedical Research, is a network of nonprofit organizations that celebrates the "people, the process, and the promise of biomedical research."

Governmental Solutions

The laws that deal with animals vary from country to country. In this volume we examine closely the laws of England and the United States. In the United States, the main legislation dealing with animals is the Animal Welfare Act and its amendments (see discussion). The Department of Agriculture is responsible for promulgating rules and regulations and for enforcing these rules under the terms of the Animal Welfare Act. The Department of Agriculture is also responsible for enforcing the rules and regulations of the Humane Slaughter Act. As discussed in chapter 2, there are relatively complex rules and regulations to deal with the waste generated by concentrated animal feeding organizations, but there are no laws that deal with the treatment of the animals held in these facilities.

United States

Background

As described later, the major U.S. legislation dealing with animal welfare is the Animal Welfare Act of 1966, commonly referred to as the Research or Experimentation—Cats and Dogs Act, and its amendments. The act makes the secretary of agriculture responsible for promulgating and enforcing the rules and regulations included in the Act, and it is the Animal and Plant Inspection Service, commonly referred to as APHIS, that is the agency within the U.S. Department of Agriculture (USDA) that is directly charged with enforcing these rules and regulations. Most of the focus is on animals used in scientific research. Organizations that display animals, such as zoos, aquaria, and roadside attractions, are required to register with APHIS. Farm animals and animals used for agricultural research are specifically excluded, as are birds and cold blooded animals (e.g., reptiles and amphibians). Animals bought and sold through retail pet stores are also not covered.

The first bill to regulate animal welfare in the United States was introduced, in 1896, by Representative McMillan, a Republican from Michigan. This bill would have regulated vivisection in the District of Columbia. After a public hearing, the vote was delayed by the Spanish-American War and was never passed. A similar bill was proposed by Senator Jacob Gallinger, a New Hampshire Republican, but it languished in committee and was never passed.

After World War II, there was a rapid growth in research using animal subjects, but no regulatory activity was attempted until the 1960s. Although animal welfare, especially as applied to animals used in biomedical research, had been discussed from time to time since the turn of the 20th century, there were no real efforts to initiate or pass legislation. One of the tipping points occurred in 1965 with the story of Pepper, a five-year-old Dalmatian, as reported by Coles Phinizy in *Sports Illustrated*, on November 27, 1965. Pepper was the family pet of the Lakavage family and disappeared from her home on a Pennsylvania farm. In an unrelated incident, William Miller was arrested for improperly loading a shipment of dogs and goats. The animals were temporarily housed at a Northampton animal shelter, where a local SPCA worker took photographs of the animals. When shown the photos, Mrs. Lakavage was sure that one of the Dalmatians shown was Pepper. Mrs. Lakavage tracked Miller to a dog farm in High Falls, New York. Miller would not let Mrs. Lakavage see his dogs because she did not have a search warrant. In what may be an apocryphal story, Representative Joseph Resnick (D, New York) was contacted and was also refused access to the animals. Unfortunately, it was a moot point because Miller had dropped the dog at Montefiore Hospital, where it was used in an experiment, euthanized, and cremated.

The cover of *Life* magazine on February 4, 1966 warned, "Your Dog Is in Cruel Danger." The article, titled "Concentration Camps for Dogs," showed graphic images of sick, lethargic, and skeletal dogs, photographed by Stan Wayman on the White Hill, New York property of Lester Brown. This article brought an avalanche of letters to *Life*, reportedly more mail than was inspired by stories dealing with the Vietnam War or human rights violations.

Federal Regulations (Nonagricultural)

On July 9, 1965, Representative Resnick introduced House Bill 9743, and, after a hearing on September 30, 1965, a similar bill was introduced in the Senate by Senators Warren Magnuson (D, Washington) and Joseph S. Clark (D, Pennsylvania).

Drafting of legislation is a complex task. Typically, an Act is fit into a part of the U.S. Federal Code. For example, to amend the Animal Welfare Act, it would be Title 7, which deals with agriculture, Chapter 54 which deals with the transportation, sale, and handling of certain animals, Sections 2131–2159 which deals with the Animal Welfare Act. The legislation must spell out the changes exactly and in detail. Often this means changing punctuation marks, single words, sentences, or sections, either by omitting existing ones or inserting new ones.

Since writing legislation is a relatively technical task, it is handled by specialists employed by Congress, often with help from people outside Congress, notably people with a stake in the legislation, such as lobbyists. Judges and bureaucrats often complain about the fact that much of the legislation is open to interpretation. This is a result of the political processes at work; in order for a piece of legislation to pass, it needs to be rather vague so that it can garner the votes needed. A bill is sponsored by one or more representatives or senators; often, essentially parallel bills are started in the House and in the Senate.

Because of the amount and complexity of modern legislation, both the House of Representatives (http://www.house.gov/) and the Senate (http://www.senate.gov/) have a number of committees and subcommittees to "monitor on-going governmental operations, identify issues suitable for legislative review, gather and evaluate information; and recommend courses of action to their parent body." The committee structure "allows members of the legislature to develop specialized knowledge of the matters under their jurisdiction." According to the Senate Web site's information page describing the Senate Committee System (http://www.senate.gov/general/common/generic/about_com mittees.htm):

> First, [the committee or subcommittee] asks relevant ex-
> ecutive agencies for written comments on the measure.
> Second, it holds hearings to gather information and views
> from non-committee experts. At committee hearings,
> these witnesses summarize submitted statements and then
> respond to questions from the senators. Third, a committee
> meets to perfect the measure through amendments, and
> non-committee members sometimes attempt to influence
> the language. Fourth, when language is agreed upon, the
> committee sends the measure back to the full Senate, usu-
> ally along with a written report describing its purposes
> and provisions.

Government bureaucrats can be invited to attend a hearing and to answer questions, provide documents, and offer com-ments. If they refuse, they can be subpoenaed. Citizens who are experts in some relevant area can also be invited to attend and can be subpoenaed if they refuse. Experts can also volunteer to provide information about and insights into issues of interest. In general, a hearing is not just a fact-finding forum but also politi-cal theater, since the representatives and senators are, after all, politicians.

Theoretically, once drafted, the bill is sent to the appropri-ate subcommittee in the Senate or the House, where hearings about the topic may or may not be conducted. It is then sent on to the full committee with recommendations. Some legislation dies in subcommittee or committee. Some, however, is passed through the appropriate committee, again generally with recom-mendations; it then reaches the floor of the House or the Senate, where, after debate, it is voted on. If enough members vote yes, by the time it reaches this point, the versions in the House and the Senate may and probably do vary. The next step is a House-Senate conference, where these issues are resolved. If the revised bill wins approval of both houses of Congress, it is then passed along to the White House, where the president has the option of signing it, which means that it becomes the law of the land, or vetoing it, which means that the process stops or the bill is sent back to Congress to rework. This overview is accurate, but it oversimplifies the actual process, an explanation of which is outside the scope of this book.

The first federal law based on Bill 9743 is commonly referred to as the Animal Welfare Act (AWA). It became Public Law 89–544 (80 Stat. 350) when it was signed by President Lyndon Johnson on August 24, 1966.

Animal Welfare Act of 1966

The purpose of the Animal Welfare Act, commonly called the Research or Experimentation—Cats and Dogs Act of 1966, is to protect the owners of dogs and cats from the theft of such pets, to prevent the sale or use of stolen dogs or cats for the purpose of research or experimentation, and to establish humane standards for the treatment of dogs (*Canis familiaris*), cats (*Felis catus*), monkeys (nonhuman primates), guinea pigs, hamsters, and rabbits by animal dealers and medical research facilities. Animal dealers who transport animals over state lines are required to be licensed by and research facilities must be registered with the secretary of agriculture. Research facilities that receive funds from the federal government are required to follow the rules promulgated under the authority of the Act. There are minimum requirements with respect to housing, feeding, watering, sanitation, ventilation, shelter from extremes of weather and temperature, separation of species, and adequate veterinary care, as well as requirements for the humane handling, care, treatment, and transportation of animals by dealers and research facilities.

No dealer is allowed to sell or dispose of any dog or cat within five business days after acquisition of an animal. Dogs and cats must be marked for identification in some humane manner, and dealers and research facilities must make and maintain records of the sale and purchase of dogs and cats.

The Act does not authorize the secretary to promulgate rules, regulations, or orders for the handling, care, treatment, or inspections of animals during actual research or experimentation by a research facility as determined by such research. The Act describes civil and criminal procedures and penalties for violations of its provision.

Animal Welfare Act of 1970

The Animal Welfare Act of 1970 was signed by President Richard Nixon on December 24, 1970, and became Public Law 91–579 (84 Stat. 1560).

This Act amended the Animal Welfare Act to broaden the definition of "animal" to include any live or dead warm-blooded animal, and expanded its jurisdiction to organizations that do not engage in interstate transport. The rules do not apply to horses not used for research purposes or to other farm animals, such as livestock or poultry, that are used as food or fiber or for improving animal nutrition, breeding, management, or production efficiency or for improving the quality of food or fiber.

This Act requires persons or organizations that hold animals for exhibition and for sale as pets, excluding retail pet stores, to follow the rules promulgated under the authority of the Act. Exhibitors include carnivals, road shows, circuses, and zoos but do not include state or county fairs, livestock shows, rodeos, purebred dog or cat shows, and any other fairs or exhibitions that are intended to advance agricultural arts and sciences

The Act does not authorize the secretary to promulgate rules, regulations, or orders with regard to the design, outlines, guidelines, or performance of actual research or experimentation. However, each research facility must show that professionally acceptable standards governing the care, treatment, and use of animals during actual research or experimentation are being followed, including the appropriate use of anesthetic, analgesic, and tranquilizing drugs. The Act describes civil and criminal procedures and penalties for violations of its provisions.

Horse Protection Act of 1970

This act and its amendments are also administered by APHIS. The purpose of this Act was to prevent a painful practice, called scoring, used to accentuate a horse's gait. Scoring involves irritating the horse's forelegs with injections and applying chemicals or mechanical restraints. Tennessee walking horses and other high-stepping breeds are the most frequent victims of this abuse. The Act provides both civil and criminal penalties for violators.

Animal Welfare Act Amendment of 1976

The Animal Welfare Act Amendment of 1976 was signed by President Gerald Ford on April 22, 1976, and became Public Law 94–279 (90 Stat. 417).

This Act amended the Animal Welfare Act of 1970 to make it unlawful for any person to knowingly sell, buy, transport, or deliver to another person any dog or other animal for the purpose of having the dog or other animal participate in an animal-fighting venture or to sponsor or exhibit an animal in any animal-fighting venture. It does not include the use of one or more animals in hunting another animal or animals, such as waterfowl, birds, raccoons, or in fox hunting. It also prohibits the use of the U.S. Postal Service or any interstate instrumentality to promote or otherwise further an animal-fighting venture. The activities prohibited by the Act with respect to animal-fighting ventures involving live fowl are illegal only if the fight is to take place in a state where it would be illegal.

The Act also promulgated rules for the transport of animals by intermediate handlers (express companies, forwarders, and other persons or facilities that handle live-animal shipments) and carriers (airlines, railroads, motor carriers, shipping lines, or other enterprises engaged in the business of transporting any animals for hire). The rules provide minimum standards for the size of shipping containers, impose feed and water requirements, regulate the temperature and ventilation of the containers, and contain species-specific guidelines for the amount of rest to be provided for the animals.

The Act prohibits the transportation of any dog, cat, or other animal that is less than eight weeks old. A licensed veterinarian's certificate that the animal appears free of infectious disease or physical abnormality that would endanger the animal(s) or other animals or endanger human public health must be issued before an animal can be transported. The Act prohibits transportation of animals covered by the Act on a C.O.D. basis unless the consignor guarantees the round-trip fare, care, and handling charges for any animal not claimed within 48 hours. The Act includes under its provisions persons or organizations that merely negotiate the purchase of animals covered by the Act. Any person who grosses less than $500 from the sale of animals other than wild animals, dogs, and cats, as well as retail pet stores, except those stores that sell any animals to a research facility, an exhibitor, or a dealer, are excluded from the provisions of the Act. It extends the definition of the word "animal" as used in the Act to include all dogs, including dogs for hunting, security, or breeding purposes. The Act describes civil and criminal procedures and penalties for violations of its provisions.

Food Security Act of 1985

Two hearings were held as this bill was under consideration. One of the hearings, titled "Improved Standards for Laboratory

Animals," was conducted before the Senate Committee on Agriculture, Nutrition, and Forestry on July 20, 1983. The second was conducted on September 19, 1984 by the Subcommittee on Department Operations, Research, and Foreign Agriculture and was titled "Improved Standards for Laboratory Animals Act; and Enforcement of the Animal Welfare Act by the Animal and Plant Health Inspection Service." A variety of government bureaucrats and experts testified at these hearings, both for and against the bill. Other than the House Conference Report No. 99–447, titled "1985 Amendments, Joint Explanatory State of the Committee of Conference" (to accompany H.R. 2100, which is available online at http://www.animallaw.info/administrative/adush confrep99_447.htm), it is difficult to determine if there were any House and Senate floor debates or other actions, such as markups or other Conference Committee reports. Senator Dole tacked the bill onto the Food Security Act of 1985, which established the framework for the secretary of agriculture to administer agriculture and food programs for the years 1986–1990. It consisted of 18 titles dealing with dairy; wool and mohair; wheat and feed grains; cotton; rice; peanuts; soybeans; sugar, general commodity provisions; trade; conservation; credit; agricultural research, extension, and teaching; food stamp and related programs; marketing; and other miscellaneous matters. Title 17 of the bill consists of 19 subtitles that deal with: Processing, Inspecting, and Labeling; Agricultural Stabilization and Conservation Committees; National Agricultural Policy Commission Act of 1985; National Aquaculture Policy Improvement Act of 1985; Special Study and Pilot Project on Futures Trading; Animal Welfare; CCC Storage Contracts; Emergency Feed Program; Controlled Substances Production Control; Unleaded Fuel in Agricultural Machinery; Potato Advisory Commission; Viruses, Serums, Toxins, and Analogous Products; Federal Insecticide, Fungicide, and Rodenticide Act; Users Fees for Reports, Publications, and Software; Confidentiality of Information; Land Conveyance to Irwin County, Georgia; National Tree Seed Laboratory; Control of Grasshoppers and Mormon Crickets; and Study of a Strategic Ethanol Reserve

Senator Dole inserted the Animal Welfare Act into this long and complex bill, as indicated, just prior to the Senate adjournment for the 1985 Christmas holiday. The vote in the House for the Food Security Act of 1985, taken December 18, 1985, was 325 for and 39 against, and in the Senate the vote was 55 for and 38 against. The bill, commonly called the Improved Standards for Laboratory Animals Act, was signed into law on December 23, 1985, by President Ronald Reagan and became Public Law 99–198 (99 Stat. 1645).

These amendments are a significant departure from the original Animal Welfare Act and its earlier amendments, which all stopped at the laboratory doors and had no influence over the actual research. They fundamentally changed the way biomedical research is conducted. The new Act mandated the establishment of an Institutional Animal Care and Use Committee at each institution whose function would be to evaluate experimental protocols to determine if the protocols followed made the best use of the animals. The Committee could require changes if it found they were necessary.

Health Research Extension Act of 1985

The Health Research Extension Act of 1985 was signed into law by President Ronald Reagan and became Public Law 99–158. It provides guidelines for the National Institutes of Health and for scientists and clinicians who receive grants from the Institute. The Act establishes guidelines for the proper care of animals used in biomedical and behavioral research. It mandates the proper use of tranquilizers, analgesics, anesthetics, paralytics, and euthanasia, as well as appropriate pre- and postsurgical care of research animals. The Act also requires the formation of an animal care committee that essentially parallels the work of the Institutional Animal Care and Use Committee described in detail in chapter 6.

Food, Agriculture, Conservation, and Trade Act of 1990

The Food, Agriculture, Conservation, and Trade Act of 1990 was signed by President George H. W. Bush on November 28, 1990, and became Public Law 101–624, Section 2593, Protection of Pets.

The Act provides that every pound or shelter owned by the state, county, or city, every shelter that is under contract to a state, county, or city, and every private shelter established for the purpose of caring for animals, such as a humane society, must hold and care for any dog or cat that comes into its care for a period of not less than five days to enable that dog or cat to be recovered by its original owner or adopted by other individuals before it is sold to a dealer.

Animal Enterprise Protection Act of 1992

The Animal Enterprise Protection Act of 1992 was signed by President George H. W. Bush and became Public Law 102–346 (106 Stat. 928).

This Act amends Title 18 of the U.S. Code (Crimes and Criminal Procedure) by adding Section 43, Animal Enterprise Terrorism. This Act makes it a federal crime for anyone who crosses national or state borders and/or uses the mails to cause a physical disruption in the functioning of an animal enterprise by stealing, damaging, or causing the loss of property, including animals and records, that causes economic damage exceeding $10,000. An animal enterprise is defined as a commercial or academic enterprise that uses animals for food or fiber production, agriculture, research, or testing; a zoo, aquarium, circus, rodeo, or lawful competitive animal event; or a fair intended to advance agricultural arts and sciences. This Act mandates restitution in the form of the reasonable cost of repeating any experimentation that was interrupted or invalidated as a result of the offense and the loss of food production or farm income attributable to the offense. It also outlines the penalty for infractions. If the violators did not instill a reasonable fear of serious bodily injury or death and the offense resulted in no economic damage or injury, they are subject to a fine, imprisonment of not more than one year, or both. If no bodily injury occurred and the economic damage exceeded $10,000 but was less than $100,000, the punishment is a fine and imprisonment of five years or less. If the damage exceeds $100,000 or the violation resulted in serious bodily injury, the punishment is a fine and a prison term not exceeding 10 years. If the offense resulted in bodily injury or damages of $1 million, the punishment is a fine and a prison term not exceeding 20 years. If the offense resulted in the death of another individual, the violator will be imprisoned for life.

Farm Bill (2002)

Farm Bill 2002, Title 10, Miscellaneous Provisions, Section D, was signed into law on May 13, 2002, by President George W. Bush.

The Act excludes birds, mice of the genus *Mus*, and rats of the genus *Rattus* bred for research purposes, as well as horses not used for research purposes, from the definition of an "animal" in the Animal Welfare Act. It makes it a misdemeanor to ship a bird in interstate commerce for the purpose of fighting or to sponsor a fight using birds shipped via interstate commerce. The bill also requires the National Research Council to provide a report to Congress on the implications of including rats, mice, and birds within the definition of "animal" in the Animal Welfare Act.

Animal Fighting Prohibition Enforcement Act of 2007
This Act, signed into law by President Bush on May 3, 2007, makes it illegal to buy, sell, transport, or deliver into interstate or foreign commerce any sharp instrument meant to be attached to a bird's leg for use in an animal-fighting venture. It amends the federal criminal code to impose a fine and/or a prison term of up to three years for violating the provisions of the act.

The Guide for the Care and Use of Laboratory Animals
The Guide for the Care and Use of Laboratory Animals (which is available at http://www.nap.edu/openbook.php?record_id+5140 was published by the National Research Council, Commission of Life Sciences, Institute of Laboratory Animal Research, in 1996 (ISBN 0–309–05377–3). The *Guide* provides day-to-day methods for implementing the rules and regulations promulgated under the Animal Welfare Act and its amendments and under the Health Extension Act, which are published in the U.S. Code. The *Guide* has been published in French, Spanish, Chinese, Russian, Taiwanese, and Korean. An international workshop was held in Washington, DC, in 2003 to develop science-based guidelines for laboratory animal care, and these proceedings can be viewed online. It is likely that this information will be used to update the *Guide*. The National Academies Press also published *Guidelines for the Care and Use of Mammals in Neuroscience and Behavioral Research*, in 2003; the text can be viewed online at http://books.nap.edu/catalog.php?record_id=10732#toc.

Federal Regulations (Agricultural)
Background
Ruminants (dairy cows, cattle, and sheep) are the single largest source of methane emissions that result from human activity. Methane is a greenhouse gas that is produced during the normal digestive process of the animal.

Because of the concentration of animals in a CAFO, more than 1 billion tons of manure are produced in a year, which is about 130 times the amount of human waste produced in the same time period. AFO and CAFO ammonia emissions represent approximately half of all ammonia emissions. Manure also contains nitrogen, phosphorus, undigested organic matter, spilled feed, bedding/litter materials, pathogens, antibiotics, and odorous/volatile compounds, such as methane, carbon dioxide, hydrogen sulfide, and ammonia. It also tends to increase the concentration of trace elements such as arsenic and copper. Stored manure also draws insect pests and rats.

Federal legislation and rules for AFOs or CAFOs deal only with the handling of wastes. The Environmental Protection Agency (EPA) has estimated that approximately 70 percent of the pollution in U.S. rivers and streams comes from farms, especially intensive feeding operations. The 1972 Clean Water Act was designed "to restore and maintain the chemical, physical, and biological integrity of the Nation's waters." The EPA has promulgated rules for AFOs and especially CAFOs under the authority of this Act. Section 502 of the Act defines these operations as "point sources" for pollutants. It created a federal permit program, the National Pollutant Discharge Elimination System, which regulates the quantity and character of the discharge of pollutants into U.S. waters. These rules have been revised and updated several times, most recently in 2003. The goals of these rules seek to limit fish kills, nutrient loading, and offensive odors. It is not currently clear if manure is regulated under the Environmental Recovery, Compensation and Liability Act (commonly called the Superfund) or the Environmental Protection and Community Right-to-Know Act.

There is no federal legislation to deal with the treatment of animals in AFOs and CAFOs. Each state has developed CAFO statutes dealing with animal wastes, some of which are more stringent than the federal rules. These rules are quite technical and complex. They deal with how CAFOs obtain permits that allow them to operate, how and where they are allowed to release wastes, and the penalties for failure to follow these rules. Some states cover some agricultural animals in their anticruelty laws.

Humane Methods of Livestock Slaughter

The Humane Slaughter Act was sponsored by Senator Hubert Humphrey (D, Minnesota) and signed into law by President Dwight Eisenhower in 1958. This law, which is enforced by 700 inspectors of the Food Safety and Inspection Service of the U.S. Department of Agriculture, requires cattle, calves, horses, mules, sheep, swine, and other livestock to be rendered unconscious (i.e., insensible to pain) by a single blow or gunshot or an electrical, chemical or other means that is rapid and effective. An animal is considered unconscious if it fails to display a "righting reflex"; that is, it does not attempt to stand and right itself. The Act also allows slaughtering in accordance with the ritual requirements of the Jewish faith or any other religious faith where the animal is rendered unconscious by simultaneous and instantaneous severance of the carotid arteries with a sharp instrument.

The Act was updated in 1978 and gave U.S. Department of Agriculture (USDA) inspectors the authority to stop a slaughtering line when it observed cruelty until the cruelty was corrected. The USDA later withdrew this authority because of costs to the industry. If inspectors are not allowed to respond to cruelty, then it seems likely that even the minimal requirements of the Act are not being enforced. The Farm Bill of 2002 included a Resolution that the Humane Slaughter Act should be fully enforced, but it is not clear if this has caused a change in enforcement of the Act. There are efforts to develop methods for dealing with nonambulatory livestock, that is, animals that cannot walk to the slaughter station. It is likely that these animals are diseased or have been injured during transport or at the slaughterhouse. These animals are sometimes called "downer cows." Agriculture Secretary Ed Schafer, testifying before a Senate Appropriations subcommittee in February 2008, would not endorse an outright ban on the use of downer cows. This means that they still may be slaughtered and moved into the food chain.

The Humane Slaughter Act does not cover poultry, fish, rabbits, and other animals that are used for food; therefore, there are no rules covering their slaughter. The Act deals only with the last few minutes of an animal's life and does not focus on how the animals are treated while in the slaughterhouse.

The Act also does not cover the slaughter of horses. Horsemeat is considered a delicacy in France, Italy, Belgium, and Japan, and approximately 90,000 horses were slaughtered each year for human consumption. This includes both wild caught and domestic horses (e.g., ponies, retired show horses, family horses). In part because of controversy and bad publicity, three horse slaughter operations in the United States were closed in 2006. Horseflesh is also used in making pet food. The Wild Free-Roaming Horses and Burros Act (Public Law 92–195 [85 Stat. 649], see U.S.C. 1331) protects the included animals from capture, branding, harassment, or killing.

The Endangered Species Act of 1973 (Public Law 93–205 [87 Stat. 884]) and its amendments mandate that the secretary of the interior promulgate rules and regulations to protect threatened and endangered species of plants and animals. The Act does not deal directly with animal welfare except as it applies to these species.

United States—State and Local Regulations

In the United States, state, country and local governments have enacted animal welfare laws to prohibit cruelty to animals. The wording of the Texas statute (available at http://www.statutes.legis.state.tx.us/SOTWDocs/HS/htm/HS.821.36163.31446.htm) is fairly typical and can be found in Title 10 of "Health and Safety of Animals, Chapter 821, Treatment and Disposition of Animals, Subchapter A, Treatment of Animals" (http://www.statutes.legis.state.tx.us/Docs/HS/htm/HS.821.htm). The statute requires a peace officer or animal control officer of a county or city who believes that an animal has been or is being mistreated to apply to a court or magistrate to obtain a warrant to seize the animal. When executing the warrant, the officer causes the animal to be impounded and gives written notice to the owner for the time and place of a hearing.

The wording of the San Antonio anticruelty ordinance is fairly typical and can be found at "Code of Ordinances of City of San Antonio, Chapter 5, Animals and Fowl, Article 1 In General, Sec. 5-4. Cruelty to Animals." This ordinance states that it shall be unlawful for an owner of an animal to beat, cruelly treat, overload or otherwise abuse an animal, fail to provide that animal with humane care and treatment, access to an adequate supply of fresh water, and appropriate veterinary care when needed to prevent suffering.

Most local ordinances also provide a humane sanctuary or shelter for abandoned or unwanted animals. The wording of the San Antonio ordinance (http://www.municode.com/resources/gateway.asp?pid=11508&sid=43) is fairly typical and can be found at "Code of Ordinances of City of San Antonio, Chapter 5, Animals & Fowl, Article 1, In General, Sec. 5–2 Animal Care Services Facility; Erection, Maintenance; Care of Animals, Euthanasia Service." This ordinance requires the city to maintain a sanitary facility to house all animals seized, impounded, or surrounded and to provide adequate care and feeding.

Unfortunately, the number of unwanted pets (mostly cats and dogs, but also birds, amphibians, reptiles, and other exotic animals) taken into shelters generally exceeds the numbers that are adopted out, so the excess are "put to sleep" or "put down," which are euphemisms for euthanasia or being killed. The precise number of animals that are killed is controversial, but estimates put it at 6 to 8 million cats and dogs per year. The method of euthanasia varies from place to place. Many of these shelters require pets that are adopted to be spayed or neutered. Local authorities also have licensing laws to help control diseases such as rabies.

One of the controversial aspects of some local ordinances is commonly called "pound seizure." It provides that "surplus" cats or dogs that might be euthanized can be released or sold to research, testing, or educational institutions. Fourteen states (Connecticut, Delaware, Hawaii, Illinois, Maine, Maryland, Massachusetts, New Hampshire, New Jersey, New York, Pennsylvania, Rhode Island, Vermont, and West Virginia) have laws banning pound seizures, while three states (Minnesota, Oklahoma, and Utah) require pounds to release animals to research and educational institutions (American Anti-Vivisection Society 2009). The remaining states do not have specific laws dealing with this issue, so it is left to each county or city to determine whether its shelters will release cats and dogs to research or educational institutions. The San Antonio ordinance mentioned earlier prohibits pound seizures.

England

As indicated earlier, the first animal welfare act enacted was the Act to Prevent Cruel and Improper Treatment of Cattle of 1822. This Act was amended by the Cruelty to Animals Act of 1835 to include as "cattle" bulls, bears, dogs, and sheep. The Act also prohibited bear baiting and cockfighting. The Cruelty to Animals Act of 1849 (An Act for the More Effectual Prevention of Cruelty to Animals) repealed the 1822 and 1835 Acts and penalties for beating, ill-treating, overdriving, abusing, and torturing animals.

The Cruelty to Animal Act of 1876, which applies to vertebrate animals, amended the 1849 Act and set up a licensing system for animal experimentation administered by the secretary of state. The application for a license must be signed by the president of the Royal Society, the Royal Society of Edinburgh, the Royal Irish Academy, the Royal College of Surgeons, the Royal College of Physicians, the General Medical Council, the Faculty of Physicians and Surgeons of Glasgow, or a professor of physiology, medicine, anatomy, medical jurisprudence, material media, or surgery in a university. The Act required that the research be designed to further knowledge of physiology or knowledge useful for saving or prolonging life or alleviating suffering. The Act required that test animals be anaesthetized, except where insensibility would frustrate the object of the experiment. Animals could be used for research only once. Paralytics, such as curare, are not considered anesthetics, as they do not prevent painful sensations. The Act also provides that animals must be euthanized at the end of the experiment. A person who takes part in an experiment likely to cause pain and who lacks the appropriate license is fined 50 pounds for the first offense; any second or succeeding offense is punishable by a fine of 100 pounds or imprisonment for three months or less.

The Animal (Scientific Procedures) Act of 1986 extended the meaning of protected animal to include all living vertebrates other than humans. Developing vertebrates are covered after the first half of gestation. This Act gives the secretary of state the right to extend protection to invertebrates. Animals are considered alive until there is permanent cessation of circulation or destruction of the brain. A regulated procedure is defined as a scientific procedure that may cause the animal pain, suffering, distress, or lasting harm and includes the administration of an anesthetic or analgesic, decerebration, or any other method for rendering an animal insentient. All experiments are required to be conducted under general or local anesthetics. If anesthesia is not possible, analgesics and other methods should be used to ensure as far as possible that pain, suffering, distress, or harm are limited and that the animals are not subjected to severe pain, distress, or suffering.

The person who performs a regulated procedure, the project under which the procedure is performed, and the organization in which the procedure is performed must be licensed by the secretary of state. The project license will be granted if the secretary determines that the research is intended to further the prevention, diagnosis, or treatment of disease, ill health, or abnormality or their effects in humans, animals, or plants. Licenses are also granted for the assessment, detection, regulation, or modification of physiological conditions in humans, animals, or plants, as well as for the protection of the natural environment in the interests of the health and welfare of humans or animals. Licenses can also be granted for the advancement of knowledge of biological or behavioral sciences, for education or training in primary or secondary schools, for forensic inquiries, and for breeding animals for experimental or other scientific uses. The secretary will not grant a license unless the project cannot be satisfactorily achieved without the use of protected animals. The secretary will also not grant a license for the use of cats, dogs, primates, horses, or related animals unless he is satisfied that no other species is suitable for the program. Institutions are required to have a certificate issued by the secretary of state and must specify the person responsible for the day-to-day care of the animals and a veterinary surgeon or other suitably qualified person to provide advice on the health and welfare of the animals. At the conclusion of the procedures allowed by the license, the animal is euthanized by the appropriate method. These include exposure to overdose of an anesthetic, exposure to carbon dioxide in rising concentration, or dislocation of the neck or concussion of the brain by striking the cranium. The use of neuromuscular blocking agents is prohibited unless expressly authorized by the license, and they cannot be used instead of an anesthetic.

This Act established an Animal Procedures Committee, which consists of a chair and at least 12 members appointed by the secretary. One of the members must be a barrister, solicitor, or advocate. At least half of the members must hold or have held within the past six years any license under the Act. Two-thirds of the committee must have full registration as a medical practitioner or veterinary surgeon. No one may serve on the Committee for more than four years. The Committee advises the secretary on matters concerned with the Act and its functions. The secretary issues codes of practice related to the care of protected animals. The Act mandates that no endangered species will be used or any protected animal taken from the wild and imposes civil and criminal penalties for those who violate its provision.

The Animal Welfare Act of 2006 brings together and updates legislation to promote the welfare of vertebrate animals, except for those in the wild. The Act aligns welfare standards for farm and nonfarm animals that were formulated in the early part of the 20th century and modified to incorporate scientific findings as they occur.

References

Act to Prevent Cruel and Improper Treatment of Cattle. http://www.animalrightshistory.org/library/mar-richard-martin/1822-britian-cattle.htm. Accessed April 16, 2009.

American Anti-Vivisection Society. http://www.aavs.org/ campPoundSeizureState.html. Accessed April 16, 2009.

American Association for the Advancement of Science. http://www. aaas.org. Accessed April 16, 2009.

American Humane Association. http://www.americanhumane.org/. Accessed April 16, 2009.

Americans for Medical Progress. www.amprogress.org/. Accessed April 16, 2009.

American Society for the Prevention of Cruelty to Animals. http:// www2.aspca.org/. Accessed April 16, 2009.

Animal Defense Militia. http://www.animaldefense.org. Accessed April 16, 2009.

Animal Liberation Front. http://www.animalliberationfront.com/ ALFront/lab.htm. Accessed April 16, 2009.

Animal (Scientific Procedures) Act of 1986. http://www.archive. official-documents.co.uk/document/hoc/321/321-xa.htm. Accessed April 16, 2009.

Animal Welfare Act of 2006. http://www.animallaw.info/nonus/statutes/ stat_pdf/UKAnimalWelfareAct2006.pdf. Accessed August 20, 2009.

Animal Welfare Institute. 2009. http://dynamodata.fdncenter.org/990_ pdf_archive/135/135655952/135655952_200706_990.pdf. Accessed April 16, 2009.

Bernard, C. 1957. *An Introduction to the Study of Experimental Medicine.* Trans. H. C. Greene. New York: Dover.

British Union for the Abolition of Vivisection. http://www.buav.org/. Accessed April 16, 2009.

Cruelty to Animal Act of 1876. http://web.archive.org/ web/20061214034848/; http://homepage.tinet.ie/~pnowlan/ Chapter-77.htm. Accessed April 16, 2009.

European Coalition to End Animal Experiments. http://www.eceae. org/. Accessed April 16, 2009.

Foundation for Biomedical Research. http://www.fbresearch.org/. Accessed April 16, 2009.

Jamison, W. V., and W. M. Lunch. 1992. "Rights of Animals, Perceptions of Science, and Political Activism: Profile of American Animal Rights Activists." *Science, Technology, & Human Values* 17(4): 438–58.

Massachusetts Society for the Prevention of Cruelty to Animals. http:// www.mspca.org. Accessed April 16, 2009.

National Antivivisectionists Society. http://www.navs.org. Accessed April 16, 2009.

National Association for Biomedical Research. http://www.nabr.org. Accessed April 16, 2009.

National Institutes of Health. http://www.nih.gov/. Accessed April 16, 2009.

National Research Foundation. http://www.nsf.gov/. Accessed April 16, 2009.

New York Times. 1989, January 14.

Nicoll, C. S., and Russell, S. M. 1991. "Mozart, Alexander the Great, and the Animal Rights/Liberation Philosophy." *Federation of the American Society of Experimental Biology Journal* 5 (14): 2008–2892. http://www.fasebj.org/cgi/reprint/5/14/2888. Accessed April 16, 2009.

Organization for Economic Cooperation and Development. http://www.oecd.org/home. Accessed April 16, 2009.

People for the Ethical Treatment of Animals. http://www.peta.org; http://dynamodata.fdncenter.org/990_pdf_archive/521/521218336/52 1218336_200607_990.pdf. Accessed April 16, 2009.

Royal Society for the Prevention of Cruelty to Animals. http://www.rspca.org.uk/. Accessed April 16, 2009.Science-Based Guidelines for Laboratory Animal Care. Available at: http://www.nap.edu/openbook.php?isbn=0309093023. Accessed April 16, 2009.

Society for Neuroscience. http://www.sfn.org. Accessed April 16, 2009.

States United for Biomedical Research. http://www.statesforbiomed.org/. Accessed April 16, 2009.

Vogue Magazine September, 1989.

Washingtonian Magazine August, 1986.

4

Chronology

This chronology provides a historical overview of the relationship between humans and animals. Since animal activists focus much of their attention on the use of animals in education, research, and testing, it highlights the major events in the history of science as they relate to animal use, such as the formation of organizations related to animals.

The Nobel Prize, generally regarded as the most prestigious award a scientist can receive, was instituted by Alfred Nobel, the inventor of high explosives, and the first Nobel Prize for physiology and medicine was awarded in 1901. Winners of the Nobel Prize are indicated by a single asterisk (*); many of them used animals in their research.

John D. MacArthur, who owned Bankers Life and Casualty and other businesses, left 92 percent of his estate, valued at more than $1 billion, to fund the John D. and Catherine T. MacArthur Foundation. Fellowships (commonly called Genius Awards), first granted in 1981, are given to between 20 and 40 citizens of the United States, of any age and working in any field, who "show exceptional merit and promise for continued and creative work." Each fellow is awarded $500,000 a year for five years, with no strings attached. Winners of the MacArthur Award who have utilized animals in their research are indicated by two asterisks (**).

Chronology

10000–7000 B.C.E.	The dog is domesticated in Mesopotamia; goats and sheep are domesticated in Persia; the pig and

10000–7000 B.C.E. *(cont.)*	water buffalo are domesticated in eastern Asia; chickens are domesticated in southern Asia.
5000 B.C.E.	Horses are domesticated in Ukraine.
3000 B.C.E.	Donkeys and mules are domesticated in Israel, camels in Iran, and elephants in India.
2950 B.C.E.	Imhotep, an Egyptian physician and architect, is the first scientist whose name has come down to us. He is also the only scientist to ever become a god.
2500 B.C.E.	Cats are domesticated in Egypt.
520 B.C.E.	Anaximander introduces the idea of evolution.
500 B.C.E.	Alcmaeon dissects a human cadaver for scientific purposes.
400 B.C.E.	Hippocrates develops the ethical oath named after him.
323 B.C.E.	Aristotle is considered to be the father of the life sciences, especially embryology; he observes and describes the development of embryos in different species. He is the first to engage in large-scale classification of plants and animals. He introduces the inductive-deductive method of reasoning.
40 C.E.	Pedanius Dioscorides publishes the *De Materia Medica*, which describes the medicinal properties of herbs.
159	Galen, a Greek medical scientist, is one of the first scientists to perform experiments on living animals.
1140	Roger II, a Norman king, decrees that only physicians with a license from the government can practice medicine.

1193   Albertus Magnus describes his dissection of animals.

1620   Bacon publishes *Novum Organum*, in which he recommends induction and experimentation as the basis of the scientific method.

1621   Fabricius's *De Formatione Ovi et Pulli* (On the Formation of the Egg and the Chick) is published.

1628   Harvey publishes *Exercitatio Anatomica de Motu Cordis et Sanguinis in Animalibus* (On the Motion of the Heart and Blood in Animals).

1637   Descartes publishes *Discours de la Méthode pour Bien Conduire la Raison et Chercher la Vérité dans les Sciences* (Discourse on the Method of Rightly Conducting Reason and Seeking Truth in the Sciences), in which he argues for the deductive method in science. Descartes, a mechanist, believes that lower animals lack a pineal gland, which he believes serves as a channel and valve to regulate the flow of thought. Therefore, he maintains, lower animals are mere living machines.

1651   Harvey publishes *Exercitationes de Generatione Animalium* (Experiments Concerning Animal Generation), which describes organ differentiation in the developing embryo.

1667   Robert Boyle demonstrates that an animal can be kept alive by artificial respiration.

1676   Nehemiah Grew coins the term "comparative anatomy."

1683   Thomas Tryon publishes *The Way To Health, Long Life and Happiness*, which is the first book in the English language to use the term "rights" in regard to animals.

1735–1737   Carl Linnaeus publishes *Systema Naturae*, in which he describes the classification of animals, and

1735–1737 (*cont.*)	*Genera Plantorum,* which introduces the classification of plants that is used to this day.
1747	Albrect von Haller publishes *Primae Lineae Physiologiae,* the first textbook of physiology.
1761	The first school of veterinary medicine is founded at Lyons, France.
1766	Albrecht von Haller, the father of modern experimental neurology, is the first to show that nerves stimulate muscles.
1775	Sir Percival Potts discovers that environmental factors can cause cancer.
1779	Jeremy Bentham, a utilitarian philosopher, publishes *An Introduction to the Principles of Morals and Legislation,* in which he writes of animals, "The question is not, can they reason? Nor can they talk? But, can they suffer?" This statement becomes the battle cry of both the Victorian and the modern animal protection movements.
1790	Luigi Galvani determines the effects of electrical stimulation on frog legs.
	Antoine Lavoisier experiments on the relationship between maintenance and generation of body heat and oxygen in the air.
1796	Edward Jenner performs the first inoculation against smallpox. This is the beginning of the development of vaccines that prevent disease.
1817	Heinz Christina Pander discovers the three different layers that form in the early development of the chick embryo.
1822	An Act to Prevent Cruel and Improper Treatment of Cattle (a.k.a Martin's Act) is passed by Parliament and becomes the first law against cruelty to

animals. It seeks to prevent cruel and improper treatment of horses, mares, geldings, mules, asses, oxen, cows, heifers, steers, sheep, and cattle. It does not cover dogs, cats, other mammals, or birds.

1824   Henry Hill Hickman uses carbon dioxide as a general anesthetic in an animal.

The Society for the Prevention of Cruelty to Animals is founded in London by Richard Martin with the help of Sir Samuel Romilly and Sir William Wilberforce.

1834   If the drugs in common use were to be, in the words of Dr. Oliver Wendell Holmes, "sunk to the bottom of the sea, it would be all the better for mankind—and all the worse for the fishes."

1835   Parliament amends the 1822 Cruelty to Animals Act to include bulls, bears, dogs, and sheep.

Princess Victoria extends patronage to the Society for the Prevention of Cruelty to Animals, and it becomes the Royal Society for the Prevention of Cruelty to Animals.

1839   Jan Evangelista Purkinje, a Czech anatomist, becomes the director of the world's first Department of Physiology, at the University of Breslau in Prussia.

1843   Sir David Ferrier uses the brains of living primates and other animals to locate motor and sensory regions in the brain and to map them.

1849   The Cruelty to Animals Act of 1849 (An Act for the More Effectual Prevention of Cruelty to Animals) repeals the 1822 and 1835 Acts and provides penalties for ill-treating, overdriving, abusing, and torturing animals.

1852   Hermann von Helmholtz determines the speed of transmission of a nerve impulse in a frog's nerve cell.

1856	Carl Ludwig is the first to keep animal organs alive outside the body.
1859	Charles Darwin publishes *On the Origin of Species.*
1863	Wilhelm Wundt publishes *Lectures on the Minds of Men and Animals.*
	The National Academy of Science is founded in the United States.
1865	Claude Bernard publishes *Introduction à la médicine expérimentale* (An Introduction to Experimental Medicine).
1866	Gregor Mendel publishes his discoveries in genetics using peas (*Pisum sativum*) in the *Proceedings of the Natural History Society of Brunn,* a relatively obscure scientific journal. He describes the law of segregation and the law of independent assortment.
	The American Society for the Prevention of Cruelty to Animals is founded in New York City by Henry Bergh, and the first state charter for an animal protection society is granted in New York in the same year.
1866–69	Boston, Philadelphia, and San Francisco incorporate humane societies.
1872	Charles Darwin publishes *The Expression of the Emotions in Man and Animals,* in which he argues that the similarity of expression of emotions in humans and in animals argues for the evolution of humans from lower forms of life.
1875	The Society for the Protection of Animals Liable to Vivisection is founded by Frances Power Cobbe in England.
1876	The Cruelty to Animals Act of 1876 amends the Cruelty to Animals Act of 1849 and sets up a

licensing system, administered by the secretary of state, for those who wish to engage in animal experimentation.

1877   The American Humane Association is founded by representatives of 27 humane organizations from 10 states.

1878   The *Home Chronicler*, a publication of one of the London antivivisectionist societies, publishes a list of marginal seats in the House of Commons held by members who voted against the bill to abolish vivisection.

1879   Louis Pasteur discovers that a weakened cholera organism fails to cause the disease in chickens and that chickens infected with the weakened organism are immune to the disease.

1880   Sir William Pulteney proposes a bill to ban bull baiting. It is defeated in the House of Commons.

1881   Louis Pasteur produces the first artificially produced vaccine by heating a preparation of anthrax germs to weaken them and then injecting them into sheep. Sheep treated in this manner fail to develop anthrax.

1882   The Association for the Advancement of Medicine by Research is founded.

1883   The first veterinary school in the United States is founded at the University of Pennsylvania.

The American Anti-Vivisection Society is founded in Jenkinton, Pennsylvania, by Caroline Earle White and Mary Frances Lovell.

1887   Wolfgang Kohler, one of the founders of the Gestalt school of psychology, studies chimpanzee problem-solving abilities.

1889   Ivan Petrovich Pavlov demonstrates classical conditioning in dogs.

Oskar Minkowski and Joseph von Mering discover that the pancreas supplies a hormone (insulin) that is essential for normal glucose metabolism by removing the pancreas of dogs and noting the results.

The American Humane Education is founded.

1892   The American Psychological Association is founded.

1898   The British Union for the Abolition of Vivisection is founded by Frances Power Cobb to protest the use of dogs in vivisection.

1900   Mendel's work on the basic laws of heredity are "rediscovered" by Hugo de Vriet, Carl Correns, and possibly by Erich von Tschermak.

1901   The Public Health and Marine Hospital Service is founded.

Emil von Behring receives the first Nobel Prize for Physiology or Medicine for his work using rats, rabbits, guinea pigs, cows, and horses in the development of diphtheria antiserum and for ascertaining its usefulness.*

1902   Ronald Ross uses pigeons and other birds to study how malaria enters the organism. His work is the foundation for our ability to combat the disease.*

1904   Ivan Petrovich Pavlov receives the Nobel Prize for his work on the physiology of digestion. His work on conditioned reflexes, which made him famous, is an offshoot of this work.*

1905   Robert Koch uses cow and sheep in the study of the pathogenesis of tuberculosis.*

1906   Representative James McMillan introduces a bill into Congress to control vivisection in Washington, DC The bill never comes to a vote.

Neuroanatomists Camillio Golgi and Santiago y Cajal use mice, rabbits, cats, dogs, and a variety of birds and reptiles to study the structure of the nervous system.*

1907   Alphonse Laveran uses cows, horses, mice, guinea pigs, and birds to demonstrate that protozoa cause disease.*

Ross Granville Harrison demonstrates the in vitro growth of living animal tissues.

1908   Paul Ehrlich and Ilya Metchnikov use fish, birds, and guinea pigs in the study of immune reactions and phagocytes (cells that engulf other cells).*

1910   Albrecht Kossel uses rats, guinea pigs, and birds to study proteins and nucleic acids.*

1912   The Public Health and Marine Hospital Service's name is changed to the Public Health Service.

Alexis Carrel uses dogs to study the rejoining of severed blood vessels, which is the first step in organ transplantation.*

1913   Charles Richet uses dogs and rabbits to study the mechanism of anaphylaxis.*

John Watson publishes his first paper on behaviorism.

1914   Joseph Goldberger of the Public Health Service begins a study of pellagra.

1916   The National Research Council is formed.

1919   Jules Bordet uses rabbits, guinea pigs, and horses to study the function of white blood cells.*

1923   Frederick Banting and John MacLeod use dogs, rabbits, and fish in the study of insulin and the mechanism of diabetes.*

Otto Warburg develops a method for studying respiration in thin slices of tissue.

1924   Willem Einthoven develops the electrocardiograph, using dogs.*

1925   R. A. Fisher publishes *Statistical Methods for Research Workers*, and Alfred J. Lotka publishes *Elements of Physical Biology*, which contains simple mathematical models of biological phenomena.

The Scopes "monkey trial" is held in Dayton, Tennessee; John Scopes, a high school teacher, is prosecuted for teaching evolution.

1926   Johannes Andreas Grib Fibiger demonstrates that the nematode *Spiroptera carcinoma* causes cancer in rats and mice.* (It is discovered later that this specific organism does not cause cancer.)

George Richards Minot, William P. Murphy, and George H. Whipple establish the use of liver as a successful treatment for anemia; the treatment is based on work in dogs.*

1927   Thomas Hunt Morgan publishes *Experimental Embryology*.

Ivan Pavlov publishes *Conditioned Reflexes*.

Henry Copley Green translates Claude Bernard's *Introduction a la médicine expérimentale* into English.

1928   Alexander Fleming discovers penicillin in molds. The clinical use of penicillin starts only after Howard Florey and Ernst Boris Chain learn how to manufacture it in quantity and test its curative effects in mice in the 1940s. The chemical structure of penicillin is studied by x-ray diffraction, and it is so complex that an electronic computer is needed to work out the tedious mathematics involved.*

1929   Christian Eijkman and Frederick Gowland Hopkins use rats, mice, and chickens to discover the importance of vitamins.*

The National Anti-Vivisection Society is founded in Chicago by Clarence E. Richards.

Walter Vogt publishes the first 'fate map' of a vertebrate embryo.

Joseph Henry Woodger publishes *Biological Principles,* an analysis of theoretical biology.

1930   The Laboratory of Hygiene is enlarged and reorganized as National Institute of Health is formed.

1931   Ernest William Goodpasture demonstrates that viruses can be grown in eggs. This is the first step in the development of vaccines for viral diseases.

1932   Charles Scott Sherrington and Edgar Douglas Adrian use frogs, dogs, and cats to study the functions of nerves.*

1933   Thomas Hunt Morgan uses fruit flies to demonstrate the role of chromosomes in heredity.*

1935   Hans Spemann uses frogs to discover the "organizer effect," a process in which parts of an embryo direct the development of groups of cells, tissues, and organs.*

Konrad Lorenz describes the social life of animals.

The first commercial electron microscope becomes available.

1936	Henry Dale and Otto Loewi use cats, frogs, birds, and reptiles to study the chemical transmission of nerve impulses.*
	Alexis Carrel and Charles Lindbergh develop an artificial heart that is used during cardiac surgery.
1938	The Federal Food, Drug, and Cosmetic Act (Public Law 75–717 [52 Stat. 1040]) is signed into law by Franklin D. Roosevelt.
	B. F. Skinner publishes *The Behavior of Organisms.*
1939	Gerhardt Domagk, using mice and rabbits, discovers the antibacterial effects of protosil, the first sulfa drug.*
1940	Karl Landsteiner discovers the Rhesus factor in human blood.
1943	Selman Waksman uses guinea pigs to demonstrate the antibacterial effects of streptomycin, an antibiotic that is effective against gram-negative bacteria.
1944	Joseph Erlanger and Herbert Spencer Gasser use frogs and cats to demonstrate the role of nerve cells.*
1945	Alexander Fleming, Howard Walter Florey, and Ernst Brois Chain use mice to demonstrate that penicillin can be used against infectious disease.*
1946	Hermann Joseph Muller, using fruit flies, demonstrates that x-rays can produce mutations.*
	The Office of Naval Research is formed.
1948	The National Institutes of Health is created.
	Morris Animal Foundation is founded.
1949	The American Association for Laboratory Animal Science is founded.

Kenneth S. Cole and George Marmont invent the voltage "clamp" for controlling cell membrane potential.

Walter Rudolf Hess uses cats in his studies of the midbrain.*

1950   Edward Calvin Kendall, Tadeus Reichstein, and Philip Showalter Hench use rats to discover the structure and biological effects of hormones secreted by the adrenal cortex.*

The National Science Foundation is founded.

1951   The Animal Welfare Institute is founded in New York City by Christine Stevens.

1952   Selman Abraham Wakesman uses mice, guinea pigs, and chickens to demonstrate the effectiveness for streptomycin in treating tuberculosis.*

The Institute of Laboratory Animal Resources is founded.

Alan Lloyd Hodgkin and Andrew Huxley, using neurons from squid and crab, formulate the theory of excitation of nerves, which is based on changes in sodium and potassium ions.

A polio epidemic affects more than 47,000 people in the United States.

Jonas Salk develops the killed-virus vaccine against polio. It comes into wide use in 1954.

1953   Evarts Graham and Ernest L. Wydner demonstrate that tar from tobacco smoke cause cancer in mice.

1954   The Humane Society of the United States is founded.

John Franklin Enders, Thomas Huckle Weller, and Frederick Chapman Robbins discover that the poliomyelitis viruses will grow in cultures of tissues from animals.*

1955   Axel Hugo Theodor Theorell uses horses to dis-
            cover and understand the mode of action of
            oxidative enzymes.*

1957   Daniel Bovet uses rabbits and dogs to discover an-
            tihistamines that are used in allergy medications.*

            The Society for Animal Protective Legislation is
            founded in New York City by Christine Stevens.

            Albert Sabin develops the live, weakened virus
            vaccine for polio.

1958   The Humane Slaughter Act is signed into law by
            President Dwight Eisenhower.

1959   The National Trappers Association is founded.

1961   Georg von Bekesy uses guinea pigs and frogs to
            discover how the inner ear works.*

1962   The Harris-Kefauver Amendment to the Federal
            Pure Food, Drug, and Cosmetics Act is signed into
            law. This Amendment requires extensive pharma-
            cological and toxicological research before a drug
            could be tested in humans.

1963   John Carew Eccles, Alan Lloyd Hodgkin, and Andrew
            Fielding Huxley use squid to understand the mecha-
            nism of excitation and inhibition of nerve cells.*

            The *Guide for the Care and Use of Laboratory Animals* is
            published, and the U.S. Public Health Service begins
            to require all recipients to adhere to its guidelines.

1964   Konrad Bloch and Feodor Lynen use rats to deter-
            mine the mechanism and regulation of cholesterol
            and fatty acid metabolism.*

1965   An article about a five-year-old Dalmatian named
            Pepper who had been stolen from her home ap-
            pears in *Sports Illustrated* and is one of the events

that causes Representative Joseph Resnick to introduce the bill that ultimately becomes the Animal Welfare Act of 1966.

The American Association for the Accreditation of Laboratory Animal Care is founded.

Harry Harlow demonstrates that monkeys that are raised in isolation show emotional impairment for the rest of their lives.

1966   A cover story of *Life* magazine titled "A Concentration Camp for Dogs" causes a stir and creates a demand for protection for pets.

The Animal Welfare Act of 1966 (commonly referred to as the Research or Experimentation—Cats and Dogs Act of 1966) (Public Law 89–544 [80 Stat. 350]) is signed into law by President Lyndon Johnson.

1967   Ragnar Granit, Haldan Keffer Hartline, and George Wald use rats, guinea pigs, cats, frogs, and crustaceans to discover the primary physiological and chemical processes of the eye.*

1968   Robert W. Holley, Har Gobind Khorana, and Marshcall W. Nirenberg use rats, guinea pigs, and frogs to determine how the genetic code is involved in protein synthesis.*

The Humane Slaughter Act is amended.

1970   Bernard Katz, Ulf von Euler, and Julius Axelrod discover the mechanism of storage, release, and inactivation of neurotransmitters, using mice, rats, rabbits, cats, dogs, and cows.*

The Animal Welfare Act of 1970 (Public Law 91—579 [84 Stat. 1560]) is signed into law by President Richard Nixon.

The Horse Protection Act of 1970 is signed into law by President Nixon.

1972   The Animal and Plant Health Inspection is established in the U.S. Department of Agriculture and is charged with enforcement of the Animal Welfare Act of 1966 and its amendments.

The Clean Water Act is signed into law. This is one of the federal laws that regulates wastes from concentrated animal feeding operations.

1973   Karl von Frisch studies the social behavior of honeybees, and Konrad Lozenz and Nikolass Tinbergen study the social behavior of birds.*

The Endangered Species Act of 1973 (Public Law 93–205 [87 Stat. 884]) is signed into law.

1975   Peter Singer publishes *Animal Liberation: A New Ethics for Our Treatment of Animals.*

The National Congress of Animal Trainers and Breeders is founded.

1976   Baruch S. Slumberg discovers the hepatitis B virus and develops a diagnostic test and vaccine for it.

D. Carleton Gajdusek describes the first prion disease, kuku.*

The Animal Welfare Act Amendments of 1976 (Public Law 94–279 [90 Stat. 417]) is signed into law by President Gerald Ford.

1977   Roger Guillemin and Andrew V. Schally discover the role and effects of peptide(small chains of amino acids) hormone production of the brain using mice, rats, hamsters, guinea pigs, and sheep.*

1978   The Humane Slaughter Act is amended.

1979   Peter Singer publishes *Practical Ethics.*

Allan M. Cormack and Godfrey N. Hounsfield develop computer-assisted tomography (CAT) scans, which allow three-dimensional images of the body. They initially use pigs in their research.*

The National Association for Biomedical Research is founded by Francine Trull in Washington, DC.

The Animal Liberation Front first appears in England and claims responsibility for a break-in at an animal research facility.

1980   The People for the Ethical Treatment of Animals is founded in Norfolk, Virginia, by Ingrid Newkirk and Alex Pacheco.

Raymond Gillespie Frey publishes *Interests and Rights: The Case against Animals*, in which he argues that animals do not have rights.

1981   The Foundation for Biomedical Research is founded by Francine Trull in Washington, DC.

The disease AIDS is officially recognized.

Roger W. Sperry works on the functional specializations of the cerebral hemispheres using monkeys, and David H. Hubel and Torsten N. Wiesel study how information processing occurs in the visual system in cats.*

1982   Sune K. Bergstrom, Bengt L. Samuelsson, and John R. Vance, using rabbits, guinea pigs, and sheep, discover prostaglandins, which influence blood pressure, body temperature, and allergic reactions.*

1983   David Feltman studies the relationship between the nervous and the immune systems and the role of neurotransmitters in cancer.**

Raymond Gillespie Frey, a utilitarian, like Jeremy Bentham and Peter Singer, rejects the claims of moral vegetarianism in *Rights, Killing, and Suffering: Moral Vegetarianism and Applied Ethics.*

1983 (*cont.*)   Tom Regan publishes *The Case for Animal Rights.*

Scientists demonstrate that a genetically engineered yeast can protect chimpanzees from hepatitis B.

1984   George Archibald pioneers methods for saving cranes, which are on the verge of extinction.**

Arnold Mandell applies nonlinear dynamics to biological systems.**

Carl Woese revises the phylogenic tree to include archaea, a single-cell microorganism.**

Roger Payne discovers whale songs and is active in attempts to end commercial whaling.**

Arthur Winfree applies mathematical modeling to biological phenomena.**

The Laboratory Animal Management Association is founded.

1985   George Oster studies the basic physics and chemistry of protein motors, which allow single-cell organisms to move.**

The Food Security Act of 1985—Subtitle F, Animal Welfare (Public Law 99–198 [99 Stat. 1645]) is signed into law by President Ronald Reagan. This law causes a major change in the way biomedical and psychological research in animals is conducted.

The Health Research Extension Act of 1985 is signed into law by President Reagan.

Incurably Ill for Animal Research is founded.

The National Association for Biomedical Research is founded.

The Fur Farm Animal Welfare Coalition is founded.

1986   Rita Levi-Montalcini and Stanley Cohen discover nerve growth factors in mice, chickens, and other animals.*

Michael A. Fox publishes *The Case for Animal Experimentation: An Evolutionary and Ethical Perspective.*

Robert Shapley gains recognition for studying visual processing in cats and monkeys.**

Parliament passes the Animal (Scientific Procedures) Act of 1986, which extends the term "protected animal" to cover all living vertebrates and which provides rules and regulations for conducting animal research.

1987   Ira Herskowitz studies cell function and gene regulation in yeast.**

Eric Lander studies the relationship between complex genetic systems and disorders like cancer and diabetes.**

Roger Morris Sapolsky studies the relationship between stress and neural degeneration.**

Jon Seger studies the evolutionary genetics of whales and vertebrate smell receptors.**

Richard Wrangham studies chimpanzee behavior in Kibale Forest National Park and draws comparisons to human behavior.**

1988   James W. Black synthesizes propranolol and discovers that it can be used to treat high blood pressure and migraine headaches; Gertrude B. Elion invents drugs to treat a variety of disorders; and George H. Hitchings discovers drugs to treat cancer. They use rats, guinea pigs, dogs, and cats in their research.*

1988 (*cont.*)   Naomi Pierce studies the relationship between butterfly larvae and ants and genetic trends in butterflies.**

1989   J. Michael Bishop and Harold E. Varmus, using chickens, discover the role of viruses in the development of cancer.*

1990   M.A.R. Koehl studies how body structure affects mechanical function.**

The Food, Agriculture, Conservation, and Trade Act of 1990 is signed into law by President George H. W. Bush.

The first animal rights march is held in Washington, DC.

The European Coalition to End Experiments is founded.

The Organization for Economic Cooperation and Development is founded and develops international standards for animal testing.

Medical Scientists' Legal Defense Fund is founded.

1991   The Coalition for Animals and Research is founded.

Martin Kreitman studies molecular genetics in Drosophila (fruit flies).**

1992   Edmond H. Fisher and Edwin G. Krebs, using mice and rabbits, describe how cells regulate proteins and various cellular processes.*

Geerat J. Vermeij studies living and fossil marine mollusks. Dr. Vermeij is blind.**

Gunter Wagner uses mathematical modeling to understand the development of control genes.**

The Animal Enterprise Protection Act of 1992 (Public Law 102–346 [106 Stat. 928]) is signed into law by President George H. W. Bush.

1993   Victoria Foe studies the timetable of early development of Drosophila.**

Heather Williams studies the evolution of bird song.**

1995   Edward B. Lewis, Christiane Nusslein-Volhard, and Eric F. Wieschaus discover how genes control early embryonic development in the fruit fly.*

Sharon Emereson studies predator-prey interactions.**

Nicholas J. Strausfeld studies the function of and analyzes insect visual systems and publishes an atlas of an insect brain.

1996   Peter C. Dolherty and Rolf M. Zinernagel, using mice, discover how the immune system protects the body from viruses.*

An updated edition of the *Guide for the Care and Use of Laboratory Animals* is published.

Barbara Block studies the cellular mechanisms that underlie heat production of force production in tuna and billfishes.**

Thomas Daniel studies flight control in dragon flies, using implantable microelectrodes.**

1997   Stanley B. Prusiner studies and characterizes prions in knockout mice and hamsters. Prions are a new infective agent, responsible for "mad cow disease."*

Russell Lande studies the relationship among morphological, behavioral, and physiological characteristics and genetic and environmental factors.**

1997 (*cont.*)   Nancy A. Moran studies symbiosis between multi-cellular hosts and microbes.**

1998   Robert F. Furchgott, Louis J. Ignarro, and Ferid Murad discover that nitric oxide is a signaling molecule in mice, rats, rabbits, guinea pigs, and snails.*

Leah Krubitzer studies sensory integration in animal models.**

1999   David M. Hillis studies the evolutionary history of organisms, focusing on amphibians.**

2000   The Farm Bill, Title 10, Miscellaneous Provisions, Section D, is signed into law by President George W. Bush.

2001   Timothy Hunt, Paul Nurse, and John Sulston discover the cyclin molecule, which regulates cell division, in the sea urchin egg.*

Michael Dickinson studies underlying physical and biological principles of insect flight, focusing on the fly.**

Geraldine Seydoux studies key developmental processes called polarization in the round worm *C. elegans*, which establishes distinct anterior and posterior regions in the single-celled embryo.**

2002   Sydney Brenner, H. Robert Horvitz, and John E. Sulston discover how genes regulate the development of organs and the mechanism of programmed cell death, using the nematode *C. elegans.*

Bonniee Bassler studies how bacteria communicate.**

2003   Paul C. Lauterbur and Sir Peter Mansfield receive recognition for their work with magnetic resonance imaging, initially using rats.*

Xiaowei Zhyang uses advanced optical imaging techniques to study the behavior of individual biological molecules.**

An international symposium to develop science-based guidelines for laboratory animal care is held in Washington, DC.

The National Academies Press publishes *Guidelines for the Care and Use of Mammals in Neuroscience and Behavioral Research.*

2004   Richard Axel and Linda B. Buck analyze the anatomy and physiology of odor receptors and the organization of the olfactory system in the mouse, rat, and fruit fly.*

Joseph DeRisi profiles gene expression in the protozoan that causes malaria.**

2005   Barry J. Marshall and J. Robin Warren, using pigs and gerbils, discover the bacterium *Helicobacter pylori* and its role in gastritis and peptic ulcers.*

Nicole King uses molecular processes to determine the relationship between organisms in the "tree of life."**

2006   Andrew Z. Fire and Craig C. Mello, using the nematode worm, *C. elegan,* discover RNA interference and gene splicing by double-stranded RNA.*

Parliament passes the Animal Welfare Act of 2006, which brings together and updates legislation to promote the welfare of vertebrate animals.

Kenneth C. Carania studies the organization and function of mammalian sensory systems, focusing on star-nosed moles and shrews, which are among the smallest mammals, and naked mole rats.**

Kevin Eggan studies the reasons that cloned animals have organ defects and immunological problems.**

2007   Mario R. Capecchi, Martin J. Evans, and Oliver
                  Smithies discover how to introduce specific genes
                  into mice by the use of embryonic stem cells.*

                  The Animal Fighting Prohibition Enforcement Act
                  of 2007 is signed into law by President George
                  W. Bush.

                  Yoky Matsuoka combines neuroscience and robot-
                  ics to develop more realistic prosthetics (functional
                  artificial limbs).**

2008   Francoise Barre-Sinoussi and Luc Montagnier dis-
                  cover treatments for the human immunodeficiency
                  virus (HIV), which causes AIDS. Work on the nude
                  mouse, sheep, house (standard lab mouse), and
                  goat (begun in 1983) helps lead to a better under-
                  standing of the mechanisms of how HIV develops
                  and possible treatments.*

                  Susan Mango studies organogenesis (the forma-
                  tion of organs).**

                  Sally Temple studies how neuro-progenitor cells
                  develop into numerous and diverse cells in the
                  nervous system.**

5

Biographies

I n this chapter, we present biographies of both historical and contemporary individuals involved with animal rights and animal welfare.

Animal rights activists claim that animal research does not help either animals or humans. However, animal research has played a large role in, for example, heart-transplant surgery and open-heart surgery. Described in this chapter are some, but not all, of the key scientists and physicians who developed the techniques needed to perform these valuable surgical procedures (Drs. Alexis Carrell, Frank C. Mann, Vladimir Petrovich Demikhov, and E. Marcus). Both Drs. Barnard and Shumway, who performed the first and the second human heart transplant, respectively, performed numerous experiments on animals, mostly dogs, before moving on to perform the surgery on humans. Animals were also used to develop the heart-lung machine that allows surgeons to stop the heart of the recipient so that it can be removed safely and then to implant the donor heart (Leland C. Clark) or an artificial heart (Robert K. Jarvik). When these surgical techniques were perfected, patients still faced a significant problem—rejection of the donor heart by the recipient's body. Animal experiments played a key role in the development of the first antirejection drug, cyclosporine (Jean François Borel).

Cleveland Amory
(Sept. 2, 1917–Oct. 14, 1998)

Cleveland Amory was born in Nahant, Massachusetts. He was a freelance writer, lecturer, and television commentator. Amory was on the board of directors of the Humane Society of the United States from 1962 to 1970 He founded the Fund For Animals in 1967, which he said is committed to "litigation, legislation, education, and confrontation," and was its first president. The Fund is famous for painting baby seals on the ice floes off the Magdalene Islands in Canada with red organic dye that did not harm the seals but made their coats worthless to the sealers who kill them for their coats. The Fund is also known for its rescue of the burros in the Grand Canyon; it owns and runs the Black Beauty ranch for abused and injured horses and other animals. Amory was the president of the New England Anti-Vivisection Society from 1987 to 1998. He is the author of *The Cat Who Came for Christmas* (Little Brown, 1987), which describes his rescue of his feline companion, Polar Bear, and of *Man Kind?: Our Incredible War on Wildlife* (Harper, 1974). Amory recruited celebrities like Doris Day, Angie Dickinson, and Mary Tyler Moore for his campaign for compassionate clothing.

George Thorndike Angell
(June 5, 1823–March 16, 1909)

George Thorndike Angell was born in Southbridge, Massachusetts. He graduated from Dartmouth College, studied law at the Harvard Law School, and was admitted to the bar in 1851. He founded the Massachusetts Society for the Prevention of Cruelty to Animals in 1868 and served as its president. In 1889, he founded and served as president of the American Humane Education Society.

Aristotle
(384 B.C.E.–322 B.C.E.)

Aristotle was born in Stageira, Chalcidice. The earliest naturalist whose writings have survived, he dissected animals but not humans. He studied the sea life around Lesbos. In *Generation of Animals,* he described the embryological development of the chicken by breaking open a fertilized egg to visualize the development of the embryo.

Bob Barker (b. Dec. 12, 1923)

Bob Barker, whose full name is Robert William Barker, was born in Darrington, Washington. He had a long career as the host of various television game shows, most notably *The Price Is Right*. Barker became a vegetarian in 1979 and promoted animal rights, ending each episode of *The Price Is Right* with the phrase "Help control the pet population; have your pet spayed or neutered." Barker founded the DJ&T Foundation in 1995. The goal of the Foundation is to fund spay/neuter clinics and voucher programs to relieve pet overpopulation.

Christiaan Neethling Barnard (Nov. 8, 1922–Sept. 2, 2001)

Barnard was born in South Africa and received his Ch.B. (Bachelor of Surgery) at the University of Cape Town Medical School in 1946. He received a two-year scholarship for postgraduate training at the University of Minnesota, where he became acquainted with the work of Dr. Norman Shumway. He received his Master of Science in Surgery degree in 1958 for a thesis titled "The Aortic Valve—Problems in the Fabrication and Testing of a Prosthetic Valve" and his Ph.D. in the same year for a dissertation titled "The Aetiology of Congenital Intestinal Astresia." When he returned to Cape Town, he performed more than 50 heart transplants in dogs. He performed the first human heart transplant on December 3, 1967. The recipient, a 54-year-old male, survived for 18 days before he succumbed to pneumonia caused by the immunosuppressive drugs he was taking to prevent the rejection of the heart. Barnard continued to perform experiments and transplants until his retirement in 1983 because of rheumatoid arthritis in his hands that prevented him from performing surgery.

Jeremy Bentham (Feb. 15, 1748–June 6, 1832)

Jeremy Bentham was born at Red Lion Street, Houndsditch, London, and attended Queen's College, Oxford, as a young man. His first book, *Fragment on Government*, published in 1776, is credited with marking the beginning of philosophic radicalism. In his book *An Introduction to the Principles of Morals and Legislation*, he defined the principle of utility: "that property in any object whereby it tends to produce pleasure, good, or happiness, or to prevent the happening of mischief, pain, evil, or unhappiness to the party whose interest is considered" (Bentham 1907, pg. 2).

Bentham claimed that humanity was governed by two sovereign motives, pain and pleasure, and that the principle of utility recognized this subjection. Bentham argued that humans are hedonistic (pursue personal pleasure and avoid pain) and pursue general happiness. Crime should be punished swiftly by sanctions, such as arrest (political sanction); ostracism (moral or social sanction); or punishment hereafter (theological sanction). Bentham wrote of animals, "The question is not, can they reason? Nor can they talk? But, can they suffer?" Bentham maintained that because they can suffer, they have a right to life, liberty, and the pursuit of happiness. This argument became the centerpiece for and the battle cry of both the Victorian and the modern animal protection movements.

Henry Bergh
(Aug. 29, 1811–March 12, 1888)

Henry Bergh studied at Columbia College and received an inheritance on the death of his father. He traveled extensively in the United States and Europe and founded the American Society for the Prevention of Cruelty to Animals in April 1866. Bergh, with Elbridge T. Garry and John D. White, founded the New York Society for the Prevention of Cruelty to Children in 1875.

Claude Bernard
(July 12, 1813–Feb. 10, 1878)

Claude Bernard was born in Saint-Julien, France. In 1841, he joined the laboratory of François Magendie at the College de France. Bernard wrote, "La fixité du milieu intérieur est la condition d'une vie libre et indépendante" ("The constancy of the internal environment is the condition for a free and independent life"). This is still the underlying principle of homeostasis today. Bernard believed that medical knowledge, like other forms of scientific knowledge, could be won by systematic experiments. He was the first to state the principle of scientific determinism, that is, that identical experiments should yield identical results. The real beginnings of animal research probably date from the publication of his book, *Introduction à la médicine expérimentale*, in 1865. This book was translated into English (*An Introduction to Experimental Medicine*) by Henry Copley Green in 1927.

Jean François Borel (b. 1933)

One of the fundamental problems with organ transplants, including heart transplants, is that the recipient's body's immunological system attacks the "foreign" organ. While screening fungi for active compounds, Borel isolated cyclosporine from a fungus (*Tolypocladium inflatum*). Working at Sandoz Laboratories, Borel discovered that cyclosporine allowed selective immunoregulation of T cells in the recipient's body, without excessive toxicity. Borel continued experiments to identify side effects and to determine the correct dose and method of administration. These experiments were completed within four years. Clinical trials demonstrated that cyclosporine could prevent rejection of kidney transplants and bone marrow transplants in humans. It continues to be used today as an immunosuppressant.

Alexis Carrell
(June 28, 1873–Nov. 5, 1944)

Carrell was born in Sainte-Foy-les-Lyon, France, and received his medical degree from the University of Lyon. Carrell joined the Rockefeller Institute for Medical Research in New York. He developed a method to suture (sew) two blood vessels together end-to-end, which is called an anastomosis. He used this technique to transplant whole organs. For example, he attempted to transplant the kidney of a dog to the neck, using the carotid artery and the jugular vein to provide blood flow to the kidney. He also performed the first heart transplant, severing the carotid artery and using it to provide blood flow to the pulmonary veins of the transplanted heart and returning blood to the body via the transplanted heart's aorta sutured to the jugular vein. Carrell attempted to keep organs or portions of organs alive by passing blood through the organ's own blood vessels. He developed the perfusion pump with Charles A. Lindbergh, the famed pilot. Carrell and Lindbergh published their results in a book entitled *The Culture of Organs*. This pump was a crucial step in the development of the heart-lung machine, which made it possible for open-heart surgery and heart transplants to be performed. Carrell kept an embryonic chicken heart alive in culture for more than 34 years, far longer than the lifetime of a chicken. This proved his contention that all cells could grow indefinitely. More recent researchers claim that this was an anomalous result, that is, that differentiated cells can undergo only a limited number of division before dying. This phenomenon is commonly called the Hayflick limit. Carrell received the Nobel Prize in Physiology or Medicine in 1912 in recognition of his work.

Joseph Sill Clark
(Oct. 21, 1901–Jan. 12, 1990)

Joseph Clark was born in Philadelphia, Pennsylvania. He received a B.A. from Harvard University in 1923 and his law degree from the University of Pennsylvania in 1926. He was admitted to the bar and started a law practice in Philadelphia in 1926. Clark served with the U.S. Army Air Corps during World War II, achieved the rank of colonel, and acted as the deputy chief of staff for the Eastern Air Command. He received the Bronze Star, the Legion of Merit, and the Order of the British Empire.

Clark served as the controller for the city of Philadelphia from 1950 to 1952 and as mayor from 1952 to 1956. He was sworn in to the U.S. Senate on January 3, 1957, and served until January 3, 1969, when he was defeated for re-election. During his tenure in the Senate, Clark, a Democrat, was one of the sponsors of Public Law 89–544 (the Animal Welfare Act). After his Senate career, he was the president of the World Federalists, U.S.A., and the chairman of the Coalition on National Priorities and Military Policy.

Leland C. Clark
(Dec. 4, 1918–Sept. 25, 2005)

Clark was born in Rochester, New York, and received his Ph.D. in biochemistry from the University of Rochester in 1948. In the early 1950s, Clark began experiments that would ultimately lead to the development of a heart-lung machine that would allow blood to be pumped through the machine, where it was oxygenated, and then pumped back into the body. This allowed surgeons to stop a heart patient's heart, remove it, and replace it with a donor heart. Clark's experiments utilized dogs as the subjects. Clark and his colleagues tested their machine by placing cannuli into the vena cava (arteries that carry deoxygenated blood from the body back to the heart), bypassing the heart and lungs. The dog's blood pressure remained constant, and its reflexes and pupils were normal. Clark initially used the machine for patients who needed assistance with oxygenation of their blood (e.g., a fireman with damaged lungs). By the mid-1950s, the heart-lung machine was in common use.

Frances Power Cobbe
(Dec. 2, 1822–April 5, 1904)

Frances Power Cobbe was born in Dublin, Ireland. She was a social reformer, feminist theorist, and animal rights activist. Cobbe founded the Society for the Protection of Animals Liable to Vivisection in 1875, which was the world's first organization to campaign against animal experimentation. She also founded the British Union for the Abolition of Vivisection, in 1898. She is the author of *Vivisection in America* (Swan Sonnenschein, London, 1890).

Carl Cohen (?–)

Carl Cohen is a professor of philosophy at the Residential College of the University of Michigan in Ann Arbor. Cohen is perhaps best known for his participation in the events that led to a Supreme Court ruling that race could not be given substantial weight when deciding which students should be admitted to the University.

Cohen engaged in a point-counterpoint debate with Tom Regan on the issue of animal rights, which was published as *The Animal Rights Debate*. Cohen defends the use of animals in research ("The Case for the Use of Animals in Biomedical Research," *New England Journal of Medicine*, October 2, 1986). He also defends the limited use of prisoners as research subjects ("Medical Experimentation on Prisoners," *Perspectives in Biology and Medicine*, Spring 1978).

Doris Day (b. April 3, 1924)

Doris Day was born Doris Mary Anne von Kappelhoff, in Cincinnati, Ohio. Day was a recording, radio, and movie star, as well as a television singer and actress. In 1971, she co-founded Actors and Others for Animals and appeared in a series of advertisements with Mary Tyler Moore, Angie Dickinson, and Jayne Meadows, who were also television celebrities, to promote a ban on the wearing of fur. Throughout the 1970s and 1980s, Day promoted the annual Spay Day, USA. She provides funds for the Doris Day Animal League, which uses Day's celebrity to lobby for the humane treatment of animals. The League merged with the Humane Society of the United States in September 2006.

Vladimir Petrovich Demikhov (July 18, 1916–Nov. 22, 1998)

Demikhov was born at the Kulini Farm in Russia. He developed an artificial heart that was too large to fit inside the chest cavity of a dog but that kept a dog alive for more than five hours. Demikhov also transplanted a "piggyback" heart by performing an end-to-side anastomoses of the donor aorta, pulmonary artery, and vena cavae. That is, he opened the recipient's aorta and sutured the aorta of the donor's aorta to it. The pulmonary veins of the donor heart were joined together and attached to the left atrium of the recipient. His dogs survived for as long as 15 hours and demonstrated that an allograft could provide pumping function for the recipient heart. Demikhov is perhaps most famous for his head transplantations. He removed the head of one dog and transplanted it to the neck of another, using an anastomoses of the carotid artery and jugular vein.

Walter Elias (Walt) Disney
(Dec. 5, 1901–Dec. 15, 1965)

A mouse in a kitchen or restaurant is considered vermin and is killed with poison or a trap. But Disney, who was born in Chicago, Illinois, provided the world with an anthropomorphic mouse with a personality in 1928 when he created a silent animated cartoon, *Plane Crazy*, starring Mickey Mouse and his girlfriend, Minnie. Initially, Mickey had some mouse-like characteristics, like the tail and paw-like "hands" he showed in *Steamboat Willie*, one of the first cartoons with a sound track. Gradually, Mickey morphed into a human-like character that wore red shorts, stood on two legs, wore yellow shoes, and used his forepaws like hands, wearing white gloves with a thumb and three fingers. In *The Karnival Kid*, in 1929, Mickey spoke for the first time, saying, "Hot dogs, hot dogs"; Disney provided his voice. Over the years, Mickey became more and more human-like. In addition to Minnie, Donald Duck, a whole family of ducks, and Goofy, an anthropomorphized dog, were added to the human-like pantheon of cartoon characters. Pluto, on the other hand, was Mickey's dog and did not speak; he was not as anthropomorphized as the other characters but did have a wide range of facial expressions.

Bambi is a cartoon based on the book *Bambi: A Life in the Woods*, by Felix Salten, published in 1923. Bambi and other characters, like Thumper (a rabbit) and Flower (a skunk), were not as anthropomorphized as Mickey and his friends. Bambi and the others spoke but otherwise remained fairly animal-like.

When Disneyland opened, in Anaheim, California, in 1955, Mickey, Donald and the other cartoon characters morphed again into human-size characters that strolled the streets of the amusement park, interacting with guests and providing photo ops.

Robert Joseph Dole
(b. July 22, 1923)

Robert Joseph Dole was born in Russell, Kansas. He graduated from Russell High School in 1941 and enrolled in the University of Kansas, but his studies were interrupted by World War II. He joined the Army in 1942 and was wounded in his upper right back and arm by German machine gun fire in April 1945. After the war, Dole attended the University of Arizona and earned his law degree from the Washburn University School of Law in 1952. Dole was elected to the Kansas House of Representatives for a two-year term beginning in 1950. He became the county attorney for Russell County in 1952 and served until 1960, when he was elected to the House of Representatives from the First Congressional District. He was elected to the Senate in 1968 and re-elected in 1974, 1980, 1986, and 1992. While in the Senate, Dole was the ranking Republican on the Agriculture Committee from 1975 until 1978 and the chairman of the Finance Committee from 1981 to 1985. He served as the Senate Majority Leader from 1985 to 1987 and again from 1995 to 1996. With no specific committee reports and no real debate on the House or Senate floor, Dole tacked Subtitle F, Animal Welfare, onto the Food Security Act of 1985, which is a very long law dealing with all aspects of federal farm subsidies, just prior to the Senate adjournment for the 1985 Christmas holidays. It is not clear where the language of the Act came from or whether Dole had any knowledge of or interest in animal research or animal welfare (see chapter 6).

Muriel Dowding
(March 22, 1908–Nov. 20, 1993)

Muriel Dowding was born in London and married Lord Hugh Dowding on August 24, 1936, making her Lady Dowding. Lord Dowding was a longtime British politician and commander-in-chief of the Royal Air Force, as well as a vegetarian and anti-vivisectionist. Lady Muriel Dowding founded Beauty Without Cruelty. She was the president of the National Anti-Vivisection Society and the International Association Against Painful Experiments in Animals. In November, 1998, the British Government announced that it would no longer license the testing of cosmetics or their ingredients on animals.

Michael Allen Fox (b. 1940)

Michael Allen Fox was born in Cleveland, Ohio. He received his B.A. from Cornell University and his M.A. and Ph.D. from the

University of Toronto. He has worked at the University of Toronto as an instructor and is currently a full professor of philosophy at Queen's University, Kingston, Ontario. He published *The Case for Animal Experimentation: An Evolutionary and Ethical Perspective* in 1986. He later repudiated the views expressed in this book and has written articles and books favoring vegetarianism and animal rights, such as *Deep Vegetarianism*, published in 1999.

Michael Wilson Fox
(b. Aug. 13, 1937)

Michael Wilson Fox was born in Bolton, England and received his B. Vet. Med. from the Royal Veterinary College in 1962, his Ph.D. from the University of London in 1967, and his D.Sc. in 1976. Fox was employed as a medical research associate at State Research Hospital, Galesburg, Illinois (1964–1967); as an associate professor of psychology at Washington University, St. Louis, Missouri (1967–1976); as vice president of bioethics of the Humane Society of the United States, Washington, DC (1976–1998), and as a senior scholar in bioethics at the Humane Society of the United States, Washington, DC (1998–). He has also served as a senior adviser to the Office of the President of the Humane Society of America.

He published *Between Man and Animals: The Key to the Kingdom* in 1976 and *Returning to Eden: Animal Rights and Human Responsibilities* in 1980; he edited *On the Fifth Day: Animal Rights and Human Obligations* in 1977.

Ann Cottrell Free
(June 4, 1916–Oct. 30, 2004)

Ann Cottrell Free was born in Richmond, Virginia. In the late 1950s, Free began writing about animal protection. Her exposure of the mistreatment of beagles used for testing color dye at the Food and Drug Administration (FDA) in the U.S. Department of Agriculture (USDA) building helped start the debate about laboratory animal welfare. Free was a supporter of Rachel Carson's environmental work and was responsible for the establishment of the

Rachel Carson National Wildlife Refuge in Maine. In 1982, Free testified about a plan to allow hunters to hunt deer in a fenced facility of the National Zoo. Because of her testimony, the hunt was canceled. She also authored two books: *Forever the Wild Mare* and *Animals, Nature and Albert Schweitzer*, as well as a volume of poetry titled *No Room, Save in the Heart*. The National Press Club established the Ann Cottrell Free Animal Reporting Award in her honor.

Robert K. Jarvik
(b. May 11, 1946)

Jarvik was born in Midland, Michigan, and graduated from Syracuse University in 1968 with a bachelor's degree in zoology. He attended the medical school at the University of Bologna in Italy and returned to the United States to obtain a M.A. degree in occupational biomechanics from New York University. In 1967, he joined the Institute of Biomedical Engineering at the University of Utah, where he began developing an artificial heart. In the mid-1970s, Jarvik developed a plastic and aluminum device that could replace the functions of the right ventricle (which pumps deoxygenated blood from the body to the lungs) and the left ventricle (which pumps oxygenated blood to the body). On December 2, 1982, the Jarvik-7 artificial heart was implanted in Barney Clark, who survived for four months. A number of other patients were implanted with modified Jarvik hearts, and the longest survival time exceeded 620 days. The heart was also used as a stopgap measure for patients who were awaiting natural heart transplants.

Joseph Rudyard Kipling
(Dec. 30, 1865–Jan. 18, 1936)

Kipling was at Bombay, India. One of the most popular authors in English and a master of the short story, he won the Nobel Prize for Literature in 1907. The prize citation praised Kipling's talent for narration, observation, and imagination and the virility of his ideas. Kipling published *Jungle Book* in 1894 and the *Second Jungle*

Book in 1895. These books consisted of a series of short stories or fables about a feral child, Mowgli, who was raised by anthropomorphized wolves with the help of Baloo, a bear, and Bagheera, a panther. The villain is a tiger named Shere Kahn. The anthropomorphism was limited to allowing the animals to speak, but Kipling otherwise maintained their animal-like characteristics. In one of the stories, "Tiger! Tiger!" Mowgli returns to live with humans but has a hard time adjusting and soon returns to the jungle. The books were the basis for a number of live-action and animated movies; perhaps the best-known version is Walt Disney's cartoon, which appeared in 1967 and was one of his most popular and successful films.

John Cunningham Lilly
(Jan. 6, 1915–Sept. 20, 2001)

Lilly was born in St. Paul, Minnesota. He studied physics and biology at the California Institute of Technology and received an M.D. from the University of Pennsylvania in 1942. Lilly was involved in a variety of controversial projects to study the dimensions of human consciousness, including experiments with hallucinogenic drugs and isolation tanks. In the 1960s, Lilly opened Communication Research Institute on the island of St. Thomas in the Caribbean to study large-brained marine mammals. He especially focused on dolphins in an effort to understand their communications and to attempt to communicate with them. His book *The Mind of the Dolphin* (also titled *The Mind of the Dolphin: A Nonhuman Intelligence*; Doubleday, 1967) describes these experiments.

Warren Grant Magnuson
(April 12, 1905–May 20, 1989)

Magnuson was born in Moorhead, Minnesota, and attended the University of North Dakota at Grand Forks and North Dakota State College. He received a B.A. from the University of Washington in 1926 and a J.D. degree from its law school in 1929. He was admitted to the bar in 1929 and started a law practice in Seattle. He served in the U.S. Navy during World War II and attained the rank of Lieutenant Commander. He was sworn in to the House of Representatives on January 3, 1937, and served until December 13, 1944, when he resigned and was appointed to the Senate the next day, December 14, 1944, to fill a vacancy caused by the resignation of Homer T. Bone. Magnuson was sworn in to the Senate on January 3, 1945, and served until January 3, 1975. During his tenure, he was one of the sponsors of Public Law 89–544 (the Animal Welfare Act).

Frank C. Mann
(Sept. 11, 1887–Sept. 30, 1962)

Mann was born on a family farm in Indiana. He received his M.D. degree in 1913 from Indiana University. He joined the Mayo Clinic as the Director of Experimental Medicine and Pathological Anatomy in 1914. He and his colleagues developed methods to remove the heart of an animal and transplant it to a site on the neck. They used the carotid artery to supply blood through the aorta to the heart, which also allowed blood to circulate through the coronary system. The blood flowed to the right atrium and into the right ventricle and through the pulmonary vein into an anastomosed jugular vein. They were able to keep the heart alive for as long as eight days.

Emanuel Marcus (?–)

Marcus and his team, S. N. Wong and A. A. Luisada, at the Chicago Medical School, modified Mann's technique and anastomosed both ends of the recipient's common carotid artery to the donor aorta, allowing the donor coronary arteries to function. They also anastomosed the common carotid artery to the left atrium.

Richard Martin
(Jan. 15, 1754–Jan. 6, 1834)

Richard Martin was born in Ballynahinch, County Galway, Ireland. The Act to Prevent the Cruel and Improper Treatment of

Cattle was sponsored by Martin and passed in Parliament on July 22, 1882. Martin was one of the founders of the Society for the Prevention of Cruelty to Animals in 1824.

James McMillan
(May 12, 1838–Aug. 10, 1902)

McMillan was born in Hamilton, Ontario, Canada, and was educated in the public schools of Hamilton. He moved to Detroit in 1855 and started the Michigan Car Co. In 1863, he built and was the president of the Duluth, South Shore, and Atlantic Railroad. He was a member of the Detroit Board of Park Commissioners and the Board of Estimates. McMillan became a member of the Michigan Republican State central committee in 1876 and served as its chairman. He was later elected to the U.S. Senate, where he served from March 3, 1889, until his death. While in the Senate, he was the chairman of the Senate Committee on the District of Columbia. He was appointed the chairman of a commission that was to develop a plan to beautify Washington, DC, for the celebration of the city's centennial, in 1900. McMillan and other members of the commission, architects Daniel H. Burnham and Charles F. McKim; sculptor Augustus Saint-Gaudens; and landscape architect Frederick Law Olmsted, Jr., recommended that railroad tracks and a stone depot be removed from the Mall. This was accomplished and yielded the large landscaped area that is a major attraction for visitors to Washington, DC to this day. Senator McMillan also introduced a bill to regulate vivisection in Washington, DC in 1896. The bill was defeated.

Mark L. Morris, Sr.
(Nov. 18, 1900–July 8, 1993)

Mark L. Morris, Sr., was a veterinarian, humanitarian, and visionary. He was concerned about the poor quality of pet food and began preparing his own pet food. It became popular, and Morris teamed with Burton Hill, the owner of the Hill Packing Co., to begin producing Prescription Diet pet foods, which are available only through veterinarians. A portion of the price of each can goes to the Morris Animal Foundation, which sponsors humane animal research.

Adrian R. Morrison
(b. Nov. 5, 1936)

Morrison was born in Philadelphia, PA. He received his Doctor of Veterinary Medicine degree from Cornell University in 1960 and his Ph.D. from the University of Pennsylvania in 1964. A neuroscientist who studied the sleep-wakefulness cycle, he also published a series of articles dealing with the animal rights controversy. These include "A Scientist's Perspective on the Ethics of Using Animals in Behavioral Research" (in M. E. Carroll and J. B. Overmier, eds., *Animal Research and Human Health: Advancing Human Welfare through Behavioral Science* [American Psychological Association, 2001], pp. 341–56); "Perverting Medical History in the Service of 'Animal Rights'" (*Perspectives in Biology and Medicine* 45 [2002]: 606–19); "Unscientific American: Animal Rights or Wrongs" (with Jack H. Bottling) (Biomednet [http://biomednet. com/hmsbeagle/]; and "Animal Research Is Vital to Medicine" (with J. H. Botting) (*Scientific American* [February 1997]; available at http://www.sciamdigital.com/index.cfm?fa=Products. ViewIssuePreview&ISSUEID_CHAR=F1C2CBCD-B61D-4FDF-9 F7E-9E8CCB2A04A&ARTICLEID_CHAR=02EA00AB-617F-40 F7–98ED-D09F652DA20).

Ingrid Newkirk
(b. June 11, 1949)

Ingrid Newkirk was born in Surrey, England. In 1967, she settled in Maryland, where she volunteered in the local animal shelter, working her way up to director. By 1978, Newkirk was an assertive cruelty investigator for the Humane Society in Washington, DC Reading Peter Singer's *Animal Liberation* changed her life. In 1980, she and Alex Pacheco formed People for the Ethical Treatment of Animals. PETA advocates that people stop eating meat and wearing fur; opposes experimentation and the breeding of cats and dogs; and would retire circus animals and close zoos.

"Companion animals," a term Newkirk coined, would be adopted from shelters and the streets.

Charles S. Nicoll
(b. April 11, 1937)

Nicoll was born in Toronto, Ontario, and became an American citizen in 1975. He received his Ph.D. from Michigan State in 1962. Nicoll is an endocrinologist and has been a professor of physiology at the University of California, Berkeley, since 1974. Nicoll has written a series of articles dealing with the animal rights controversy. "A Physiologist's Views on the Animal Rights/Liberation Movement" appeared in *The Physiologist* in 1991 (http://www.the-aps. org/publications/tphys/legacy/1991/issue6/303.pdf). Nicoll has also written a series of articles with his wife, Sharon Russell. "Analysis of Animal Rights Literature Reveals the Underlying Motives of the Movement: Ammunition for Counter Offensive by Scientists" appeared in *Endocrinology* in 1990 (vol. 127, pp. 985–89). Another article, this one titled "Animal Research vs. Animal Rights," appeared in the Federation of American Societies for Experimental Biology journal (http://www.fasebj.org/cgi/reprint/3/5/1668. pdf). "Mozart, Alexander the Great, and the Animal Rights/Liberation Philosophy" was a special feature that appeared in the same journal in 1991 (vol. 5, pp. 2888–92; http://www.fasebj.org/cgi/ reprint/5/14/2888.pdf). A series of letters to the editor about this article appeared in the journal in April 1992 (http://www.fasebj. org/cgi/reprint/6/7/2489.pdf.). "Critical Perspective: The Unnatural Nature of the Animal Rights/Liberation Philosophy" appeared in the *Proceedings of the Society of Experimental Biology* in 1994 (https:// dspace03.it.ohio-state.edu/dspace/bitstream/1811/23580/1/ V093N5_118.pdf). Responses to this article can be found at http:// www.ebmonline.org/cgi/reprint-embargo/205/4/269.

Coles Phinizy (?–)

Coles Phinizy was a graduate of the Hill School and Harvard College, where he was the chairman of the Harvard *Lampoon*. He began his journalist career at *Life* magazine and in 1954 joined the staff of *Sports Illustrated*. As a reporter for *Sports Illustrated*, he covered the story of Pepper, the family pet of the Lakavage family, which disappeared from the family farm. This article was one of the tipping points that led to the development of the Animal Welfare Act.

Thomas Howard Regan (b. 1938)

Thomas Howard Regan was born in Pittsburgh, Pennsylvania. He received his B.A. from Thiel College and his M.A. and Ph.D. from the University of Virginia. He was an assistant professor of philosophy at Sweet Briar College from 1965 to 1967. He joined the faculty of North Carolina State University at Raleigh in 1967 and is currently a full professor in the philosophy department. In 1983, Regan published *The Case for Animal Rights*, which provides a scholarly defense of the controversial claim that animals have rights. Regan argued that animals have rights that humans are morally obligated to recognize and respect. Regan disagrees with utilitarians (e.g., Bentham, Singer) that the ability to feel pleasure and pain does not provide a strong case for animal rights. Regan edited *Animal Rights and Human Obligations* (1976) and *Matters of Life and Death* (1980).

Joseph Yale Resnick (1924–1969)

Joseph Yale Resnick was born in Ellenville, New York. He was the founder and chairman of the board of the Channel Master Corporation, which engaged in electronics and plastics research and development. Resnick was a Democrat and was elected to the House of Representatives for the 89th and 90th Congresses. While a member of the House, Resnick introduced the bill that ultimately became the Animal Welfare Act of 1966 (a.k.a the Research or Experimentation on Cats and Dogs Act of 1966) (Public Law 89–544 [80 Stat. 350]). Resnick unsuccessfully sought nomination to the U.S. Senate.

Sharon M. Russell (b. May 14, 1944)

Russell received her Ph.D. from Stanford University in 1971. Russell specializes in the study of hormones in development. She has been an associate research physiologist at the University of California, Berkeley, since 1989. Russell is married to Charles S. Nicoll (see Nicoll biography), and they have collaborated on research.

Norman Shumway (Feb. 9, 1923–Feb. 10, 2006)

Shumway was born in Kalamazoo, Michigan, and received his M.D. from Vanderbilt University in 1949. Shumway perfected a way to cool a donor heart to minimize damage to it and was the first to use a rotating disk oxygenator. He performed numerous experiments on dogs. He was the first to carry out a human heart transplant in the United States, in 1968. The recipient was a 54-year-old male who lived for 14 days after the surgery.

Peter Singer (b. July 6, 1949)

Peter Singer was born in Melbourne, Australia. Singer attended Scotch College and the University of Melbourne, where he received his B.A. in history and philosophy and an M.A. degree in philosophy. He then studied at University College, Oxford, where he received a B.Phil. degree in 1971. Singer remained at the university as the Radcliffe lecturer. Several of Singer's fellow students (Stanley and Rosalind Godlovitch and John Harris) at Oxford gathered a series of articles providing information about factory farming and animal experimentation and calling for the ethical treatment of animals. The resulting book, *Animals, Men, and Morals*, was published in England in 1971. Singer wrote a long review of the American edition in which he combined the views of the contributors into a single coherent philosophy of animal liberation, and this appeared as the article "Animal Liberation" in the *New York Review of Books*. Singer wrote the book *Animal Liberation* in 1973 and 1974, during his last year at Oxford and while he was a visiting professor of philosophy at New York University. (The 1990 edition of *Animal Liberation* includes an account of the programs and campaigns that the book inspired.) Singer returned to Australia in 1974 and joined La Trobe University in Bundoora, Victoria, as a senior lecturer of philosophy. He reportedly does not object to illegal measures, such as raiding animal laboratories, when results cannot be obtained in any other way. But, he stands firmly against violence that harms other people. Singer and Jim Mason published *Animal Factories*, in which they describe the use of animals as biomachines to produce food, in 1980. In 1977, Singer joined the faculty of Monash University as a professor of philosophy and became the director of the university's Center for Human Bioethics in 1987. Singer, with Helga Kuhse, published *Should the Baby Live? The Problem of Handicapped Infants*, in 1985. He received considerable attention from the press when he lectured at several universities in Germany for euthanasia for severely handicapped newborn babies. He has served on the editorial boards of the *International Journal for the Study of Animal Problems*, the *Australian Journal of Philosophy*, and *Ethics*. He is the co-editor of *Bioethics*. He is currently the Ira W. DeCamp Professor of Bioethics at Princeton University and laureate professor at the Centre for Applied Philosophy and Public Ethics (CAPPE), University of Melbourne.

Christine Stevens (1918–2002)

Christine Gesell was born in St. Louis and attended the University of Michigan. Her father, a physiologist who headed the physiology department at the University of Michigan, was a pioneer in the compassionate treatment of research animals. He helped shape his daughters views on animals and animal welfare. Gesell married Roger Lacey Stevens, a New York real estate magnate, Broadway producer, fundraiser, and arts patron and the founding chairman of the John. F. Kennedy Center for the Performing Arts. A syndicate led by Stevens bought the Empire State Building and provided free office space for the founding of the Animal Welfare Institute in 1951. The Stevenses moved to Washington, DC, where Stevens formed the Society for Animal Protective Legislation in 1955. She originated the Save-the-Whales-Campaign, in 1971. Stevens lobbied Congress to promote animal welfare legislation; for example, on September 19, 1984, she gave extensive testimony at a hearing, titled "Improved Standards for Laboratory Animals Act; And Enforcement of the Animal Welfare Act by the Animal and Plant Health Inspection Service," before the House of Representatives Committee on Agriculture, Subcommittee on Department Operations, Research, and Foreign Agriculture; she also testified on July 20, 1983, before the Senate Committee on Agriculture, Nutrition, and Forestry, on improved standards for laboratory animals. Her testimony was instrumental in the passage of the Food Security Act of 1985, which caused a major change in the way biomedical research is conducted. It is likely that Steven's organization helped draft the Act and the regulations promulgated under its authority.

Frankie Trull (?–)

Trull received her undergraduate degree from Boston University and her master's degree from Tufts University. She is the founder and president of the Foundation for Biomedical Research. She is also president of the National Association for Biomedical Research (NABR), the nation's leading advocate for sound public policy on the role of animal models in biomedical research and testing. Trull is also the founder and president of Policy Directions, Inc., a Washington, DC-based government relations/strategic government communications firm, which assists corporations and nonprofits in addressing legislative and regulatory initiatives and influencing policy development.

A frequent guest speaker and media resource, Trull has written numerous articles on the importance of biomedical research and the threat posed to the American research community by animal rights extremism. She played an instrumental role in coordinating congressional consensus for the passage of the Animal Enterprise Terrorism Act (AETA), landmark legislation signed by the president in 2006 that provides greater protections for researchers from animal rights extremists.

Thomas Tyron
(Sept. 6, 1634–Aug. 21, 1703)

Thomas Tyron was probably the first author to use the word "right" with regard to animals; he did so in *The Way to Health, Long Life and Happiness* (Andrew Sowle, London, 1683), in which he also said he "would fain be an absolute monarch or arbitrary tyrant, making nothing at his pleasure to break the laws of God, and invade and destroy all the rights and privileges of inferior creatures" (Perkins 2003, p. 41). Tyron was born in Bibury, England, attended the village school, and acted as a shepherd tending his father's flock. When he was 18, he left Bibury for London, where he apprenticed himself to a castor-maker (hatter) in Bridewell Dock, Fleet Street. Following the example of his master, he became an Anabaptist (a radical movement within Protestantism that advocated Church membership and baptism for adult members only). In 1657, he broke with the Anabaptists and became a vegetarian. In 1682, he began to write and publish his convictions to the world. His writings are a curious mixture of mystical philosophy and dietetics. Lewis Gompertz, the founder of the Society for the Prevention of Cruelty to Animals, was an admirer of Tyron.

Betty White (b. Jan. 17, 1922)

Betty White was born in Oak Park, Illinois. A television star and a frequent guest on the 1960s television game show *Password*, White is a pet enthusiast and animal welfare activist. She supports the Los Angeles Zoo Commission, the Morris Animal Foundation, and Actors and Others for Animals.

References

Bentham, J. 1907. *An Introduction to Principles of Morals and Legislation.* Oxford: Clarendon Press.

Perkins, D. 2003. *Romanticism and Animal Rights.* Cambridge: Cambridge University Press.

6

Data and Documents

This chapter provides an overview of federal legislation dealing with animals, especially those used in scientific research. Selected sections of the Animal Welfare Act (AWA) are presented to allow the reader to understand the scope of the federal legislation, which gives the secretary of agriculture limited authority over animal welfare, beginning with cats and dogs. This authority was expanded and increased by amendments to the Act, as shown by the key sections of several of the amendments to it.

Congress obtains information about issues under consideration by holding hearings. Two congressional hearings about the 1985 amendments to the AWA are provided to give the reader insight into the type of information provided at such hearings. The chapter also provides statistics on the use of animals in agriculture and science.

Documents

Although animal welfare legislation was first proposed in 1896, it was not until the 1960s that the first federal animal welfare legislation was passed. This came in response to fears that unscrupulous animal dealers were stealing pets and then selling them to laboratories to be used in experiments. The full text of the Animal Welfare Act and its amendments, as well as the text of the Animal Welfare Regulations, can be found at the USDA National Agricultural Library Web site (http://awic.nal.usda.gov/nal_display/index.php?info_center=3&tax_level=3&tax_subject=182&topic_id=1118&level3_id=6735&level4_id=0&level5_id=0&placement_default=0).

Animal Welfare Act of 1966 (Public Law 89–544)

Commonly called the Research or Experimentation—Cats and Dogs Act of 1966, this is the first federal law to regulate the treatment of animals and how animals will be used in research and experimentation.

Section 1. Congressional Statement of Policy
Be it enacted by the Senate and House of Representatives of the United States of America in Congress assembled. That, in order to protect the owners of dogs and cats from theft of such pets, to prevent the sale or use of dogs and cats which have been stolen, and to insure that certain animals intended for use in research facilities are provided humane care and treatment, it is essential to regulate the transportation, purchase, sale, housing, care, handling, and treatment of such animals by persons or organizations engaged in using them for research or experimental purposes or in transporting, buying, or selling them for such use.

Section 2. Definitions
When used in this Act—

(a) The term "person" includes any individual, partnership, firm, joint stock company, corporation, association, trust, estate, or other legal entity;
(b) The term "Secretary" means the Secretary of Agriculture;
(c) The term "commerce" means commerce between any State, territory, possession, or the District of Columbia, or the Commonwealth of Puerto Rico, but through any place outside thereof; or within any territory, possession, or the District of Columbia;
(d) The term "dog" means any live dog (Canis familiaris);
(e) The term "cat" means any live cat (Felis catus);
(f) The term "research facility" means any school, institution, organization, or person that uses or intends to use dogs or cats in research, tests, or experiments, and that (1) purchases or transports dogs or cats in commerce, or (2) receives funds under a grant, award, loan, or contract from a department, agency, or instrumentality of the United States for the purpose of carrying out research, tests, or experiments;
(g) The term "dealer" means any person who for compensation or profit delivers for transportation, or transports, except as a common carrier, buys, or sells dogs or cats in commerce for research purposes;
(h) The term "animal" means live dogs, cats, monkeys (nonhuman primate mammals), guinea pigs, hamsters, and rabbits.

Section 3. Licenses to Dealers

The Secretary shall issue licenses to dealers upon application therefor in such form and manner as he may prescribe and upon payment of such fee established pursuant to section 23 of this Act: *Provided,* That no such license shall be issued until the dealer shall have demonstrated that his facilities comply with the standards promulgated by the Secretary pursuant to section 13 of this Act: *Provided, however,* That any person who derives less than a substantial portion of his income (as determined by the Secretary) from the breeding and raising of dogs or cats on his own premises and sells any such dog or cat to a dealer or research facility shall not be required to obtain a license as a dealer under this Act. The Secretary is further authorized to license, as dealers within the meaning of this Act upon such persons' complying with the requirements specified above and agreeing, in writing, to comply with all the requirements of this Act and the regulations promulgated by the Secretary hereunder.

Section 4. License Requirements

No dealer shall sell or offer to sell or transport or offer for transportation to any research facility any dog or cat, or buy, sell, offer to buy or sell, transport or offer for transportation in commerce to or from another dealer under this Act any dog or cat, unless and until such dealer shall have obtained a license from the Secretary and such license shall not have been suspended or revoked.

Section 5.

No dealer shall sell or otherwise dispose of any dog or cat within a period of five business days after the acquisition of such animal or within such other period as may be specified by the Secretary.

Section 7. Purchase Restrictions

It shall be unlawful for any research facility to purchase any dog or cat from any person except a person holding a valid license as a dealer issued by the Secretary pursuant to this Act unless such person is exempted from obtaining such license under section 3 of this Act.

Section 12. Humane Standards Promulgation

The Secretary is authorized to promulgate humane standards and recordkeeping requirements governing the purchase, handling, or sale of dogs or cats by dealers or research facilities at auction sales.

Section 13.

The Secretary shall establish and promulgate standards to govern the humane handling, care, treatment, and transportation of animals by dealers and research facilities. Such standards shall include minimum requirements with respect to the housing, feeding, watering, sanitation, ventilation, shelter from extremes of weather and temperature, separation by species, and adequate veterinary care. The foregoing shall not be construed as authorizing the Secretary to prescribe standards for the handling, care, or treatment of animals during actual research or experimentation by research facility as determined by such research facility.

Section 16. Investigations or Inspections

The Secretary shall make such investigations or inspections as he deems necessary to determine whether any dealer or research facility has violated or is violating any provision of this Act or any regulation issued thereunder. The Secretary shall promulgate such rules and regulations as he deems necessary to permit inspectors to confiscate or destroy in a humane manner any animals found to be suffering as a result of a failure to comply with any provision of this Act or any regulation issued thereunder if (1) such animals are held by a dealer, or (2) such animals are held by a research facility and are no longer required by such research facility to carry out the research, test, or experiment for which such animals have been utilized.

Section 18.

Nothing in this Act shall be construed as authorizing the Secretary to promulgate rules, regulations, or orders for the handling, care, treatment, or inspection of animals during actual research or experimentation by a research facility as determined by such research facility.

Source: http://www.nal.usda.gov/awic/legislat/pl89544.htm. Accessed May 15, 2009.

Animal Welfare Act Amendments of 1970 (Public Law 91–579)

Section 3.

(e) The term "research facility" means any school (except an elementary or secondary school), institution, organization, or person that uses or intends to use live animals in research, tests, or experiments, and that (1) purchases or transports live animals affecting commerce, or (2) receives funds under a grant, award, loan, or contract from a department, agency, or instrumentality of the United States for the purpose of carrying out research, tests, or experiments: *Provided,* That the Secretary may exempt, by regulation, any such school, institution, organization, or person that does not use or intend to use live dogs or cats, except those schools, institutions, organizations, or persons, in biomedical research or testing, when in the judgement of the Secretary, any such exception does not vitiate the purpose of this Act; . . .

(g) The term "animal" means any live or dead dog, cat, monkey (nonhuman primate mammal), guinea pig, hamster, rabbit, or such other warm-blooded animal, as the Secretary may determine is being used, or is intended for use, for research, testing, experimentation, or exhibition purposes, or as a pet; but such term excludes horses not used for research purposes and other farm animals, such as but not limited to livestock or poultry used or intended for use for improving animal nutrition, breeding, management, or production efficiency, or for improving the quality of food or fiber.

Source: http://www.nal.usda.gov/awic/legislat/pl91579.htm. Accessed May 15, 2009.

Animal Welfare Act Amendment of 1976 (Public Law 94–279)

Section 17. Animal Fighting Venture, Prohibition

(a) It shall be unlawful for any person to knowingly sponsor or exhibit any animal in any animal fighting venture to which any animal was moved in interstate or foreign commerce.
(b) It shall be unlawful for any person to knowingly sell, buy, transport, or deliver to another person or receive from another person for purposes of transportation, in interstate for foreign commerce, any dog or other animal for purposes of having the dog or other animal participate in an animal fighting venture.
(c) It shall be unlawful for any person to knowingly use the mail service of the United States Postal Service or any interstate instrumentality for purposes of promoting or in any other manner furthering an animal fighting venture except as performed outside the limits of the States of the United States.
(d) Not withstanding the provisions of subsection (a), (b), or (c) of this section, the activities prohibited by such subsection shall be unlawful with respect to fighting ventures involving live birds only if the fight is to take place in a State where it would be in violation of the laws thereof.

Source: http://awic.nal.usda.gov/nal_display/index.php?info_center=3%20 &tax_level=4&tax_subject=182&topic_id=1118&level3_id=6735&level4_ id=11094&level5_id=0&placement_default=0. Accessed May 15, 2009.

Food Security Act of 1985

There were two committee hearings on the proposed Bill that would remain the Animal Welfare Act of 1966. These committee hearings were to determine what changes should be made, and are the source of expert testimony about the Bill. Government bureaucrats can be invited to attend a hearing and be prepared to answer questions, provide documents, and comments. Citizens who are experts in some area of the Bill under consideration can also volunteer to provide information about and insights into issues of interest.

Prior to the subsequent amendment to the bill, the authority of the secretary of agriculture stopped "at the laboratory door"; that is, the secretary could not regulate the conduct of the research or experimentation. This amendment allowed the secretary to have each research institution appoint an Institutional Animal Care and Use Committee (see later discussion), which would review experimental protocols and, if necessary, require that investigators modify the protocol.

Senate Hearing 161–4, "Improved Standards for Laboratory Animals"

The first of the hearings (July 20, 1983), Senate Hearing 161–4, "Improved Standards for Laboratory Animals," was conducted before the Senate Committee on Agriculture, Nutrition, and Forestry in 1983. The entire hearing is available on microfiche at Federal Depository Libraries; the location of the libraries can be found at http://catalog.gpo.gov/fdlpdir/FDLPdir.jsp.

Senator Robert Dole (R, Kansas) was presiding, and Senator Melcher was present. They were the only two Senators reported to be present. This hearing was on Senate Bill 657, which was introduced as an amendment to the Animal Welfare Act, "to help insure a more humane and uniform treatment of lab animals."

In his opening remarks, Senator Dole commented on the content of Senate Bill 657. This bill would ask that alternative methods to using animals for research or testing be considered. It would encourage an information service to be established at the USDA National Library of Agriculture and the National Library of Medicine. It would establish an animal studies committee within each institution that would consist of at least three persons, one of whom would be an outside person not related to the institution and one a veterinarian. This committee would review the ongoing care, treatment, and practices of the facility, focusing on minimizing animal pain and distress. The bill would allow committee members to review practices of the facility during experimentation but preserve the institution's right to design its own experiments. Senator Dole reported that he had received letters that supported and opposed animal welfare legislation. A repeated comment was "although it is important to treat animals humanely, we must not impede scientific research."

Bert Hawkins, the Administrator of the Animal Plant Health Inspection Service (APHIS), reported that APHIS is responsible for registration and inspection of approximately 3,300 research sites. The current bill would require APHIS to expand the definition of research facility to include each federal department, agency, or instrumentality. Since federal agencies are required to comply with the same standard of care, Mr. Hawkins questioned the need to expand the definition of research facility to include federal agencies. Mr. Hawkins also questioned the change in standards for veterinary care from "minimum" to "proper." Mr. Hawkins said, "This change would require us to develop standards considered proper for the different segments of the industry and various animal species covered by the act. The term 'proper' would have to be qualified, that is, proper requirements with respect to the type of animal, the species, the use of the animal, its immediate environment, and other factors. The term 'minimum,' on the other hand, is more definitive and more enforceable in a court of law." Mr. Hawkins also did not favor adding "adequate exercise" as a required standard, as it would be difficult to determine what amount of exercise was adequate for each species. Mr. Hawkins believed that the determination of whether an animal is suffering for momentary pain or discomfort during the actual research should be left to the professional judgment of a veterinarian.

William F. Raub, Associate Director for Extramural Research and Training for the National Institutes of Health, testified with regard to how oversight of the use of animals by the National Institutes of Health and its grantees is managed. The Institutes require all of its intramural staff and grantees to provide a written description of the uses of all vertebrate animals and to ensure that the institution has an animal care committee with a veterinarian as one of its members. Mr. Raub also testified that the NIH was cooperating and funding the Institute of Laboratory Animal Resources of the National Academy of Science to update its *Guide for the Care and Use of Laboratory Animals*.

Senator John Melcher reported that the current AWA standards were minimum standards, meaning that they were open to interpretation by APHIS, the research facility, and Congress. It was the intent of Congress and the public that animal facilities be very clean and adequate in size. Senator Melcher was concerned about how appropriations were handled. Senator Melcher also mentions that Christine Stevens had started to coordinate and expedite all the various groups that were affected by this bill.

The Department of Health and Human Services, National Institutes of Health, provided a list of institutions that acknowledged use of warmblooded animals in their activities and had received approval of their proposed standard of animal care.

Stuart Proctor, Assistant Director, National Affairs Division of the American Farm Bureau Federation, claimed that farmers were under attack by individuals and organizations that made false and inaccurate statements about how things are done on farms. These individuals and organizations, he asserted, present emotional arguments and exaggerated examples of how animals are raised, treated, and slaughtered. He was concerned that these organizations might be successful in passing legislation based on emotion. Many of the animal rights activists who challenge laboratories also challenge the farming industry, he said.

Dr. Orr E. Reynolds, Executive Vice President of the American Physiological Society, reported that physiologists use more than half of the animals required for biomedical and behavioral research and for teaching. He suggested that deviations in research protocols could be discussed with the animal studies committee. He also suggested that the decision to replicate an experiment should be left in the hands of scientists and teachers.

Dr. Walter Randall, Professor of Physiology, Loyola University of Chicago, Stritch School of Medicine, reminded the subcommittee that physiology is the study of how living beings function and that more than half of the animals used in research are used for cardiovascular, neurophysiological, endocrinological and respiratory research. He mentioned that he had undergone quadruple bypass surgery and argued that 80 percent of the diagnostic techniques and treatment he benefited from were not known to medicine 5 or even 15 years ago. He further stated that the bypass surgery was based entirely on animal experimentation. He claimed that there is significant evidence that researchers and scientists using live animals follow the standards of the AWA and the guidelines of NIH. In addition to these standards, the American Physiological Society and other professional societies have published their own guidelines. The Society does not support review of research protocols or interference with the actual research. Dr. Randall stated that the definition of "methodologies and procedures" is something that requires real expertise. An individual who has only textbook knowledge is simply not qualified to make this judgment. Research is at the forefront of knowledge and interjection by the staff of the secretary could have a stultifying effect on progress.

Dr. Frank Standaert, Chairman of the Department of Pharmacology, Georgetown University School of Medicine, spoke for the American Association of Medical Colleges, which represents 127 accredited medical schools and 400 major teaching hospitals. Dr. Standaert believed that advances in patient care are totally dependent on progress in biomedical research using laboratory animals. He said, "Over the last four decades, medical school research capacity has grown very rapidly and the application of that new knowledge has resulted in profound improvements in the understanding as well as in the prevention, diagnosis and treatment of human disease." The Association was not aware of any deficiencies in the care of laboratory animals within academic medical centers.

Charles Chambers, Executive Director of the American Institute of Biological Sciences, reported that the Institute is a federation of three dozen biological, medical, and agricultural societies. The Institute believes that the use of replicable experiments "is an indispensable element of scientific validation, and, in order to ensure that the knowledge that is obtained in the laboratory is sound enough to be used for the improvement of human welfare, the validation of that data through replication of the experiments is essential." Mr. Chambers was concerned about the use of a public representative as a member of the animal use committee. He cited the general decrease in science literacy and said that good research data can be obtained only with good animal care. Use of animals in student teaching laboratories enhances the student's sensitivity to and understanding of living creatures.

Dr. Herbert Rackow, of the Scientists' Group for the Reform of Animal Experimentation, found that the provisions for adequate exercise and appropriate pre- and postsurgical care are long overdue for revision. He says that if animals are to be used as a model for humans, then the medical and nursing care should be similar. Rackow believed that the training for scientists and for those who care for the animals that was called for under the bill should be mandatory.

Dr. Bennett Derby, Professor of Clinical Neurology and Pathology at New York University, agreed that that a veterinarian should be responsible for dealing with animal pain. The bill went beyond the stay of the animal and provided for the need for euthanasia. He mentioned a particularly sensitive practice that exists in neurophysiology in which an animal is in a stereotaxic holder (a device that holds the skull in a fixed position that allows an electrode to be placed in a specific location in the brain) without general anesthesia, which would interfere with the electrical activity of the brain as it was being recorded.

The American Psychological Association and the Association for the Advancement of Psychology argued that a study should be conducted prior to enacting the proposed amendments to the AWA. They believed that many of the provisions would impose an extra regulatory burden on researchers without necessarily improving animal welfare. One of the major concerns was that there are few alternative methods for studying behavior.

Emily F. Gleockler, President of Humane Information Services, St. Petersburg, Florida, believed that the small possible additions to medical knowledge should not be achieved at the expense of morally unjustified cruelties to lesser forms of life. She said, "At last it is recognized that preoccupation with the problems of human welfare does not justify ignoring the problems of animal welfare." She continued, "So, it will no longer serve to defend unnecessary suffering by laboratory animals because it is a broad effort to improve public health and save human lives. The public, to a constantly increasing extent, wants to know how and why some particular source of animal suffering is required to serve some socially desirable purpose, and whether or not the end justifies the means." She reported that a random sample of the research included in the Index Medicus studied by independent research analysts found that 74.6 percent of these studies could have used fewer animals, if proper statistical design had been used.

The Cosmetic, Toiletry and Fragrance Association represents 240 companies that manufacture or distribute more than 90 percent of the finished cosmetic products marketed in the United States and has 220 members that provide cosmetic raw materials and testing laboratories. The Association agreed that animal testing should be conducted in a humane manner and said that it had been in the forefront in identifying alternatives to animal research. In 1981, the Association established the Center for Alternatives to Animal Testing at Johns Hopkins University. The Association believed that having an "unaffiliated community representative" is unworkable because this person may have difficulty appreciating the need for a particular study.

Steve Kopperud, Legislative Director for the American Feed Manufacturers Association, reported that members of the

Association produce more than 70 percent of formula livestock and poultry feed. The Association, he said, was committed to the humane treatment of animals. While the Association commended the motivation behind the bill, it questioned the need for it. The Association, he added, believed that animal rights and welfare activists are well meaning but argued there is no verifiable evidence to support their claims.

C. Leon Hirsch, President of the United States Surgical Corporation, asserted that most research organizations' animal care standards far exceeded the existing statutory and regulatory "minimum" requirements. He believed that the committee and Congress should "deliberate very carefully" to avoid "unintentional results which could hamper medical research, developing technology or essential training." He was also concerned about the protection of trade secrets and other proprietary rights. Last, he was concerned about the costs of good-faith compliance with the requirements of the bill. He reported that U.S. Surgical was subject to inspections by two federal and two state agencies in addition to having to meet the stringent requirements for American Association for Laboratory Animal Care (AALAC) certification. He questioned the need for an additional inspection by an "institutional animal studies committee." He was particularly concerned about the requirement that one member of this committee not be affiliated with the organization, which he claimed might jeopardize proprietary rights to the treatments or devices that are the subject of the research. He was also concerned about the time and funds required for the committee to provide annual training for personnel involved with animal care and treatment.

John McArdle, Director of the Laboratory Animal Welfare at the Humane Society of the United States, reported that there should be a reduction of pain and suffering endured by animals used in research. He believed that everything that an animal experiences has a real or potential impact on the validity of the results of the research. Any attempt to compare results between two or more institutions must assume equivalent care of the animals involved. He argued that the standards set by the AWA and the NIH are minimum standards that may not be sufficient to establish and maintain normal behavioral and physiological responses. Dr. Michael Fox, the Scientific Director of the Society, endorsed a change from "adequate" to "proper" species-specific requirements, including the need for physical exercise and the opportunity to engage in natural behavioral repertoires.

Christine Stevens, Secretary of the Society for Animal Protection Legislation, supported the bill. She said that remarkable progress had been made in the use of alternatives to animals. For example, the Pharmaceutical Manufacturers Association and the National Society for Medical Researchers have stated that the routine use of the quantitative lethal dose 50 percent (i.e. the level of drug that kills 50% of the subjects exposed to it) is not scientifically justified. The lethal dose 50 percent is used to determine the lethal dose of a drug or chemical. Ms. Stevens believed that animal study committees are important. She suggested that these committees include a veterinarian and someone not associated with the facility. She argued that this committee would be similar to one intended to protect human subjects, the Institutional Review Board. She provided USDA reports of inspections of medical schools and other scientific institutions that she had obtained under the Freedom of Information Act. She proceeded to provide quotes from these documents that suggest that the inspections were inadequate. She argued that an animal should be used in no more than one major operation and reported seeing animals that had been subjected to as many as seven operations. She was also in favor of the exercise provision of the bill and the provision forbidding discrimination against those who report violations, as well as the requirements for training for scientists and animal care technicians. She mentioned that even though farm animals are exempt from the bill, some farm organizations still opposed the bill. She reported that the Association for Biomedical Research, reportedly funded by Charles River Breeding Laboratories, in Wilmington, Massachusetts, favored a study of the state of animal welfare and asserted that this was a stalling tactic

Peyton Hawes Dunn, Chairperson of Working for Animals Used in Research, Drugs, and Surgery (WARDS), argued that the USDA had failed to enforce the AWA and believed that the Department of Health and Human Services, which was the source of most of the funding for biomedical research, should be tasked with enforcing animal welfare. Mr. Dunn presented a discussion of the Silver Springs monkey case. After discussing this case, Mr. Dunn said that "one of the main purposes of NIH is to prevent interference with research by laws and inspectors ignorant of the purposes and procedures of research." He asserted that professional handling of animals is vital to meaningful research. He was also in favor of developing alternatives and proposed to create a Center for Alternatives that would include representatives of government agencies concerned with research. Mr. Dunn did not believe that the current method for reporting the number of animals used in painful experiments had no value. Mr. Dunn reports that a 1978 survey by the Institute of Laboratory Animal Resources reported that only 14 of the 21 research organizations working with the NIH were following NIH guidelines. This survey found that 77 percent of the laboratories that responded claimed that they were following the NIH guidelines, and 23 percent admitted they were not.

Dr. John F. Kullberg, Executive Director of the American Society for the Prevention of Cruelty to Animals, said that the Society supported the bill. He reported that the Director of the National Center of Toxicological Research was committed to the development of alternatives to animals, that Bristol Myers had committed itself to reducing the number of animals it used and to use nonanimal tests when possible, that Revlon was using computer searches to determine whether products similar to its own were in use to minimize animal testing, and that Johnson and Johnson was using a cell culture as a preliminary screen for potential irritants. He found that Johns Hopkins University, Rockefeller University, and the University of Texas were also seeking alternatives. He strongly recommended the use of research committees and was in favor of language in the bill that changed "minimum standards" to "appropriate standards."

Dr. Kenneth J. Shapiro, Executive Director of the Psychologists for the Ethical Treatment of Animals, reported that his organization supported the bill, especially the provision for including an outside member on the animal use committee.

Dr. W. M. Decker of the American Veterinary Medical Association recommended that the AWA be adequately enforced before new legislation is considered.

Orville K. Sweet, Executive Vice President of the National Pork Producers Council, supported the exclusion of farm and food animals from the bill.

Tom Gustafson, Chairman of the National Cattlemen's Association Subcommittee on Animal Care, said that cattlemen were interested in animal welfare and had an economic interest in animals. The Association supported the idea that farm animals should not be included under the bill. The Association was concerned that the animal use committee might try to derive solutions to a problem without really understanding the nature of the problem. The Association also believed that the wording of the section concerning in vitro testing, encourages but does not legislate their use.

Virginia Chipuroni, President of the New York Humane Society, maintained that animals kept in relatively small cages should have an opportunity to exercise and that adequate veterinary care is vital. The Society also was in favor of constructive steps toward the development of alternative research methods and of training of researchers.

John Gleiber, Executive Secretary of the Society for Animal Protection Legislation, provided resolutions by the Lycoming County SPCA, Williamsport, Pennsylvania; the Animal Rescue Foundation, Middlebury, Connecticut; Defenders of Animals, Inc., West Allis, Wisconsin; the Orlando Humane Society, Orlando, Florida; and the Humane Society of Rochester and Monroe County, Fairport, New York, all in support of the bill.

Dr. Claude Migeon, Chairman of the Public Affairs Committee of the Endocrine Society, which represents more than 4,000 scientists and physicians, argued that adequate animal care is essential to excellent research. But the Society felt that it was important to determine the current status of animals before initiating new legislation.

The Academy of Clinical Laboratory Physicians and Scientists endorsed the further study of animal welfare before enacting new legislation.

Jean Harper, President of the Leon County Humane Society of Tallahassee, Florida, supported the bill.

Robert Markmann, President of the Society for the Protection and Preservation of Animals, supported the bill.

Dr. Samuel M. Peacock, of Psychopharmacology Research, Inc., supported the bill and said, "It has been my experience, based on almost 40 years of research at seven institutions, that the individual investigators and the science administrator, for a variety of reasons, will not be concerned with the human treatment of research animals. It is not that these people are in-humane, but rather that there is a certain overriding zeal to get the research done, coupled with frequent budget limitations which dictate that the funds be spent elsewhere."

Dr. Jay Glass of Pittsburgh, Pennsylvania, supported the bill.

Bianca Beary, President of the Washington Humane Society, said that lab animal facilities should be inspected by the USDA and that the inclusion of a member of the public provides important oversight.

Alex Pacheco, of People for the Ethical Treatment of Animals, believed that the bill would prevent abuses that were causing pain and distress to animals. He also believed that the Animal Studies Committee would provide valuable assistance to the USDA.

Dr. Marjorie Anchel, President of the New York State Humane Association, maintained that the bill should be enacted. The Association, she said, was familiar with the effects of small cages for companion animals and believed that the requirement for exercise is essential. The Association also was familiar with the misuse of paralytics and suggested that these agents should not be used for euthanasia.

House of Representatives Hearing 161–27, "Improved Standards for Laboratory Animals Act; and Enforcement of the Animal Welfare Act by the Animal and Plant Health Inspection Service"

A second hearing was before the House Subcommittee on Department Operations, Research, and Foreign Agriculture on September 19, 1984. A transcript of the entire hearing is available on microfiche at the Federal Depository Libraries; the location of the libraries can be found at http://catalog.gpo.gov/fdlpdir/FDLP-dir.jsp.

The subcommittee chairman was George E. Brown. The members present for this hearing were Representatives Harvey O. Staggers, Timothy J. Penny, Thomas S. Foley, Harold J. Volkmer, Pat Roberts, Steve Gunderson, Cooper Evans, and Webb Franklin. Representative Charles Rose, a member of the full committee, and Cristobal P. Aldrete, special counsel, were also present.

The hearing dealt with H.R. 5725, a revised version of S. 657 introduced by Senator Dole. Congressman Brown reported that there was no law that required researchers to use painkillers during experiments that cause pain to animals. The bill would require the use of painkillers unless it specifically interfered with the research protocol. This bill would also establish a voluntary national database to help reduce unintended duplication of research and to ensure that researchers are aware of alternatives (e.g. lower animals, in vitro methods, and computer simulations). The bill, said the congressman, "would not interfere with the freedom of the decision of a scientist to conduct an experiment but instead takes precautions to ensure that humane handling of animals occurs whenever possible." Brown maintained that no field should be free of scrutiny or improvement. Each witness before the committee was asked to limit testimony to five minutes; additional information could be added to the official record.

Dr. James B. Wyngaarden, Director of the National Institutes of Health, asserted "that the bill reflects a general understanding of some of the fundamental concerns and needs of the biomedical research community." He believed that existing law and administrative authority were satisfactory and that new legislation was not needed. Institutions that receive support from NIH must provide assurances that they will comply with NIH guidelines; approximately one-third are accredited by the American Association for Accreditation of Laboratory Animal Care, and the remaining institutions are either in full compliance or working toward full compliance. In 1983, NIH inspectors visited 10 randomly selected institutions and found no abuses of animals; the institutions were in compliance with the guidelines. NIH added a requirement that the animal use committee have one member not affiliated with the institution, required more frequent updating of institutional assurance statements, and initiated an educational campaign. NIH also sponsored a series of workshops on the subjects of "alternative" or "adjunct" methods of research.

Gretchen Wyler, Vice Chairman of The Fund for Animals, which has 250,000 members, reported that her members were surprised that the requirements outlined in the proposed bill were not already laws. She claimed that current enforcement was grossly deficient, that the budget of APHIS was too low to do an adequate job, and that, because of budgetary restrictions, inspectors might not be well enough trained. She reported that a comprehensive survey by Dr. Michael Glannelli, a member of the American Psychological Association and science adviser to the Fund, found that "1984 animal research published in the APA journals raises reasonable questions about the necessity of much of the published work and removes all reasonable doubt that animals are routinely made to bear suffering and despair." The Fund supported the bill.

Christine Stevens, Secretary of the Society for Animal Protective Legislation, noted that the biomedical research organizations supported the AWA and its amendments. The data collected by the Society showed "major and repeated deficiencies or alleged violations of the minimum standards of the Animal Welfare Act by 23.7 percent of a sample of 186 institutions whose inspection reports and annual reports have so far been examined. Another 22 percent had less frequent major violations, and 28.5 percent have minor ones; 1.6 percent are under investigation and the rest, according to the USDA veterinary inspectors' records, are abiding by the, and I repeat, minimum standards." Ms. Stevens suggested that USDA inspectors have overlooked serious violations in the past. This means that only 24.2 percent of registered research institutions were regularly meeting the AWA standards. Ms. Stevens argued that the number of animals used in research was not diminishing. She provided a list of research institutions and showed video sequences taken by the Lifeforce Foundation. She also mentioned tapes stolen by the Animal Liberation Front of scientists at the University of Pennsylvania Head Injury Clinical Research Center; People for the Ethical Treatment of Animals prepared a half-hour of excerpts from a 60-hour-long tape. Ms. Stevens showed this tape with commentary. After presenting the tape, she reported that the University of Pennsylvania had claimed in its annual report to have caused no unrelieved pain to animals. She discussed "learned helplessness" experiments. She then went on to report that the current bill was the product of a years' work and involved meetings with the American Physiological Society, the American Psychological Association, the Association of American Medical Colleges, the Society of Animal Protective Legislation, the Humane Society of the United States, the American Humane Society, and the People for the Ethical Treatment of Animals. This process led to S. 657, sponsored by Senator Dole. She believed that two statements—"and shall concern themselves with the welfare of animal subjects" and "an outside member who shall be responsible for the welfare for representing community concerns regarding the welfare of animal subjects". She acknowledged the controversy around defining standards that are "proper" and those that are "minimum" and suggested that "proper" would be a better term to use in the standards. She indicated that the USDA was asking for additional guidance on the standards for exercise for dogs and that the agency questioned the need for veterinarians to visit other federal agencies, which she believes would be highly beneficial. She reported that the Association for Biomedical Research is funded by the Charles River Breeding Laboratories, which is a multinational, multi-million-dollar business that had, according to the Boston *Globe*, $45 million in sales and $6.2 million in earnings in 1983. Ms. Stevens claimed that "these sales are achieved by skillful and unrelenting promotion of the sale of the maximum number of animals to scientific institutions." She reported that NIH was a big customer of Charles River, where in 1983 it spent more than $3 million. Ms. Stevens claimed that Frankie Trull, the Executive Director of the Foundation for Biomedical Research and the Association for Biomedical Research, worked closely with NIH and that Ms. Trull had worked to convince Congress not to act on the current bill until the completion of an 18-month study by the National Academy of Sciences. Ms. Stevens stated that agricultural interests opposed the enactment of the current bill even though farm animals were exempt from its terms.

The American Heart Association asserted that animal research has had a substantial impact on the reduction of cardiovascular disease.

Representative Par Roberts maintained that the new legislation might not be required but that the USDA should actively enforce existing regulations. He asked if APHIS had sufficient funds to make the necessary inspections.

Representative Charles Rose asserted that the bill was fair and realistic.

Bert W. Hawkins, Administrator of the Animal and Plant Inspection Service, argued that to administer the AWA required judgment. He reported that inspectors visited, on average, each registered site at least twice annually. But this was not always possible or necessary, which was where judgment came into play.

Dr. Gerald van Hoosier, Jr., testifying on behalf of the National Association of State Universities and Land Grant Colleges, the American Council on Education, and the Association of American Universities, said that the bill was a thoughtful attempt to address important issues about animal care. But, he believed that new legislation should wait until the completion of the National Academy of Science study. In addition, NIH was revising its guidelines, and any differences in the language between the bill and the NIH guidelines might cause confusion. He did not believe that "alternative" research methods were reasonable, because for some forms of research there are no substitutes for animals, except possibly humans.

Dr. John McArdle, Director of Laboratory Animal Welfare for the Humane Society of America, believed that there should be consistent interpretation of inspection and enforcement requirements and that some inspectors have inadequate training. He discussed the failure of APHIS enforcement at the University of California,

Berkeley. He asked that another section be added to the bill and titled "Civil Enforcement Suits"; this section would enable any person to commence a civil suit to compel the secretary of agriculture to apply and enforce the provisions of the AWA. He argued that he was concerned about the combined use of paralytics and anesthetics.

Dr. Glenn Geelhoed, Director of Surgical Research Laboratories, speaking on behalf of the Association of American Medical Colleges, which represents 127 medical schools, 400 teaching hospitals, and 70 professional and academic societies, claimed that violations of standards were rare and that a comprehensive study should be conducted to determine if problems existed and if there was a need for future legislation and, if so, what it should contain. He believed that APHIS lacked sufficient funds to ensure full compliance with the law. He stated that three agencies were revising guidelines and that future legislation should wait until this process was complete.

Dr. Walter C. Randall, Professor of Physiology, Stritch School of Medicine, Loyola University of Chicago, speaking on behalf of the American Physiological Society, presented testimony that physiologists are the largest users of animals and that more than half of the total number of animals used in research are used for cardiovascular, neurophysiological, endocrinological, and respiratory research. Most of the spectacular advances in medicine are based on animal experiments, he said. The number of dogs, cats, and frogs used for educational purposes has declined. Dr. Randall argued that where nonanimal adjunct methods were available, they were used voluntarily by physiologists. Dr. Randall believed that the secretary of agriculture should initiate new regulations and that new legislation was not needed. The Association recommended that the AWA be amended to provide for federal prosecution of persons or organizations that either directly or indirectly interfered with federally funded research; if convicted, such persons or organizations should be held liable for punitive damages and for the cost of replacing materials, data, equipment, animals, or records, as well as the cost of repeating the experiments that were interrupted or invalidated.

Dr. Edward C. Melby, Jr., Dean of the Cornell Veterinary College and President of the Association of Bio-medical Research, which represents about 200 organizations and companies that use animal models in biomedical research and testing, said that the Association agreed with the basic premise of the bill but recommended that it wait for the outcome of the study by the National Academy of Science. He claimed that APHIS inspections were often inconsistent and lacking in uniformity. The Association believed that the current bill, because of the nonspecificity of some of the language, implied that the secretary of agriculture had the authority to interfere with actual research performance. The Association argued that this approach was full of pitfalls, especially if assumed that "that all USDA inspectors do possess a broad-based knowledge of the vast types of research being conducted in this country and enough expertise to assess the quality or necessity of this research." The Association also disagreed with wording describing an outside member of the committee as "one who represents community concerns regarding the welfare of animal subjects." This definition, the speaker said, assumes that no one else on the committee is concerned about animal welfare, and it would be difficult to determine to what extent an outside member was aware of the general community's concerns and had some understanding of the scientific process and of the ethical considerations attached to using animals in research.

Dr. Barbara Orlans, Executive Director of the Scientist Center for Animal Welfare reported that the Center was an organization of scientists concerned about the humane treatment of animals. The Center runs workshops on how to run an animal care and use committee. The Center supported the legislation and believed that training for investigators was vital.

Dr. Marshall Steinberg, Secretary of the Society for Toxicology, which has members from academia, government, and industry, reported that in vitro techniques are valuable but that they cannot replace animals. The Society suggested that the definition of "distress" needed to be clarified. The speaker said, "Safety studies are required by regulation to produce a toxic effect at a high dose." He believed that the animal use committee should be run like a quality assurance unit.

Howard C. Brown, Vice President for Scientific Affairs of the National Association of Life Sciences Industries, a trade organization of independent toxicology testing laboratories commonly referred to as "contract laboratories," was concerned about the requirement that a nonassociated community member be given access to proprietary information, with fines and imprisonment, as well as actual and consequential damages, as deterrents; the consequences to the owner may be tested in organizations where this exposure is not possible.

Marc H. Rosenberg, Executive Director of the National Coalition for Science and Technology, an organization that represents approximately 1,000 research scientists, educators, businesspeople and engineers, as well as corporations and professional societies, said that the Coalition did not support this legislation and wanted to wait for the report of the Office of Technology Assessment that was due in 1985. In a series of workshops, a consensus was reached that more could be done to reduce duplication of animal research. The Coalition was concerned that local animal use committees would be left to establish their own standards, which might lead to confusion. The Coalition also believed that a swift and definite appeals process should be available to researchers. The Coalition agreed that it would be useful to have a national clearinghouse for information about animal research and alternatives, but it suggested that this clearinghouse should have its own line item in the budget.

John H. Seamer, a member of the British Veterinary Association, representing the Humane Information Services of the United States, reported that he had read the AWA and the proposed amendments and found that they were very different from the law in Britain, which was more restrictive. The British law applied to all vertebrates, while the AWA applied only to warmblooded animals. The British law required that "If an animal at any time during any experiment is found to be suffering from severe pain, which is likely to endure, such animal shall forthwith be painlessly killed." This was the case even if the objective of the experiments had not been achieved.

Food Security Act of 1985 (Public Law 99–198)

Title XVII-Related and Miscellaneous Matters
Section 1751. Congressional Findings
For the purposes of this subtitle, the Congress finds that

(1) the use of animals is instrumental in certain research and education for advancing knowledge of cures and treatment for diseases and injuries which afflict both humans and animals;
(2) methods of testing that do not use animals are being and continue to be developed which are faster, less expensive, and more accurate than traditional animal experiments for some purposes and further opportunities exist for the development of these methods of testing;

(3) measures which eliminate or minimize the unnecessary duplication of experiments on animals can result in more productive use of Federal funds; and

(4) measures which help meet the public concern for laboratory animal care and treatment are important in assuring that research will continue to progress.

Section 1752. Standards and Certification

(1) redesignating subsections (b) through (d) as subsections (f) through (h) respectively; and

(2) striking out the first two sentences of subsection (a) and inserting in lieu thereof the following new sentences: "(1) The Secretary shall promulgate standards to govern the humane handling, care, treatment, and transportation of animals by dealers, research facilities, and exhibitors.

(2) The standards described in paragraph (1) shall include minimum requirements

   (A) for handling, housing, feeding, watering, sanitation, ventilation, shelter from extremes of weather and temperatures, adequate veterinary care, and separation by species where the Secretary finds necessary for humane handling, care, or treatment of animals; and

   (B) for exercise of dogs, as determined by an attending veterinarian in accordance with general standards promulgated by the Secretary, and for a physical environment adequate to promote the psychological well-being of primates.

(3) In addition to the requirements under paragraph (2), the standards described in paragraph (1) shall, with respect to animals in research facilities, include requirements

   (A) for animal care, treatment, and practices in experimental procedures to ensure that animal pain and distress are minimized, including adequate veterinary care with the appropriate use of anesthetic, analgesic, tranquilizing drugs, or euthanasia;

   (B) that the principal investigator considers alternatives to any procedure likely to produce pain to or distress in an experimental animal;

   "(C) in any practice which could cause pain to animals

      (i) that a doctor of veterinary medicine is consulted in the planning of such procedures;

      (ii) for the use of tranquilizers, analgesics, and anesthetics;

      (iii) for pre-surgical and post-surgical care by laboratory workers, in accordance with established veterinary medical and nursing procedures;

(iv) against the use of paralytics without anesthesia, and
(v) that the withholding of tranquilizers, anesthesia, analgesia, or euthanasia when scientifically necessary shall continue for only the necessary period of time;

(D) that no animal is used in more than one major operative experiment from which it is allowed to recover except in cases of

(i) scientific necessity; or
(ii) other special circumstances as determined by the Secretary; and

(E) that exceptions to such standards may be made only when specified by research protocol and that any such exception shall be detailed and explained in a report outlined under paragraph (7) and filed with the Institutional Animal Care Committee."

(b) Section 13(a) of such Act is further amended

(1) by designating the third and fourth sentences as paragraph (4);
(2) by designating the fifth sentence as paragraph (5); and
(3) by striking out the last sentence and inserting in lieu thereof the following:

"(6)(A) Nothing in this Act

(i) except as provided in paragraphs (7) of this subsection, shall be construed as authorizing the Secretary to promulgate rules, regulations, or orders with regard to the design, outlines, or guidelines of actual research or experimentation by a research facility as determined by such research facility;
(ii) except as provided subparagraphs (A) and (C) (ii) through (v) of paragraph (3) and paragraph (7) of this subsection, shall be construed as authorizing the Secretary to promulgate rules, regulations, or orders with regard to the performance of actual research or experimentation by a research facility as determined by such research facility; and
(iii) shall authorize the Secretary, during inspection, to interrupt the conduct of actual research or experimentation.

(B) No rule, regulation, order, or part of this Act shall be construed to require a research facility to disclose publicly or to the Institutional Animal Committee during its inspection, trade secrets or commercial or financial information which is privileged or confidential.

(7)(A) The Secretary shall require each research facility to show upon inspection, and to report at least annually, that the provisions of this Act are being followed and that professionally acceptable standards governing the care, treatment, and use of animals are being followed by the research facility during actual research or experimentation.

(B) In complying with subparagraph (A), such research facilities shall provide

(i) information on procedures likely to produce pain or distress in any animal and assurances demonstrating that the principal investigator considered alternatives to those procedures;

(ii) assurances satisfactory to the Secretary that such facility is adhering to the standards described in this section; and

(iii) an explanation for any deviation from the standards promulgated under this section.

(8) Paragraph (1) shall not prohibit any State (or a political subdivision of such State) from promulgating standards in addition to those standards promulgated by the Secretary under paragraph (1)."

(c) Section 13 of such Act is further amended by inserting after subsection (a) the following new subsections:

(b)(1) The Secretary shall require that each research facility establish at least one Committee. Each Committee shall be appointed by the chief executive officer of each such research facility and shall be composed of not fewer than three members. Such members shall possess sufficient ability to assess animal care, treatment, and practices in experimental research as determined by the needs of the research facility and shall represent society's concerns regarding the welfare of animal subjects used at such facility. Of the members of the Committee—

(A) at least one member shall be a doctor of veterinary medicine;

(B) at least one member—
    (i) shall not be affiliated in any way with such facility other than as a member of the Committee;
    (ii) shall not be a member of the immediate family of a person who is affiliated with such facility; and
    (iii) is intended to provide representation for general community interests in the proper care and treatment of animals; and

(C) in those cases where the Committee consists of more than three members, not more than three members shall be from the same administrative unit of such facility.

(2) A quorum shall be required for all formal actions of the Committee, including inspections under paragraph (3).
(3) The Committee shall inspect at least semiannually all animal study areas and animal facilities of such research facility and review as part of the inspection—
   (A) practices involving pain to animals, and
   (B) the condition of animals,

to ensure compliance with the provisions of this Act to minimize pain and distress to animals. Exceptions to the requirement of inspection of such study areas may be made by the Secretary if animals are studied in their natural environment and the study area is prohibitive to easy access."

Source: http://www.nal.usda.gov/awic/legislat/pl99198.htm. Accessed May 15, 2009

The 1985 Amendments Become Law

Once the 1985 Amendments were signed into law, the bureaucrats at the USDA Animal and Plant Protection and Inspection Service began the process of promulgating the regulations and standards that would be used to enforce this law. Generally, the secretary and other appointed officials of the USDA are only minimally involved in this process. The first step in this process is to solicit information and public comment for the drafting of regulations and standards called for in this amendment. This is accomplished by publishing a notice in the Federal Register (http://www.gpoaccess.gov/fr/), which is the official daily publication for rules, proposed rules, and notices of federal agencies and organizations, executive orders, and presidential documents.

"Animal Welfare; Final Rules, Parts 1 and 2, Final Rule" was published in the Federal Register on August 31, 1989 (vol. 54, no. 163, pp. 36112–163) and is summarized: "Often referred to as the 'Preamble' to the Animal Welfare Act amendments of 1985, the explanations of the regulations are used to identify the intent of the regulations published in Title 9, Code of Federal Regulations.

This issue contains final regulations developed to enact the 1985 amendments to the Animal Welfare Act covering the Definitions and Regulations sections. Extensive commentary is provided to respond to public comments about each of the proposed regulations. Comments and final regulations are provided in many areas including the structure and functions of the Institutional Animal Care and Use Committee; the principal investigator's consideration of alternatives that reduce, refine, or replace animal use; records; licensing; registration; stolen animals; and research facilities." This document is available at http://www.nal.usda.gov/awic/legislat/awafin.htm.

Once the comments are received and evaluated, the bureaucrats begin the process of promulgating the regulations and standards, which are published in the Code of Federal Regulations, Title 9, Chapter 1, Subchapter A—Animal Welfare.

Source: http://cfr.vlex.com/source/1058. Accessed May 15, 2009.

Food, Agriculture, Conservation, and Trade Act of 1990 (Public Law 101–624)

Section 28. Protection of Pets

(a) HOLDING PERIOD.—

(1) REQUIREMENT.—In the case of each dog or cat acquired by an entity described in paragraph (2), such entity shall hold and care for such dog or cat for a period of not less than five days to enable such dog or cat to be recovered by its original owner or adopted by other individuals before such entity sells such dog or cat to a dealer.

(2) ENTITIES DESCRIBED.—An entity subject to paragraph (1) is—

(A) each State, county, or city owned and operated pound or shelter;

(B) each private entity established for the purpose of caring for animals, such as a humane society, or other organization that is under contract

with a State, county, or city that operates as a
pound or shelter and that releases animals on a
voluntary basis; and

(C) each research facility licensed by the
Department of Agriculture.

Source: http://awic.nal.usda.gov/nal_display/index.php?info_center=3%20
&tax_level=4&tax_subject=182&topic_id=1118&level3_id=6735&level4_id=
11096&level5_id=0&placement_default=0. Accessed May 15, 2009.

Animal Enterprise Protection Act of 1992 (Public Law 102–346)

Section 2. Animal Enterprise Terrorism

(a) IN GENERAL.—Title 18, United States Code, is amended by
inserting after section 42 the following:

§ 43. Animal enterprise terrorism

(a) OFFENSE.—Whoever—

(1) travels in interstate or foreign commerce, or uses
or causes to be used the mail or any facility in
interstate or foreign commerce, for the purpose of
causing physical disruption to the functioning of
an animal enterprise; and

(2) intentionally causes physical disruption to the
functioning of an animal enterprise by intentionally
stealing, damaging, or causing the loss of, any
property (including animals or records) used by
the animal enterprise, and thereby causes economic
damage exceeding $10,000 to that enterprise, or
conspires to do so; shall be fined under this title or
imprisoned not more than one year, or both.

(b) AGGRAVATED OFFENSE.—

(1) SERIOUS BODILY INJURY.—Whoever in the
course of a violation of subsection (a) causes
serious bodily injury to another individual shall
be fined under this title or imprisoned not more
than 10 years, or both.

(2) DEATH.—Whoever in the course of a violation of subsection (a) causes the death of an individual shall be fined under this title and imprisoned for life or for any term of years.

(c) RESTITUTION.—An order of restitution under section 3663 of this title with respect to a violation of this section may also include restitution—

(1) for the reasonable cost of repeating any experimentation that was interrupted or invalidated as a result of the offense; and
(2) the loss of food production or farm income reasonably attributable to the offense.

(d) DEFINITIONS.—As used in this section—

(1) the term "animal enterprise" means—
  (A) a commercial or academic enterprise that uses animals for food or fiber production, agriculture, research, or testing;
  (B) a zoo, aquarium, circus, rodeo, or lawful competitive animal event; or
  (C) any fair or similar event intended to advance agricultural arts and sciences;
(2) the term "physical disruption" does not include any lawful disruption that results from lawful public, governmental, or animal enterprise employee reaction to the disclosure of information about an animal enterprise;
(3) the term "economic damage" means the replacement costs of lost or damaged property or records, the costs of repeating an interrupted or invalidated experiment, or the loss of profits; and
(4) the term "serious bodily injury" has the meaning given that term in section 1365 of this title.

(9e) NON-PREEMPTION.—Nothing in this section preempts any State law."

(b) CLERICAL AMENDMENT.—The item relating to section 43 in table of sections at the beginning of chapter 3 of title, United States Code, is amended to read as follows:
"43. Animal enterprise terrorism."

Farm Bill Title 10, Miscellaneous Provisions, Section D (2002)

Section 10301. Definition of Animal under the Animal Welfare Act

Section 2(g) of the Animal Welfare Act (7 U.S.C. 2132(g)) is amended in the first sentence by striking "excludes horses not used for research purposes and'" and inserting the following: "excludes (1) birds, rats of the genus Rattus, and mice of the genus Mus, bred for use in research, (2) horses not used for research purposes, and (3)."

Data

TABLE 6.1

Number of animals used in scientific research by state and species, fiscal year 2007

Species / States	All other covered species	Cats	Dogs	Guinea pigs	Hamsters	Nonhuman primates	Other farm animals	Pigs	Rabbits	Sheep	Total by state
AK	614				52		30				696
AL	2,730	211	1,904	503	214	1,463	610	1,174	1,807	28	10,644
AR	49	70	251	441	85	128	194	429	533	0	2,180
AZ	6,582	120	275	206	69	94	33	443	274	50	8,146
CA	16,380	2,195	3,498	27,774	6,175	4,470	7,241	4,970	49,396	2,056	124,155
CO	2,092	394	587	5,622	1,830	0	87	623	503	483	12,221
CT	763	36	592	622	2,408	339	10	584	525	51	5,930
DC	5,660	107	48	576	527	224	41	844	405	33	8,465
DE	932	266	377	5,158	1,481	0	507	41	16,176	570	25,508
FL	2,723	441	403	462	151	716	881	1,237	303	232	7,549
GA	7,024	1,037	1,940	1,214	10,226	3,334	166	1,269	5,043	76	31,329
HI	5	51	50	5	478	0	0	38	31	0	658
IA	1,337	2,180	2,229	5,646	43,809	23	919	974	5,163	512	62,792
ID	238	16	40	0	0	0	49	0	34	2	379
IL	4,513	975	3,074	2,788	3,046	652	761	1,792	5,051	300	22,952
IN	2,810	329	1,983	750	1,862	709	364	927	2,257	135	12,126
KS	1,350	565	1,533	670	813	220	112	138	667	0	6,068
KY	2,309	56	177	254	372	63	26	140	535	0	3,932
LA	1,029	237	380	4	240	2,561	359	83	1,032	7	5,932

MA	6,258	106	3,287	22,436	9,229	5,211	714	5,286	14,857	752	68,136
MD	8,462	87	810	19,849	5,061	6,304	1,725	1,656	7,465	377	51,796
ME	716	0	0	48	0	0	340	31	234	3	1,372
MI	6,493	463	6,784	15,291	913	3,361	286	2,912	4,482	563	41,548
MN	1,281	1,734	3,072	10,814	104	216	1,127	3,808	5,691	1,067	28,914
MO	1,440	1,874	2,413	3,978	8,126	108	450	1,813	3,373	66	23,641
MS	171	5	70	118	7	84	46	76	442	0	1,019
MT	26	9	0	28	532	5	125	0	313	84	1,122
NC	1,989	1,138	1,699	8,731	1,098	2,085	4,772	3,074	4,237	593	29,416
ND	36	149	21	3	2	81	24	952	443		1,711
NE	1,835	649	1,032	1,302	7,317	89	261	9,132	815	46	22,478
NH	394	23	9	1	265	16	0	256	7	31	1,002
NJ	3,692	135	6,427	13,668	2,193	4,461	42	1,284	8,260	0	40,162
NM	341	21	228	134	88	295	0	66	972	0	2,145
NV	1,947	0	121	163	0	0	9	0	188	380	2,808
NY	8,074	2,325	4,595	14,708	43,974	2,230	869	1,422	13,665	245	92,107
OH	4,159	1,113	6,052	13,438	3,884	2,151	192	4,304	13,827	137	49,257
OK	646	93	657	533	3	113	173	21	451	52	2,742
OR	576	46	37	1,022	101	2,369	645	708	416	299	6,219
PA	3,997	1,743	5,627	11,557	2,388	4,183	1,364	2,544	38,618	692	72,713
PR	971	0	0	0	287	3,066	0	36	14	0	4,374
RI	943	12	0	61	247	25	50	201	322	58	1,919
SC	635	238	199	248	55	471	44	289	617	0	2,796
SD	356	21	14	7	94	17	624	125	307	6	1,571
TN	2,179	120	466	161	990	171	239	1,440	732	11	6,509
TX	12,261	585	1,455	8,506	3,826	4,389	3,380	3,080	17,189	952	55,623
UT	1,418	107	291	423	4,190	16	14	214	791	198	7,662

(Continued)

TABLE 6.1

Number of animals used in scientific research by state and species, fiscal year 2007 (*Continued*)

Species	All other covered species	Cats	Dogs	Guinea pigs	Hamsters	Nonhuman primates	Other farm animals	Pigs	Rabbits	Sheep	Total by state
VA	2,109	80	283	360	321	94	125	4,389	1,212	37	9,010
VT	213	18	17	450	0	0	12	89	137	1,280	2,216
WA	2,221	162	795	4,687	359	4,596	248	795	1,949	26	15,838
WI	955	300	6,192	1,820	2,972	8,859	722	834	3,914	203	26,771
WV	230	40	20	14	27	9	0	0	307	81	728
WY	345	5	23	3	7	0	37	0	20	23	463
Species Total	136,509	22,687	72,037	207,257	172,498	69,990	31,106	65,615	236,511	13,240	
Report Total											1,027,450

Source: U.S. Department of Agriculture, Animal and Plant Health Inspection Service, *Animal Care Annual Report of Activities: Fiscal Year 2007.*

TABLE 6.2

Total number of animals used in research, 1973–2007

FY	Dogs	Cats	Primates	Guinea pigs	Hamsters	Rabbits	Farm animals	Other covered animals	Totals
1973	195,157	66,165	42,298	408,970	454,986	447,570	Not reported	38,169	1,653,345
1974	199,204	74,259	51,253	430,439	430,766	425,585	"	81,021	1,692,527
1975	154,489	51,439	36,202	436,446	456,031	448,530	"	42,523	1,625,660
1976	210,330	70,468	50,115	486,310	503,590	527,551	"	73,736	1,922,100
1977	176,430	62,311	53,116	348,741	393,533	439,003	"	46,535	1,519,669
1978	197,010	65,929	57,009	419,341	414,394	475,162	"	58,356	1,687,201
1979	211,104	69,103	59,359	457,134	419,504	539,594	"	76,247	1,832,045
1980	188,783	68,482	56,024	422,390	405,826	471,297	"	49,102	1,661,904
1981	188,649	58,090	57,515	432,632	397,522	473,922	"	50,111	1,658,441
1982	161,396	49,923	46,388	459,246	337,790	453,506	"	69,043	1,577,292
1983	174,542	53,344	54,926	485,048	337,023	466,810	"	108,549	1,680,242
1984	201,936	56,910	55,338	561,184	437,123	529,101	"	232,541	2,074,133
1985	194,905	59,211	57,271	598,903	414,460	544,621	"	284,416	2,153,787
1986	176141	54,125	48,540	462,699	370,655	521,773	"	144,470	1,778,403
1987	180,169	50,145	61,392	538,998	416,002	554,385	"	168,032	1,969,123
1988	140,471	42,271	51,641	431,457	331,945	459,254	"	178,249	1,635,288
1989	156,443	50,812	51,688	481,712	389,042	471,037	"	153,722	1,754,456
1990	109,992	33,700	47,177	352,627	311,068	399,264	66,702	257,569	1,578,099
1991	107,908	34,613	42,620	378,582	304,207	396,046	214,759	363,685	1,842,420
1992	124,161	38,592	55,105	375,063	396,585	431,432	210,936	529,308	2,134,182
1993	106,191	33,991	49,561	392,138	318,268	426,501	165,416	212,309	1,704,505
1994	101,090	32,610	55,113	360,184	298,934	393,751	180,667	202,300	1,624,649
1995	89,420	29,569	50,206	333,379	248,402	354,076	163,985	126,426	1,395,463

(Continued)

TABLE 6.2

Total number of animals used in research, 1973–2007(*Continued*)

FY	Dogs	Cats	Primates	Guinea pigs	Hamsters	Rabbits	Farm animals	Other covered animals	Totals
1996	82,420	26,035	52,327	299,011	246,415	338,574	154,344	146,579	1,345,739
1997	75,429	26,091	56,381	272,797	217,079	309,322	159,742	150,987	1,267,828
1998	76,071	24,712	57,377	261,305	206,243	287,523	157,620	142,963	1,213,814
1999	70,541	23,238	54,927	266,129	201,593	280,222	155,409	165,939	1,217,998
2000	69,516	25,560	57,518	266,873	174,146	258,754	159,711	166,429	1,286,412
2001	70,082	22,755	49,382	256,193	167,231	267,351	161,658	242,251	1,236,903
2002	68,253	24,222	52,279	245,576	180,000	243,838	143,061	180,351	1,137,580
2003	67,875	25,997	53,586	260,809	177,991	236,250	166,135	199,826	1,188,469
2004	64,932	23,640	54,998	244,104	175,721	261,573	105,678	171,312	1,101,958
2005	66,610	22,921	57,531	221,286	176,988	245,786	155,004	231,440	1,177,566
2006	66,314	21,637	62,315	204,809	167,571	239,720	105,780	144,567	1,012,713
2007	72,037	22,687	69,990	207,257	172,498	236,511	109,961	136,509	1,027,450

Source: U.S. Department of Agriculture, Animal and Plant Health Inspection Service, *Animal Care Annual Report of Activities: Fiscal Year 2007.*

TABLE 6.3

Number of cattle in the United States, 1993–2002 (in thousands)

Year	All cattle and calves[1]	Cows and heifers that have calved		Heifers 500 pounds and over			Steers	Bulls	Calves under 500 pounds
		Beef cows	Milk cows	Beef cow replacements	Milk cow replacements	Other			
1993	99,176	33,365	9,658	6,092	4,176	8,550	16,940	2,278	18,118
1994	100,974	34,603	9,507	6,364	4,125	9,104	17,086	2,312	17,873
1995	102,785	35,190	9,482	6,452	4,121	9,302	17,513	2,385	18,341
1996	103,548	35,319	9,420	6,189	4,090	9,948	17,815	2,384	18,384
1997	101,656	34,458	9,318	6,042	4,058	10,212	17,392	2,350	17,826
1998	99,744	33,885	9,199	5,764	3,986	10,051	17,189	2,270	17,401
1999	99,115	33,745	9,133	5,535	4,069	10,170	16,891	2,281	17,290
2000	98,198	33,569	9,190	5,503	4,000	10,147	16,682	2,293	16,815
2001	97,277	33,397	9,183	5,588	4,057	10,131	16,441	2,274	16,206
2002[2]	96,704	33,100	9,110	5,561	4,060	10,057	16,800	2,244	15,773

Source: U.S. Department of Agriculture, National Agricultural Statistics Service.

[1]Totals may not add due to rounding.

[2]Preliminary.

TABLE 6.4

Number of hogs in the United States, 1992–2001

		Value	
	Number	Per head	Total
Year	Thousands	Dollars	1,000 dollars
1992	58,202	71.2	4,146,646
1993	57,940	75	4,339,509
1994	59,738	53	3,178,123
1995	58,201	71	4,115,118
1996	56,124	94	5,280,742
1997	61,158	82	4,985,532
1998	62,206	44	2,765,847
1999	59,342	72	4,254,293
2000	59,138	77	4,542,493
2001[1]	58,774	77	4,549,370

Source: U.S. Department of Agriculture, National Agricultural Statistics Service.
[1]Preliminary.

TABLE 6.5

Number of sheep and lambs in the United States, 1993–2003

		Value	
	Number	Per head	Total
Year	Thousands	Dollars	1,000 dollars
1993	10,201	70.6	714,163
1994[1]	9,836	69.9	681,384
1995[1]	8,989	74.7	663,449
1996[1]	8,465	86.5	732,197
1997[1]	8,024	96	761,650
1998[1]	7,825	102	797,826
1999[1]	7,215	88	637,634
2000[1]	7,032	95	668,750
2001[1]	6,965	100	694,495
2002[1,2]	6,685	92	618,123

Source: U.S. Department of Agriculture, National Agricultural Statistics Service.
[1]Beginning in 1994 includes new crop lambs.
[2]Preliminary.

7

Directory of Organizations

This chapter highlights organizations that promote animal rights and animal welfare. Each entry contains, where available, the name, address, e-mail address, and Webpage for the organization and information about its activities. Some of these organizations are small, while others are large and have a national or international presence. When available, I have included budgets and size of membership, which allows you to have a sense of how much influence the organization may have.

Abundant Wildlife Society of North America (AWS)
P.O. Box 2
Beresford, SD 57004
Founded: 1991
Phone: (605) 751-0979
Fax: NA
E-mail: NA
URL: http://www.aws.vcn.com

This is a group of interested individuals who support multiple use of public lands and the management and protection of wildlife. It keeps members apprised of environmental and animal rights agenda.

Selected publications include *Conservation-vs.-Environmentalism: Yellowstone National Park, Wolf Predation in Alaska*, the fact sheets "Wolf Reintroduction in the United States," "Mountain Lion," "Wolf Attacks in the United States," and "Endangered Species Act: Flawed Law."

Actors and Others for Animals (A&O)
11523 Burbank Blvd.
North Hollywood, CA 91601-2309
Founded: 1971
Phone: (818) 755-6045
Fax: (818) 755-6048
E-mail: webmistress@wom-designs.com
URL: http://actorsandothers.com
Membership: NA
Budget: NA

The organization was founded by Richard and Diana Basehart. It encourages spaying and neutering of pets, helping the City of Los Angeles with its mobile sterilization services. One focus is on pit bulls and pit bull mixes. Founding members include Doris Day, Jackie Joseph, and Lucie Arnaz, who used their celebrity to promote their ideas. A variety of other celebrities are involved, including JoAnne Worley, Loretta Swit, Betty White, and Earl Holliman.

Alliance for Animals (AFA)
232 Silver St.
South Boston, MA 02127-2206
Founded: 1988
Phone: (617) 268-7800
Fax: NA
E-mail: shelter@afa.arlington.ma.us
URL: http://www.afaboston.org
Membership: 3,500
Budget: NA

It promotes animal protection, fosters human-animal bond, raises the status of animals and animal caretakers, and provides direct rescue, adoption, and affordable veterinary care. It publishes a quarterly newsletter.

**Alliance for Contraception in Cats
and Dogs (ACC&D)**
14245 NW Belle Ct.
Portland, OR 97229

Founded: 2000
Phone: (503) 358-1438
Fax: NA
E-mail: info@acc-d.org
URL: http://www.acc-d.org
Membership: NA
Budget: NA

It promotes the distribution and development of nonsurgical methods and products for dogs and cats to help control pet population control. ACC&D has joined with the Found Animal Foundation (www.foundanimals.org) to launch the Michelson Prize in Reproductive Biology, which supports research on nonsurgical methods of sterilization.

American Anti-Vivisection Society (AAVS)
801 Old York Rd., Suite 204
Jenkintown, PA 19046
Founded: 1883
Phone: (215) 887-0816 (Toll-free: 800-SAY-AAVS)
Fax: NA
E-mail: aavs@aavs.org
URL: http://www.aavs.org
Membership: NA
Budget: NA

AAVS was the first nonprofit animal and protection organization in America. It is dedicated to ending the use of animals in research, testing, and education and promoting the use of nonanimal alternatives. AAVS has two main branches, Animalearn, which focuses on ending vivisection and dissection in the classroom, and The Science Bank, which focuses on alternatives to animal experiments, from basic dissection to psychology experiments. It publishes a quarterly magazine, *AV* Magazine, which focuses on a specific topic and is available at the Web site.

It seeks to end attempts at animal cloning, especially pet cloning. It seeks to ban pound seizures and to add mice, rats, and birds to the meaning of "animal" in the Animal Welfare Act. AVVS sells a variety of items in its online shop. It also provides a free Compassionate Shopping Guide on its Web site.

**American Association for Accreditation of Laboratory
Animal Care (AAALAC)**
5283 Corporate Dr., Suite 203
Frederick, MD 21703
Founded: 1965
Phone: (301) 696-9626
Fax: (301) 696-9627
E-mail: accredit@aaalac.org
URL: http://www.aaalac.org/
Membership: NA
Budget: NA

AAALAC provides institutions involved with animal research an independent, unbiased expert assessment of their programs and accredits those that meet or exceed standards. Accredited institutions must demonstrate that they are in compliance with the *Guide for the Care and Use of Laboratory Animals* (National Research Council, 1996). The AAALAC publishes a newsletter, as well as the magazines *Animal Lab News*, *Comparative Medicine*, *ILLAR Journal*, and *Lab Animals*. AAALAC provides pdf files on animal welfare issues, rules and regulations.

**American Association for Laboratory
Animal Science (AALAS)**
9190 Crestwyn Hills Dr.
Memphis, TN 38125
Founded: 1949
Phone: (901) 754-8620
Fax: (901) 753-0046
E-mail: info@aalas.org
URL: http://www.aalas.org/index.aspx
Membership: None
Budget: NA

AALAS is the premier forum for the exchange of information and expertise in the use of laboratory animals. It provides a certification program for laboratory animal technicians. It publishes the *Journal of the American Association for Laboratory Animal Science*, *Techtalk*, and *AALAS in Action*. AALAS also provides information for members of Institutional Animal Care and Use Committees and links to other organizations.

**American Council on Science
and Health (ACSH)**
1995 Broadway, 2nd Floor
New York, NY 10023
Founded: 1978
Phone: (212) 362-7044 (Toll- Free: (866) 905-2694)
Fax: (212) 362-4919
E-mail: acsh@acsh.org
URL: http://www.acsh.org/
Membership: NA
Budget: NA

The American Council on Science and Health (ACSH) is "a consumer education consortium concerned with issues related to food, nutrition, chemicals, pharmaceuticals, lifestyle, the environment and health. ACSH is an independent, nonprofit, tax-exempt organization."

**American Association of Zoo
Veterinarians (AAZV)**
581705 White Oak Rd.
Yulee, FL 32097
Founded: 1960
Phone: (904) 225-3275
Fax: (904) 225-3289
E-mail: rhilsenrothaazv@aol.com
URL: http://www.aazv.org
Members: 1,200
Budget: NA

The AAZV seeks to advance programs for preventive medicine, husbandry, and scientific research for free-ranging and captive wild animals, as well as to promote the general welfare of these animals. Its annual meeting presents a forum for the presentation and discussion of problems related to these animals. ACZM provides a short course in zoological medicine. It publishes *Zoo News from Around the World*, which is available on its Web site, as are links to information about infectious diseases in wildlife and to worldwide veterinarian and zoological organizations. It also provides a link to the AZA Wildlife Contraception Center, located at the St. Louis Zoo.

American Cetacean Society (ACS)
P.O. Box 1391
San Pedro, CA 90733-1391
Founded: 1967
Phone: (310) 548-6279
Fax: (310) 548-6950
E-mail: info@acsonline.org
URL: http://www.acsonline.org
Membership: 1,500
Budget: NA

The ACS seeks to protect whales, dolphins, porpoises and their habitats via public education, research grants, and conservation activities. ACS sponsors whale watching trips. The ACS provides annual reports online and provides its public policy statements.

American Humane Association (AHA)
63 Inverness Dr. East
Englewood, CO 80112-5117
Founded: 1877
Phone: (303) 792-9900 (Toll-free: (800) 227-4645)
Fax: (303) 792-5333
E-mail: publicpolicy@americanhumane.org
URL: http://www.americanhumane.org
Membership: NA
Budget: $11 million

AHA supports organizations and individuals seeking to prevent cruelty to children and animals and issues position statements on a variety of topics, including but not limited to animal fighting, animals in research, and captive wild animals, that are available as downloadable PDF files. It publishes *The Link*, which discusses the relationship between animal abuse and other forms of violence. Its Los Angeles office monitors the use of animals in film and television and authorizes the *No Animals Were Harmed*® end credit disclaimer. It provides a copy of its Annual Report on its Web site. AHA offers a variety of items in its online gift shop and provides animal and child welfare information and resources. It has a Facebook site (http://www.facebook.com/pages/American-Humane-Association/5943727453).

**American Society for the Prevention of Cruelty
to Animals (ASPCA)**
424 E. 92nd St.
New York, NY 10128-6804
Founded: 1866
Phone: (212) 876-7700 (Toll-free: (800)-628-0028)
Fax: NA
E-mail: shonalib@aspca.org
URL: http://www.aspca.org
Membership: NA
Budget: NA

ASPCA was the first humane organization in the Western Hemisphere. It offers discussions of its policies and positions and responds to frequently asked questions. It provides links to its various programs and services and to information about dog fighting, puppy mills, farm animal cruelty, horse cruelty, cockfighting, circus cruelty, and animal hoarding. It sells a variety of merchandise in its online store and is a source of pet health insurance. ASPCA provides links to pending federal and state legislation and encourages its member and others to lobby on behalf of animals.

American Veterinary Medical Association (AVMA)
1931 N. Meacham Rd., Suite 100
Schaumburg, IL 60173
Founded: 1863
Phone: (847) 925-8070 (Toll-free: (800) 248-2862)
Fax: (847) 925-1329
E-mail: avmainfo@avma.org
URL: http://www.avma.org
Members: 78,000
Budget: NA

The AVMA was founded by practitioners along the East Coast, and its first meeting, in New York, was attended by delegates representing New York, Massachusetts, New Jersey, Pennsylvania, Maine, Ohio, and Delaware. AVMA is a professional society for veterinarians and is the accrediting agency for the nation's 28 schools of veterinary medicine. The AVMA conducts educational and research programs; provides animal-related scientific information in a variety of venues, including annual meetings and the *American Journal of Veterinary Research*; and offers awards to outstanding veterinarians. It also sponsors National Pet Week (www.petweek.org). The purpose of AVMA is to improve animal and human health and to advance the veterinary medical profession. AVMA publishes point papers dealing with animal issues on its Web site, including one dealing with biosecurity issues, as well as brochures and fact sheets dealing with animal and public health issues. It provides a placement service for vets seeking work.

Animal Agriculture Alliance
P.O. Box 9522
Arlington, VA 22219
Founded: 1987
Phone: (703) 562-5160
E-mail: info@animalagalliance.org
URL: http://www.animalagalliance.org
Membership: NA
Budget: $250,000

The purpose of the Alliance is to provide the public with science-based information about the role of animal agriculture in helping feed a hungry world. It uses behavioral, physiological, biochemical, and pathological criteria to assess the wellbeing of farm animals. These criteria include access to clean water and nutritionally balanced diets, access to veterinary care as needed, adequate shelter, and the use of science-based husbandry practices (handling and during transportation). The AAA Web site contains information for teachers to enable them to spread the truth about animal agriculture The site also provides extensive links to other organizations.

Animal Behavior Management Alliance (ABMA)
3650 S Pointe Circle, No. 205
Laughlin, NV 89029
Founded: NA
E-mail: sekard@sandiegozoo.org
URL: http://www.theabma.org
Membership: NA
Budget: NA

The ABMA seeks to improve animal care using enrichment and training to enhance husbandry. Its members consist of trainers, handlers, and keepers of animals. It hosts an annual meeting and has a job bank. It publishes *ABMA Wellspring*, which is available as a pdf file on its Web site.

Animal Legal Defense Fund (ALDF)
170 E. Cotati Ave.
Cotati, CA 94931
Founded: 1979
Phone: (707) 795-2533
Fax: (707) 795-7280
E-mail: info@aldf.org
URL: http://www.aldf.org
Membership: 100, 000
Budget: $3 million

ADLF uses litigation to protect the lives and advance the interests of animals. ADLF provides legal assistance to prosecutors handling animal cruelty cases and strives to strengthen anticruelty statutes. It initiates lawsuits to stop animal abuse and to expand the boundaries of animal law and encourages government agencies to enforce existing animal protection laws. It provides leadership, encouragement, and funding for student groups interested in protecting animal lives and improving and advancing the cause of animal welfare through litigation.

Animal Liberation Front (ALF)
Address: NA
Founded: 1971
Phone: NA
Fax: NA
E-mail: NA
URL: http://www.animalliberationfront.com/

The ALF uses direct action in rescuing abused animals and causing financial harm through damage and destruction of property, while minimizing harm to animals (human and otherwise). ALF's activities are illegal, and the group does not have a central organization but functions through small groups or individuals. The Web site has links to videos, slide shows, and literature dealing with animal rights.

Animal Rights Coalition (ARC)
P.O. Box 8750
Minneapolis, MN 55408-0750
Founded: 1980
Phone: (612) 822-6161
Fax: NA
E-mail: animalrightscoalition@msn.com
URL: http://www.animalrightscoalition.com
Membership: NA
Budget: NA

ARC is the oldest animal rights organization in Minnesota. It supports a furless vegan emporium. ARC has convinced the University of Minnesota Medical School to stop using dogs in its cardiology laboratory and the American Humane Society to stop using gas chambers for euthanasia. It funds the first mobile facility for spaying and neutering feral cats. It provides information about animal welfare at a variety of venues.

Animal Rights International (ARI)
P.O. Box 1292
Middlebury, CT 06762
Founded: 1974
Phone: (203) 598-0554
E-mail: info@ari-online.org
URL: http://www.ari-online.org
Membership: NA
Budget: NA

ARI was founded by Henry Spira. The organization originally targeted experiments at the American Museum of Natural History that utilized cats and sought the repeal of New York State's pound seizure law. ARI helped increase the use of alternatives to animal testing in the cosmetics industry. ARI has been attempting to stop the use of the lethal dose 50 percent test to determine the lethal dose of drugs and chemicals. ARI persuaded slaughterhouses to stop the shackling and hoisting of animals during slaughter and to replace this method of control with upright restrainer technology. The ultimate goal of ARI is to reduce animal suffering by reducing the consumption of animal products. The

Web site has links to various animal rights and vegetarian organizations.

Animal Rights Mobilization (ARM)
P.O. Box 805859
Chicago, IL 60680
Founded: 1981
Phone: (773) 282-8918
Fax: NA
E-mail: spayneuterchicago@earthlink.net
URL: http://www.animalrightsmobilization.org/
Membership: NA
Budget: NA

ARM members advocate for the elimination of animal exploitation and abuse, foster cooperation within the rights movement, and promote awareness of the natural relationship between human and animal liberation. They conduct campaigns to eliminate the wearing of fur and to end the use of animals in laboratory experiments and product testing. They also promote spaying and neutering.

Animal and Society Institute
2512 Carpenter Rd., Suite 201-A2
Ann Arbor, MI 48108
Founded: 1979
Phone: (734) 677-9240
Fax: (734) 677-9242
E-mail: bee.friedlander@animalsandsociety.org
URL: http://www.animalsandsociety.org
Membership: NA
Budget: $200,000

The ASI was a result of the merger, in 2005, of the Institute for Animals and Society and the Animal and Society Forum , which were formerly the Animal Rights Network and Psychologists for the Ethical Treatment of Animals, respectively. ASI promotes advocacy for animal rights issues in public policy development by conducting scholarly research and analysis, providing education and training, and fostering cooperation with other social movements and interests. It argues that creditable economic, political, legal, philosophical, and scientific arguments must be identified and used to change commercial, religious, and academic attitudes and actions that involve animals. The Web site provides links to other organizations and publications.

The Animal Society (TAS)
723 S Casino Center Blvd., 2nd Fl.
Las Vegas, NV 89101
Founded: 2000
Phone: (702) 477-9677 (Toll-free: (877) 227-7487)
Fax: NA
E-mail: support@animalsociety.org
URL: http://www.animalsociety.org
Membership: NA
Budget: NA

AS is "dedicated to preventing suffering, neglect, abuse, and cruelty to animals, providing information, raising public awareness of animal issues, promoting responsible pet ownership, and kindness towards all living things." Its focus is national in scope and promotes responsible pet ownership

Animal Transportation Association (AATA)
111 East Loop N.
Houston, TX 77029
Founded: 1976
Phone: (713) 532-2177
Fax: (713) 532-2166
E-mail: info@aata-animaltransport.org
URL: http://www.aata-animaltransport.org
Members: 300
Budget: $100,000

AATA is dedicated to the safe and humane transport of animals by carriers, shippers, forwarders, humane and animal welfare groups, zoos, and animal breeders. ATTA publishes a magazine, *Migrations*. The Web site provides links to animal transport professionals around the world, as well as to AATA publications. AATA provides a certification program for animal attendants of horses.

Animal Welfare Institute (AWI)
P.O. Box 3650
Washington, DC 20027
Founded: 1951
Phone: (703) 836-4300
Fax: (703) 836-0400
E-mail: awi@awionline.org
URL: http://www.awionline.org
Membership: NA
Budget: NA

In its early years, AWI focused on the needs of animals used for experimentation, on encouraging nonanimal alternatives, and on seeking a ban on the use of animals in science fair projects. AWI's focus has broadened to factory farms and the cruelty inflicted on pigs, cows, chickens, and other farm animals. AWI seeks to ban leg-hold traps and wire snare traps, as well as to minimize human-generated ocean noise and to ban commercial whaling. AWI publishes the magazine *AWI Quarterly*, which is available on its Web site, and provides links to other AWI Web sites. It also provides eAlerts called The Compassion Index, which provides information about legislative action.

Animals Voice (AV)
1354 East Ave., No. R-252
Chico, CA 95926
Founded: 2000
Phone: (530) 343-2498 (Toll-free: (800)-82-VOICE)
Fax: (530) 343-2498
E-mail: veda@animalsvoice.com
URL: http://www.animalsvoice.com
Membership: NA
Budget: NA

AV publishes the magazine *Animal Voice*; current editions are available at the Web site, as are links that describe their current concerns. Its bookstore includes the books *In Your Mouth: For Food: An Eating Animals Pictorial*; *At Our Hands: A Pictorial of Animal Exploitation*; and *All Heaven in a Rage: Essays on Eating Animals*. AV resources provide links to books and fact sheets.

Associated Humane Societies (AHS)
124 Evergreen Ave.
Newark, NJ 07114-2133
Founded: 1906
Phone: (973) 824-7080
Fax: (973) 824-2720
E-mail: contactus@ahcares.org
URL: http://www.associatedhumanesocieties.org
Membership: NA
Budget: NA

AHS is the largest animal shelter in New Jersey. It runs a federally licensed zoo for exotic animals called Popcorn Park. AHS publishes *Humane News*, which is available at its Web site, along with other publications and videotapes. AHS supports the purchase of bulletproof vests for K-9 working dogs.

Association of Veterinarians for
Animal Rights (AVAR)
P.O. Box 208
Davis, CA 95617-0208
Founded: 1981
Phone: (530) 759-8106
Fax: (530) 759-8116
E-mail: info@avar.org
URL: http://avar.org
Membership: 2,500
Budget: NA

AVAR strives to provide rights for nonhuman animals by educating the public and the veterinary profession. It provides a searchable database for alternatives to animals in education, scientific research, and product testing. It publishes two newsletters, including *Directions and Alternatives in Veterinary Medical Education*, as well as a variety of fact sheets and brochures. It provides links to other animal rights organizations and discussions of animal rights issues.

Association for the Protection of Fur-Bearing
Animals (Fur Bearer Defenders)
225 E. 17th Ave., Suite 101
Vancouver, BC, Canada V5V 1A6

Founded: 1944
Phone: (604) 435-1850
Fax: (604) 435-1840
E-mail: fbd@banlegholdtraps.com
URL: http://www.banlegholdtraps.com
Membership: 3,500
Budget: $125,000

This organization strongly opposes trapping using conibears, snares, and leghold traps. It works to end the trade in the fur of dogs and cats. It provides videos of animals struggling in traps and claims that traps do not discriminate and can trap pets and endangered species. The Association proposes to ban both padded and unpadded leghold traps. It would also ban the use of the conibear trap, which is designed to be an "instant kill" trap but often smashes down on parts of the body without killing the animal.

Beauty without Cruelty (BWC)
1340-G Industrial Ave.
Petaluma, CA 94952
Founded: 1989
Phone: (888) 674-2344
Fax: (707) 769-7342
E-mail: info@beautywithoutcruelty.com
URL: http://www.beautywithoutcruelty.com/
Membership: NA
Budget: NA

BWC's goal is to manufacture and distribute natural-color cosmetics that are not tested on animals and that do not contain animal products, but are made according to plant-based formulas. BWC also provides information about cosmetics that are not tested on animals and that do not contain animal products. BWC sells such products at its online store.

Canadian Association for Humane Trapping (CAHT)
P.O. Box 71115
Maplehurst Postal Outlet
Burlington, ON, Canada L7T 4J8
Founded: 1954
Phone: (416) 363-2614

Fax: (905) 637-3912
E-mail: caht1@cogeco.ca
URL: http://www.caht.ca/caht
Membership: NA
Budget: NA

CAHT "works constructively toward abolishing the suffering imposed on wild animals by devices or trapping systems used to capture them. It is not a trapping, anti-trapping or animal rights organization." CAHT does promote research and development of humane traps. Wild foxes have adapted to urban settings and are difficult to take in live traps, so CAHT recommends that unless the fox is ill, it should be left in place. It also has recommendations for beavers, coyotes, and other wildlife.

Center for Whale Research (CWR)
P.O. Box 1577
Friday Harbor, WA 98250-1577
Founded: 1986
Phone: (360) 378-5835
Fax: (360) 378-5954
E-mail: orcasurv@rockisland.com
URL: http://www.whaleresearch.com
Membership: 1,000
Budget: $100,000

CWR strives to "develop, promote, and conduct benign studies of free-swimming Cetaceans (Whales, Dolphins, and Porpoises) for the purpose of conserving their populations and informing governments and the public of their ecosystem needs." It provides sound recordings of whale calls, as well as links to other organizations dealing with cetaceans.

Cetacean Society International (CSI)
P.O. Box 953
Georgetown, CT 06829
Founded: 1974
Phone: (203) 770-8615
Fax: (860) 561-0187
E-mail: rossiter@csiwhalesalive.org
URL: http://www.csiwhalesalive.org

Membership: 400
Budget: NA

CSI promotes whale and dolphin watching and noninvasive research, nonlethal, and humane research. CSI seeks the cessation of all killing and captive display of whales, dolphins, and porpoises by advocating for laws and treaties to prevent commercial whaling and habitat destruction. CSI publishes a quarterly newsletter, *Whales Alive!*

Citizens to End Animal Suffering and Exploitation (CEASE)
P.O. Box 440456
Somerville, MA 02144
Founded: 1979
Phone: (617) 379-0535
E-mail: info@ceaseboston.org
URL: http://www.ceaseboston.org
Membership: 20,000
Budget: $75,000

CEASE is dedicated to ending animal cruelty and exploitation, particularly of fur-bearing animals. It provides links to Web sites with information about trapping and fur farming. It also provides information about the use of animals in entertainment and research and about pet overpopulation.

Coalition for Animals and Animal Research
University of Arizona
P.O. Box 210101
Tucson, AZ 85721
Founded: NA
Phone: NA
Fax: NA
E-mail: antrnweb@ahsc.arizona.edu
URL: http://www.swaebr.org/cfaar/index.htm
Membership: NA
Budget: NA

The Coalition seeks to provide the general public with information about the true nature of animal research and animal researchers. The Coalition is dedicated to improving human and animal health by supporting humane and responsible use of animals in research. It provides links to publications and other organizations.

Committee to Abolish Sport Hunting (CASH)
P.O. Box 13815
Las Cruces, NM 88013
Founded: 1976
Phone: NA
Fax: NA
E-mail: CASH@AbolishSportHunting.com
URL: http://www.all-creatures.org/cash/
Membership: NA
Budget: NA

CASH promotes nonconsumptive enjoyment of wildlife in its native habitat. The mission of CASH is to abolish all hunting, especially bait and shoot, where an animal is lured to a site with food and then shot, and to foster wildlife watching. CASH works to stop trapping. In order to accomplish its mission, the Association promotes letter-writing campaigns to local officials and the media. It provides sample letters, fact sheets, posters, and even chants to use at protests.

Culture and Animals Foundation (CAF)
3509 Eden Croft Dr.
Raleigh, NC 27612
Founded: 1985
Phone: (919) 782-3739
Fax: (919) 782-6464
E-mail: nancy@cultureandanimals.org
URL: http://www.cultureandanimals.org
Members: 14,000
Budget: $40,000

Philosopher Tom Regan, the author of *The Case for Animal Rights*, leads this organization, which explores the role of music, film, dance, poetry, and philosophy in understanding and promoting animal welfare. CAF provides grants to other organizations in three categories: research, creativity, and performance.

Defenders of Animals (DOA)
P.O. Box 5634

Weybosset Hill Station
Providence, RI 02903-0634
Founded: 1978
Phone: (401) 738-3710
E-Mail: dennis@defendersofanimals.org
URL: http://www.defendersofanimals.org
Membership: NA
Budget: NA

DOA strives to provide rights to companion animals and wildlife. DAO provides help and support for a low-cost spaying and neutering clinic, promotes pet adoption, and provides a reward for information leading to the apprehension, conviction, and sentencing of individuals guilty of animal cruelty. DOA protests the use of gas chambers to euthanize animals and greyhound racing. It provides links to other animal rights organizations.

European Biomedical Research Association (EBRA)
c/o Membership Secretary
25 Shaftesbury Ave.
London W1D 7EG, United Kingdom
Founded: 1994
E-mail: secretariat@ebra.org
URL: http://www.ebra.org
Membership: NA
Budget: NA

EBRA was founded by individuals and organizations to educate and provide understanding of the importance of animals in medical and veterinary research. It provides a link to European animal use regulations and statistics on animal use in Europe. It publishes the *EBRA Bulletin*, which is available on its Web site.

European Fur Breeders Association (EFBA)
Ave. des Arts 3-43-5, 8th Fl.
1210 Brussels, Belgium
Founded: 1968
Phone: 322-2091170
Fax: 322-2091179
E-mail: info@efbanet.com
URL: http://www.efba-eu.com/
Members: 6,000
Budget: NA

EFBA is an umbrella for 15 national associations of fur breeders working to give the general public a realistic image of fur farming. EFBA promotes scientific research on fur farming and strives to standardize European practices and legislation. It provides links to other fur-farming organizations.

Family Farm Defenders (FFD)
P.O. Box 1772
Madison, WI 53701
Founded: 1994
Phone: (608) 260-0900
Fax: (608) 260-0900
E-mail: familyfarmdefenders@yahoo.com
URL: http://www.familyfarmdefenders.org
Members: 1,500
Budget: $75,000

FFD's "mission is to create a farmer-controlled and consumer-oriented food and fiber system, based upon democratically-controlled institutions that empower farmers to speak for and respect themselves in their quest for social and economic justice. FFD has worked to create opportunities for farmers to join together in new cooperative endeavors, form a mutual marketing agency, and forge alliances with consumers through providing high quality food products while returning a fair price to farmers." Family farms are those on which a family provides the labor and makes management decisions. FFD publishes a newsletter, *The Defender*. It has a variety of ongoing campaigns related to agrofuels, a national animal identification system, bovine growth hormone, corporate organics, fair trade, farm workers' rights, food sovereignty, genetic engineering, irradiation, cloning, local food systems, mad cow disease, and milk protein concentrate. It sells a variety of items in its online store.

Food Animal Concerns Trust (FACT)
P.O. Box 14599
Chicago, IL 60614
Founded: 1982
Phone: (773) 525-4952
Fax: (773) 525-5226

E-mail: info@foodanimalconcerns.org
URL: http://www.foodanimalconcerns.org
Membership: NA
Budget: $400,000

FACT does on-farm research and advocacy, which it uses to make science based recommendations to agricultural, public health, and environmental organizations, as well as to the federal government (e.g., Food and Drug Administration, Department of Agriculture, and Centers for Disease Control) FACT strives to improve farm animal welfare and to address public health issues related to the safety of meat, milk, and eggs. The Web site contains links to FACT newsletters, fact sheets, and annual reports.

Foundation for Biomedical Research (FBR)
818 Connecticut Ave. NW, Suite 900
Washington, DC 20006
Founded: 1981
Phone: (202) 457-0654
Fax: (202) 457-0659
E-mail: info@fbresearch.org
URL: http://www.fbresearch.org
Membership: NA
Budget: $1.1 million

FBR is dedicated to improving human and veterinary health by promoting public understanding of and support for humane and responsible animal research in the ongoing, sometimes violent debate that surrounds animal research. FBR provides information about animal research to the news media, as well as to teachers, students, and pet owners. It also monitors the activities of animal activists. FBR publishes a number of brochures, including *Fact vs. Myth*, *Proud Achievements*, *The Importance of Being a Mouse*, *Species in Research*, *Animal Rights Activism*, and *AIDS and Animal Research*, and has a virtual library of books and other materials dealing with animal research, as well as an online store. FBR provides a radio show entitled *The Animal Research Minute* to more than 3,500 radio stations. It is the nation's oldest and largest organization dedicated to improving human and veterinary health by promoting public understanding of biomedical research.

Friends of Animals (FoA)
777 Post Rd., Suite 205
Darien, CT 06820
Founded: 1957
Phone: (203) 656-1522
Fax: (203) 656-0267
E-mail: info@friendsofanimals.org
URL: http://www.friendsofanimals.org
Membership: 200,000

FoA seeks to bring about a respectful view of animals, including both domestic animals and free-living animals, to free animals from institutionalized exploitation, and to promote a vegetarian lifestyle. Its online magazine, *ActionLine,* is available on its Web site. It sells a variety of merchandise in its online store.

Fur Commission U.S.A. (FCUSA)
826 Orange Ave.
PMB 506
Coronado, CA 92118-2698
Founded: 1994
Phone: (619) 575-0139
Fax: (619) 575-5578
E-mail: info@furcommission.com
URL: http://www.furcommission.com
Membership: 650
Budget: NA

FCUSA represents 300 fur farms throughout the United States that market more than 3 million mink pelts. It provides a certificate program for fur farmers. These farms use beef, fish, dairy, and poultry "leftovers" to feed their animals. FCUSA provides links to discussions of mink biology, real fur and the environment, animal rights vs. animal welfare, education, perspectives, and a reading list.

Fur Information Council of America (FICA)
8424A Santa Monica Blvd., No. 860
West Hollywood, CA 90069
Founded: 1958
Phone: (323) 782-1700

Fax: (323) 651-1417
E-mail: info@fur.org
URL: http://www.fur.org
Membership: 300
Budget: NA
Membership Dues: NA

FICA membership consists of wholesale and retail outlets and fur manufacturers. FICA promotes the wise use and humane care of fur-bearing animals and works closely with wildlife biologists to develop and maintain habitats for fur-bearing animals. FICA provides a discussion of fur fashion, facts about fur and fur bearers, and a searchable database of fur retailers, as well as fact sheets to counter what it sees as the distortions and misrepresentations of anti-animal-use groups.

Fur Free Alliance (FFA)
P.O. Box 22505
Sacramento, CA 95822
Founded: NA
Phone: (916) 447-3085
Fax: (916) 447-3070
E-mail: info@respectforanimals.org
URL: http://infurmation.com
Membership: NA
Budget: NA

FFA is a coalition of more than 35 animal protection groups that seeks to stop the exploitation and killing of animals for their fur and that encourages consumers to use available alternatives. FFA performs in-depth investigations of fur farming and seeks to advance legislation to ban fur farming and leghold traps. FFA proposes legislation to ban or restrict trapping, fur farming, and seal hunting and then supports the proposals with campaigns, including letter writing. FFA also provides posters, videos, and banners to help with these efforts.

Fur Takers of America (FTA)
c/o Ramona Plueger, Membership Coordinator
17453 130th Ave.
Monticello, IA 52310

Founded: 1968
Telephone: NA
FAX: NA
E-mail: ckrum2003@yahoo.com
URL: http://www.furtakersofamerica.com
Membership: NA
Budget: $70, 000

FTA members include fur trappers, fur buyers, trapping-supply people, hunters, fur dressers, conservationists, and other interested individuals. FTA seeks to educate trappers about humane methods of trapping and conservation ethics. FTA provides a professional trapping school, which covers topics like bait/lure applications, furbearer management, trap and snare placement, fur skinning, grading and marketing, and public relations.

Incurably Ill for Animal Research (IIFAR)
2510 Champion Way
Lansing, MI 48910
Founded: 1985
Phone: (517) 887-1141
Fax: (517) 887-1710
E-mail: info@iifar.org
URL: http://www.iifar.org
Membership: 2,500
Budget: NA

IIFAR is currently inactive; the URL opens a Web site called Health News, Improving Health Through Research. IIFAR was founded by persons who have health problems and interested individuals who are concerned that animal research for medical purposes will be stopped or severely limited because of the efforts of animal rights activists. It supports the use of animals for the purpose of medical research, teaching, and testing.

Institute of Laboratory Animal Resources (ILAR)
The National Academies
500 Fifth Street, N.W., Keck 687
Washington, DC 20001
Founded: NA
Phone: (202) 334-2590

Fax: (202) 334-1687
E-mail: ILAR@nas.edu
URL: http://dels.nas.edu/ilar_n/ilarhome/
Membership: No membership
Budget: NA

The purpose of ILAR is to "evaluate and disseminate information on issues related to the scientific, technological, and ethical use of animals and related biological resources in research, testing, and education. Using the principles of refinement, reduction, and replacement (3Rs) as a foundation." ILAR publishes the *Guide for the Care and Use of Animals*, which is currently being updated.

Institute of Animal Technology (IAT)
5 S Parade
Summertown
Oxford OX2 7JL, United Kingdom
Founded: 1949
Phone: (44) (0) (800) 085-4380
E-mail: admin@iat.org.uk or info@iat.org.uk
URL: http://www.iat.org.uk
Membership: 2,200, including 60 corporate organizations from the U.K. and Europe
Budget: NA

IAT's purpose "is to advance knowledge and promote excellence in the care and welfare of animals in science and to enhance the standards and status of those professionally engaged in the care, welfare and use of animals in science." IAT provides training and certification for animal technologists. It publishes the *IAT Bulletin* and the *Animal Technology and Welfare Journal*, as well as two books, *Introduction to Animal Technology* and *Manual of Animal Technology*, as well as educational videos and CD-ROMs. It also provides links to other animal welfare organizations.

International Association against Painful Experiments on Animals (IAAPEA)
P.O. Box 14
Hampshire
Hayling Island PO11 9BF, United Kingdom
Founded: 1969

Phone: (44) 2392-46-3738
E-mail: iaapea@hotmail.com
URL: http://www.iaapea.com
Members: NA
Budget: NA

The IAAPEA is the only organization dealing with animal testing that has consultative status with the UN. The Association established *World Day for Laboratory Animals* in 1979 and organizes and finances undercover work to obtain photographic evidence of the cruelty of animal research, which it supplies to other animal rights organizations. The Association also funds research into cancer, heart disease, diabetes, and other illnesses that does not rely on animal research. It publishes a newsletter, *International Animal Action*, which is available online. Its *International Charter for Health and Humane Research* is available as a PDF file in Spanish, Portuguese, English, and Italian. It also has a list, "101 Misleading Results from Vivisection," and downloadable PDF files. The Association has published two books by Dr. Robert Sharpe, Scientific Director of IAAPEA, *Alternative Strategies* and *Human Tissue*. The Association is opposed to use of animals in weapons testing.

International Association of Human-Animal Interaction Organizations (IAHAIO)
c/o Delta Society
875 124th Ave. NE, Suite 101
Bellevue, WA 98005-2531
Founded: 1990
Phone: (425) 226-7357
Fax: (425) 235-1076
E-mail: info@iahaio.org
URL: http://www.iahaio.org
Members: 22
Budget: $16,000

The IAHAIO provides a coordinating structure for national humane associations and related organizations to advance understanding of the human-animal link and the unique role animals play in human wellbeing and quality of life. The IAHAIO holds an annual conference, the proceedings of which are published, and supports two international awards, the Distinguished Scholar

Award and the IAHAIO Pioneer Award, which it presents every three years.

International Fund for Animal Welfare (IFAW)
290 Summer St.
Yarmouth Port, MA 02675-0193
Phone: (508) 744-2000
Founded: 1969.
Fax: (508) 744-2009 (Toll-free: (800) 932-4329)
E-mail: info@ifaw.org
URL: http://www.ifaw.org
Membership: 300,000
Budget: NA

IFAW was founded in Canada to ban the harp seal pup hunt. IFAW rejects the idea that the interests of humans and animals are separate. The IFAW works to protect whales; to rescue animals during disasters; to encourage marine conservation and whale watching; to protect the Mediterranean monk seal; and to protect African and Asian elephants, and it is working to create ocean sanctuaries for whales. It provides annual reports, IFAW newsletters, animal fact sheets, and program publications.

International Primate Protection League (IPPL)
P.O. Box 766
Summerville, SC 29484-0766
Founded: 1973
Phone: (843) 871-2280
Fax: (843) 871-7988
E-mail: info@ippl.org
URL: http://www.ippl.org
Membership: NA
Budget: NA

IPPL is a grassroots organization that works to protect all species of primates. It provides grants and advice to organizations seeking to protect primates in the United States and overseas. At its Summerville location, it provides a sanctuary for gibbons rescued from research, pet, and zoo backgrounds. It publishes a newsletter, which can be obtained online, along with links to other primate organizations and annual reports.

International Society for Animal Rights (ISAR)
965 Griffin Pond Rd.
Clarks Summit, PA 18411-9214
Phone: (570) 586-2200 (Toll-free: (800) 543-ISAR)
Fax: (570) 586-9580
Founded: 1959
E-mail: contact@isaronline.org
URL: http://www.isaronline.org
Membership: 50,000

ISAR was one of the first organizations to use the words "animal rights" in its corporate name. It was responsible for the first successful state and federal litigations to invoke the moral principle of animal rights. ISAR's founder, Helen Jones, believed that humans have a moral responsibility to end the suffering and exploitation of animals. ISAR originated and sponsors the International Homeless Animals' Day. It has a blog and newsletters that are available online, as well as a MySpace page (http://www.myspace.com/i_s_a_r). It has a cat spay/neuter video.

International Whaling Commission (IWC)
The Red House
135 Station Rd.
Impington
Cambridge CB24 9NP, United Kingdom
Founded: 1946
Phone: (44) 1223-233971
Fax: (44) 1223-232876
E-mail: secretariat@iwcoffice.org
URL: http://www.iwcoffice.org
Membership: 58
Budget: £624,000

IWC was set up under the International Convention for the Regulation of Whaling. The membership consists of commissioners who each represent a country with an interest in whaling. IWC strives for proper conservation of whale stocks by encouraging, coordinating, and funding whale research and works to develop humane killing techniques. The *Journal of Cetacean Research and Management* is available on its Web site.

International Wildlife Coalition—USA (IWC-USA)
70 E. Falmouth Hwy.
East Falmouth, MA 02536
Founded: 1984
Phone: (508) 457-1898 (Toll-free: (800) 548-8704)
Fax: (508) 457-1898
E-mail: iwchq@iwc.org
URL: http://www.iwc.org
Membership: 150,000
Budget: $3 million

IWC-USA was started by a group of individuals from a variety
of animal rights and environmental groups. Initially, the group
raised money for whale conservation. It advocates for prevention
of cruelty and killing of wildlife and for protection of wildlife
habitat. It also lobbies and promotes letter-writing campaigns
to protect wildlife and wildlife habitats in the United States, Sri
Lanka, Brazil, Australia, the United Kingdom, and Canada.

Japan Whaling Association (JWA)
Toyomishinko Bldg. 7F
4-5 Toyomi-cho
Chuoh-ku
Tokyo 104-0055, Japan
Founded: 1988
Telephone: NA
Fax: NA
E-mail: kujira@whaling.jp
URL: http://www.whaling.jp
Membership: NA
Budget: NA

The JWA Web site is in Japanese. Japan is one of two nations that
continue commercial whaling despite an international ban on all
whaling. JWA promotes the sound development of whaling in
Japan.

Jews for Animal Rights (JAR)
255 Humphrey St.
Marblehead, MA 01945
Founded: 1985

Phone: (781) 631-7601
E-mail: micah@micahbooks.com
URL: http://www.micahbooks.com/JAR.html
Membership: NA
Budget: NA

The JAR follows the teachings of Rabbi Avraham Kirk, the first chief rabbi of Israel, which are found in "A Vision of Vegetarianism and Peace." JAR believes that the Torah contains many examples of great leaders of the Jews who showed kindness to animals and a compassion for animal life. For example, in Genesis 24:14, Rebecca says, "Drink and I will give thy camels drink also."

Justice for Animals (JFA)
P.O. Box 33051
Raleigh, NC 27636-3051
Founded: 1993
Phone: (919) 787-5190
Fax: (919) 836-9949
E-mail: jfa_nc@juno.com
URL: http://www.justiceforanimals.org
Membership: NA
Budget: NA

JFA is a coalition of individuals and groups in North Carolina who seek to achieve more effective anticruelty laws. Its members volunteer their legal and other professional expertise.

Laboratory Animal Management Association (LAMA)
7500 Flying Cloud Drive, Suite 900
Eden Park, MN 55344
Founded: 1984
Phone: (952) 253-6235
Fax: (952) 835-4774
E-mail: NA
URL: http://www.lama-online.org/
Membership: NA
Budget: NA

LAMA seeks to advance the laboratory animal management profession (directors, managers, and supervisors) through education, knowledge exchange, and professional development. LAMA publishes the *LAMA Review*. It certifies directors, managers, and supervisors of animal care facilities.

Laboratory Animal Science Association (LASA)
P.O. Box 3993
Tamworth B78 3QU, United Kingdom
Founded: 1963
Phone: (44) 1827-259130
Fax: (44) 1827-259188
E-mail: lasa@btconnect.com
URL: http://www.lasa.co.uk
Membership: NA
Budget: NA

LASA was founded by industrial, university, ministry, and research council representatives to ensure the provision and best use of animal models, including organs, tissues, and cellular components for medical, veterinary, and other scientific purposes. It provides small grants to support training in reducing, replacing, and refining experimental techniques to minimize the use of animals. The Association also awards the LASA medal to individuals or organizations that have made a significant contribution to laboratory animal welfare. LASA publishes guidelines and point papers dealing with animal welfare issues.

Last Chance for Animals (LCA)
8033 Sunset Blvd., No. 835
Los Angeles, CA 90046
Founded: 1984
Phone: (310) 271-6096 (Toll-free: (888) 882-6462)
Fax: (310) 271-1890
E-mail: development@lcanimal.org
URL: http://www.lcanimal.org
Membership: 60,000
Budget: $1 million

LCA opposes the use of animals for entertainment, clothing, or food or to satisfy scientific curiosity. LCA uses "Direct Action" in the form of well-planned and -executed peaceful protests and supports vegan ideals. LCA's Special Investigations Unit seeks to validate information, detect suspect activity, and expose illegal or unethical practices. LCA sells a variety of merchandise in its online store.

Lehigh Valley Animal Rights Coalition (LVARK)
P.O. Box 3224
Allentown, PA 18106
Founded: 1982
Phone: (610) 821-9552
E-mail: pstacks@enter.net
URL: http://www.enter.net/~pstacks/
Membership: 600
Budget: NA

LVARC is a grassroots organization that seeks to educate the public via direct action, letter writing, and public outreach about the misuse and abuse of animals wherever and whenever it occurs. LVAR seeks to provide students with alternatives to classroom dissection, to reduce fur sales, to ban pigeon shoots in Pennsylvania, and to assist in providing low-cost spay/neutering clinics. LVARC provides rewards for the apprehension of parties involved in acts of cruelty. It supplies libraries with *Animal Agenda* magazine and other anti-abuse literature and provides links to other animal welfare organizations. Its goal is to inform the public about Pennsylvania animal rights issues, pet issues, and world and national wildlife issues.

Mercy for Animals (MFA)
P.O. Box 363
Columbus, OH 43216
Founded: 1999
Toll-free: (866) MFA-OHIO
E-mail: info@mercyforanimals.org
URL: http://www.mercyforanimals.org
Membership: 25,000
Budget: NA

MFA believes that animals are irreplaceable individuals that have a right to life free from unnecessary suffering and exploitation because they have morally significant interests. MFA provides a voice for animals through grassroots activism such as undercover investigations, rescues, and advertising campaigns. MFA focuses on promoting and advocating for cruelty-free food choices. It provides information about factory farms, including those for poultry, pork, beef, dairy and veal, eggs, and fish, as well as information about animal experimentation, animals in entertainment, and the fur industry. It publishes the *Compassionate Living* newsletter and provides a variety of merchandise in its online store.

National Association for Biomedical Research (NAFBR)
818 Connecticut Ave NW, Suite 900
Washington, DC 20006
Founded: 1979
Phone: (202) 857-0540
Fax: (202) 659-1902
E-mail: info@nabr.org
URL: http://www.nabr.org/
Membership: 300
Budget: NA

NABR provides a unified voice for the scientific community on legislative and regulatory matters dealing with laboratory animal research. It also provides information about the laws governing animal research.

National Centre for Replacement, Refinement and Reduction of Animals in Research
20 Park Crescent
London W1B 1AL
Founded: 2004
Phone: (44) 020-7670-5331
Fax: (44) 020-7670-5178
E-mail: enquiries@nc3rs.org.uk
URL: http://www.nc3rs.org.uk/
Membership: NA
Budget: NA

The Centre brings together scientists and administrators from academia, industry, government, and animal welfare organizations to disseminate and advance the principles of replacement, refinement, and reduction (the 3Rs) of animals in research. The Centre provides grants for research dealing with the 3Rs. In 2008, grants totaled £2.6 million. The Centre publishes the *NC3Rs* newsletters and has a library of articles dealing with the 3Rs, as well as a FAQ.

National Federation of Humane Societies (NFHS)
2100 L St. NW
Washington, DC 20037
Founded: 2006
Phone: (563) 582-6766
E-mail: humanejane@dbqhumane.org
URL: http://www.humanefederation.org
Membership: NA
Budget: NA

The NFHS is a fee-based national trade federation representing animal shelters, animal care and control agencies, and regional and national animal welfare organizations. It provides a unified voice of advocacy for these organizations. NFHS seeks to find consensus on issues such as pets in housing, puppy mills, novelty pets/exotics, animal fighting, and animal-friendly practices, policies, and procedures for business organizations. It also monitors legislation and promotes legislation to include pets in disaster planning.

National Pet Alliance (NPA)
P.O. Box 53385
San Jose, CA 95153
Founded: NA
Phone: (408) 363-0700
E-mail: karenj115@aol.com
URL: http://fanciers.com/npa/
Membership: NA
Budget: NA

NPA was founded by purebred dog and pedigree cat owners to promote the care and wellbeing of these companion animals. NPA recognizes that the majority of animals euthanized by humane societies and animal shelters are cats, so NPA promotes trapping, testing, vaccinating, and release programs for feral cats to minimize cat overpopulation.

New Jersey Animal Rights Alliance (NJARA)
P.O. Box 174
Englishtown, NJ 07726

Founded: 1983
Phone: (732) 446-6808
Fax: (732) 446-0227
E-Mail: njara@nj-ara.org
URL: http://www.nj-ara.org
Membership: 2,000
Budget: NA

NJARA is a statewide organization that is dedicated to ending animal exploitation. It is an educational organization that seeks peaceful, nonviolent coexistence for humans and animals. NJARA seeks to educate the public about animal abuse, to encourage activism to end cruelty, and to promote lifestyles that reduce or eliminate suffering. It provides links to information about animals and to other welfare organizations. It provides information and advice about legislation in New Jersey dealing with animals.

Northwest Animal Rights Network
902-A NE 65th St.
Seattle, WA 98115
Founded: 1986
Phone: (206) 525-2246
E-mail: info@narn.org
URL: http://www.narn.org
Membership: 1,200
Budget: NA

NARN seeks to end animal exploitation in the food, entertainment, and fashion industries, as well as animal experimentation. It publishes a weekly online newsletter containing announcements and action items for the week and news or noteworthy items, as well as a blog dealing with animal issues and links to other organizations with similar interests.

Ocean Conservancy
1300 19th St. NW, 8th Fl.
Washington, DC 20036
Founded: NA
Phone: (202) 429-5609 (Toll-free: (800) 519-1541)
E-mail: membership@oceanconservancy.org
URL: http://www.oceanconservancy.org

Membership: 150,000
Budget: NA

OC promotes the protection of marine habitat and marine wildlife by increasing public awareness and education. It has an interactive map on its Web site that provides information about ongoing problems in specific areas of the coastal United States. It publishes the *Ocean Conservancy Magazine* and e-cards you can send to a friend, as well as ocean computer wallpapers for your computer.

People for Animal Rights (PAR)
P.O Box 15358
Syracuse, NY 13215-0358
Founded: 1982
Phone: (315) 488-7877
E-mail: ldestefano3@twcny.rr.com
URL: http://www.geocities.com/par-ny
Membership: 250
Budget: NA

PAR is "a local group that educates about animal rights and protecting the earth. We host vegan meals, bring in speakers on a variety of topics, have a legislative network, produce a newsletter and other material, produce a cable TV program, and provide educational material and speakers to schools and others." PAR provides presentations on environmental protection and animal rights to schools, colleges, libraries, houses of worship, and clubs in Onondaga and nearby counties. It provides its members with alerts dealing with legislation about animals and provides links to other organizations with similar interests

People for the Ethical Treatment of Animals (PETA)
501 Front St.
Norfolk, VA 23510
Founded: 1980
Phone: (757) 622-7382
Fax: (757) 622-0457
E-mail: info@peta.org
URL: http://www.peta.org
Membership: 1 million
Budget: $27 million

PETA is likely the largest and best-funded animal rights organization in the world. It focuses on the use of animals on factory farms, in scientific research, in the clothing trade, and in the entertainment industry. PETA proposes to stop all use of animals by humans and fosters a vegan lifestyle. It provides a variety of merchandise in its online shop and has a blog, action alerts that highlight alleged abuse by specific organizations, such as Kentucky Fried Chicken, McDonalds, and Pet Marts. PETA provides a variety of videos dealing with topics such as the killing of seals. It has a channel on YouTube and provides forums on a variety of topics where you can post your comments about a topic and see comments by others.

People Protecting Animals and Their Habitats (PATH)
P.O. Box 12022
Fort Pierce, FL 34979-2022
Founded: NA
Phone: (617) 354-2826
E-mail: animalpath@aol.com
URL: http://www.ppath.org/
Membership: NA
Budget: NA

PATH is attempting to create a world where people and animals thrive together. It focuses on animal welfare in the developing world by combining animal welfare, education, and community development. PATH advocates the human treatment of animals and the conservation of areas that are vital to the survival of endangered and threatened species.

Performing Animal Welfare Society (PAWS)
P.O. Box 849
Galt, CA 95632
Founded: 1984
Phone: (209) 745-2606
Fax: (209) 745-1809
E-mail: info@pawsweb.org
URL: http://www.pawsweb.org/about_paws_
home_page.html
Membership: 45,000
Budget: $3.6 million

PAWS seeks to protect performing animals and to provide a sanctuary for abused, abandoned, and retired wildlife, to promote standards of care for captive wildlife, and to improve public awareness of captive wildlife issues. It provides sanctuary to 11 African and Indian elephants and 33 tigers, as well as primates, bears, and African and mountain lions. PAWS sells animal-related merchandise in its online store.

Primarily Primates, Inc. (PPI)
26099 Dull Knife Trail
San Antonio, TX 78255
Founded: 1978
Phone: (830) 755-4616
Fax: (830) 981-4611
E-mail: primarilyprimates@friendsofanimals.org
URL: http://primarilyprimates.org
Membership: 18,000
Budget: $1 million

PP provides sanctuary, rehabilitation, lifetime care, and shelter to abused or unwanted nonnative species of primates, birds, mammals, and reptiles. PP has videos of a variety of rare and unusual primates engaged in a variety of behaviors.

**Royal Society for the Prevention of Cruelty
to Animals (RSPCA)**
Wilberforce Way
Southwater
Horsham RH13 9RS, United Kingdom
Founded: 1824
Phone: (44) 300-1234555
Fax: (44) 303-1230284
URL: http://www.rspca.org.uk
Membership: 53,754
Budget: £37.3 million

RSPCA was founded by Richard Martin and 22 others. It was the first animal protection society in the world and provided enforcement inspectors who predated the police force. The Society also has a team of undercover inspectors that investigates illegal acts, including dog fighting, badger baiting, wild bird trapping, and puppy farming. The Society uses private prosecutions to curtail such illegal acts. The Society works closely with decision makers and politicians in support of legislation dealing with animal welfare issues. The Society provides policy statements to provide guidelines for further action and to encourage compassionate attitude toward animals.

Save the Whales (STW)
1192 Waring St.
Seaside, CA 93955
Founded: 1977
Phone: (831) 899-9957
Fax: (831) 394-5555
E-mail: maris@savethewhales.org
URL: http://www.savethewhales.org
Membership: 10,000
Budget: $80,000

STW seeks to educate children and adults about marine mammals, their environment, and their preservation. STW provides information about various species of whales. It collects information about marine mammal stranding and entanglements. Whale-related items are sold in the online store, and the Web site provides links to other sites about whales.

Scientists Center for Animal Welfare (SCAW)
7833 Walker Dr., Suite 410
Greenbelt, MD 20770
Founded: 1978
Phone: (301) 345-3500
Fax: (301) 345-3503
E-Mail: info@scaw.com
URL: http://www.scaw.com

SCAW serves as an "objective, creditable source of information for the research community, the media, and the general public" about basic and applied scientific inquiries involving animals. It sponsors conferences and workshops and provides links on its Web site to publications dealing with animals and animal research. It provides an online mechanism that enables Institutional Animal Care and Use Committee members at different institutions to communicate with one another.

Society for Animal Protective Legislation (SAPL)
P.O. Box 3719
Washington, DC 20027
Founded: 1955
Phone: (703) 836-4300
Fax: (703) 836-0400
E-Mail: sapl@saplonline.org
URL: http://www.saplonline.org
Membership: NA
Budget: $150,000

The SAPL is the legislative and litigation arm of the Animal Welfare Institute. It provides members of Congress and their staffs with information about animal welfare. It monitors state and federal legislation dealing with animals and animal welfare.

Society of Animal Welfare Administrators (SAWA)
15508 W. Bell Road, Suite 101-613
Surprise, AZ 85347
Founded: 1970
Phone: (888)-600-3648
Fax: (866)-299-1311
E-mail: SAWAconnect@ymail.com
URL: http://www.sawanetwork.org/contact.htm
Membership: NA
Budget: NA

SAWA is a nonprofit management organization composed of professional administrators of organizations involved in animal care and control. It provides a Certified Animal Welfare Administrator exam. SAWA provides a copy of its annual report and its newsletter online and sells merchandise in its online store.

Student Animal Rights Alliance (SARA)
275 Seventh Ave., 23rd Fl.
New York, NY 10001
Founded: 2001
Phone: (212) 696-7911
E-mail: info@defendanimals.org
URL: http://www.defendanimals.org

SARA is dedicated to youth mobilization, education, and leadership development to build a strong and diverse youth movement for animal protection, because animals are living, feeling individuals that deserve to live free from torture, slaughter, abuse, and exploitation. SARA recommends that students get involved with animal rights legislation at the state and local level. It hosts the National Student Animal Rights Conference, provides training for student lobbyists, and is attempting to set up a grassroots network of students interested in animal welfare and animal rights.

Tree House Animal Foundation (THAF)
1212 W. Carmen Ave.
Chicago, IL 60640-2902
Founded: 1971
Phone: (773) 784-5488
Fax: (773) 784-2332
E-mail: jschlueter@treehouseanimals.org
URL: http://www.treehouseanimals.org
Membership: 10,000
Budget: NA

THAF provides a no-kill shelter for unwanted and feral cats, as well as a low-cost spay/neuter clinic. THAF works with Chicago Animal Care and Control and other open-admission shelters to transfer cats to THAF. THAF is expanding its Trap-Neuter-Return program for feral cats. THAF adoption counselors interview prospective adopters to understand their needs, with the hope of providing a permanent loving home for all cats. THAF publishes a semiannual newsletter, *Kittenville*, and sells Tree House T-shirts on its Web site.

The True Nature Network (TTNN)
P.O. Box 20672
Columbus Circle Station
New York, NY 10023-1487
Founded: 1985
Phone: (212) 581-1120
E-mail: abull@ix.netcom.com
URL: http://www.greenpeople.org/listing/The_True_Nature_
Netw_2206.cfm
Membership: NA
Budget: NA

TNN produces and distributes educational videos about animal rights and vegetarianism, which it makes available free to schools, television stations, and libraries. The videos include *Animal Rights Concerns*, *9th Life Hawaii* (dealing with overpopulation of cats in Hawaii), and *Paws for Peace*, among others.

United Action for Animals (UAA)
P.O. Box 635
New York, NY 10021
Founded: 1967
Phone: (212) 249-9178
E-Mail: info@ua4a.org
URL: http://www.ua4a.org

UAA strives "to establish and encourage the observance of ethical standards of conduct and practices in the field of animal welfare; to educate mankind on available alternatives to the use of animals in medical research and testing methods, and to actively work to promote the use of such alternatives; to protect all living things from abuse and neglect, to conduct intensive public education on cruelties of national scope; to cooperate with other ethical societies in the U.S. and abroad whose aims are comparable with those of this society; to compile, select, disseminate and distribute data and information of all kinds which may be useful in furthering the aims and purposes of this society." UAA promotes the use of nonanimal alternatives for leather and other forms of apparel. UAA fosters adoption of stray animals from the Cayman Islands.

United Animal Nations (UAN)
P.O. Box 188890
Sacramento, CA 95818
Founded: 1987
Phone: (916) 429-2457
Fax: (916) 429-2456
E-mail: info@uan.org
URL: http://www.uan.org
Membership: 20,000
Budget: $1.5 million

UAN provides leadership in emergency animal sheltering and disaster-relief services. It provides financial assistance to Good Samaritans and rescue organizations, helps find homes for horses that might otherwise be slaughtered, and offers rewards to witnesses to animal cruelty who come forward.

United Poultry Concerns (UPC)
P.O. Box 150
Machipongo, VA 23405-0150
Founded: 1990
Phone: (757) 678-7875
Fax: (757) 678-5070
E-mail: info@upc-online.org
URL: http://www.upc-online.org
Membership: 7,000
Budget: $60,000

UPC is concerned about the treatment of chickens and other birds by commercial agricultural, scientific, and educational institutions and promotes a vegetarian lifestyle. UPC wants to stop the practice of de-beaking chickens, turkeys and other birds. It provides links to other organizations on its Web site and has a YouTube page, www.YouTube.com/upcnews.

U.S. Animal Health Association (USAHA)
P.O. Box 8805
St. Joseph, MO 64508
Founded: 1887
Phone: (816) 671-1144
Fax: (816) 671-1201
E-mail: usaha@usaha.org
URL: http://www.usaha.org
Membership: 1,400
Budget: $150,000

USAHA's "1,400 members are state and federal animal health officials, national allied organizations, regional representatives, and individual members. USAHA works with state and federal governments, universities, veterinarians, livestock producers, national livestock and poultry organizations, research scientists, the extension service and seven foreign countries to control livestock diseases in the United States. USAHA represents all 50 states, 4 foreign countries and 34 allied groups serving health, technical and consumer markets."

U.S. Sportsmen's Alliance (USSA)
801 Kingsmill Pkwy.
Columbus, OH 43229
Founded: 1978
Phone: (614) 888-4868
Fax: (614) 888-0326
E-mail: info@ussportsmen.org
URL: http://www.ussportsmen.org

USSA "provides direct lobbying and grassroots coalition support to protect and advance the rights of hunters, fishermen, trappers and scientific wildlife management professionals. This is accomplished through coalition building, ballot issue campaigning and legislative and government relations."

Universities Federation for Animal Welfare (UFAW)
The Old School
Brewhouse Hill
Wheathampstead AL4 8AN, United Kingdom
Founded: 1926
Phone: (44) 1582-831818
Fax: (44) 1582-831414
E-mail: ufaw@ufaw.org.uk
URL: http://www.ufaw.org.uk
Membership: NA
Budget: NA

UFAW seeks to develop and improve the welfare of animals through scientific and educational activities, provides information to government and regulatory bodies, and offers grants, fellowships, and training. UFAW publishes the journal *Animal Welfare*, as well as a series of books, including *Environmental Enrichment for Captive Animals*, by Robert J Young; *Physiology and Behaviour of Animal Suffering*, by Neville G Gregory; and *Animal Welfare Limping towards Eden*, by John Webster, all of which can be ordered online. UFAW's Web site provides links to other organizations.

Vegetarian Resource Group (VRG)
P.O. Box 1463
Baltimore, MD 21203
Founded: 1982
Phone: (410) 366-8343

Fax: (410) 366-8804
E-mail: vrg@vrg.org
URL: http://www.vrg.org
Membership: 20,000

VRG strives to educate the public on vegetarianism. It publishes the *Vegetarian Journal* and vegetarian cookbooks. VRG provides information about vegetarian nutrition and links to vegetarian sites. The Web site has an interactive online restaurant guide that helps readers locate vegetarian restaurants, as well a list of restaurant chains that have vegetarian items on their menus.

Vegan Action (VA)
P.O. Box 4288
Richmond, VA 23220
Founded: 1993
Phone: (804) 502-8736
Fax: (804) 254-8346
E-mail: information@vegan.org
URL: http://www.vegan.org
Membership: 1,600
Budget: $19,000

VA provides information about the vegan lifestyle and how it helps animals. VA provides suggestions on how to start and maintain a vegan lifestyle and provides links to reading material and other organizations.

Voice for Animals (VOICE)
P.O. Box 120095
San Antonio, TX 78212
Founded: 1987
Phone: (210) 737-3138
E-mail: voice@voiceforanimals.org
URL: http://www.voiceforanimals.org
Membership: 950
Budget: $2,500

VFA seeks to inform the public about animal rights issues and to advance the compassionate treatment of animals. VFA's Web site provides links for compassionate shopping

Wild Animal Orphanage (WAO)
P.O. Box 690422
San Antonio, TX 78269
Founded: 1983
Phone: (210) 688-9038
Fax: (210) 688-9514
E-mail: wao@stic.net
URL: http://www.wildanimalorphanage.org
Membership: 50,000
Budget: $656,000

WAO provides a permanent home and lifetime care for unwanted, neglected, and abused animals, including animals from the exotic pet trade, roadside zoos, and breeding facilities. It also provides a home for primates retired from medical research, the pet industry, and the entertainment industry. Its publications include the bimonthly *Wild Means Wild* and a newsletter, available online, that contains stories about animal rescues and discourages the keeping of wild animals as pets.

8

Resources

This chapter provides selected print resources that allow the reader to follow up on topics of interest. It highlights classic books from the beginnings of the animal rights movement to modern treatments of the topic, including books on vegetarianism. It includes selections that deal with the specific ways humans use animals and that focus on nonhuman primates and whales and dolphins. Also included are books that deal with legal issues, the U.S. Code and the Code of Federal Regulations, and selected congressional hearings. Finally, it suggests selected sources of nonprint information, such as databases and videos.

Print Resources

Alternatives to Animals

The Food Security Act of 1985 (see chapter 6) mandates that the principal investigator in research consider alternatives to any procedures that are likely to cause pain or distress to an animal used in an experiment. This Act also mandates that each scientist consider methods that could reduce or replace animal use or minimize animal pain and distress.

Stratmann, G. C., Stratmann, C. J., and Paxton, C. L. *Animal Experiments and Their Alternatives*. Braunton, UK: Merlin Books, 1987.

This is the classic reference on how to achieve the three R's: refinement, replacement, and reduction. Stratmann recommends a careful examination of existing experimental protocols and careful

243

planning when developing new protocols. "Refinement" means improvement of experimental technique to reduce the possible suffering and stress of the animal and to avoid poor experimental results due to improper handling and care of the animals. "Replacement" means the use of techniques that eliminate the use of animals while still permitting the researcher to obtain the desired result. "Reduction" means the use of fewer animals to achieve the desired results by improving experimental methods and through critical examination of statistical methods.

Animal Rights

Animal rights activists argue that animal rights is an ethical concept and that the issues of animal rights are philosophical issues. The definition of animal, in its broadest sense, refers to an organism that possesses sensorimotor abilities and that can sense changes in its environment and respond to them. By this definition, "animal" includes humans and other primates, as well as mammals, birds, reptiles, amphibians, fish, and many invertebrates. Further, several themes reoccur in the animal rights literature. Animals, humans and nonhumans, are sentient (have the capacity to enjoy and suffer, to experience pleasure and pain), and their lives have significant value. To obstruct an animal, to cause it pain, distress, suffering, misery, or terror; to mutilate an animal; or to kill an animal is to harm the animal. We have a duty not to harm animals, and animals have a right not to be harmed by us.

Bentham, Jeremy. *An Introduction to the Principles of Morals and Legislation.* New York: Dover, 2007.

This is a reprint of Bentham's book, which was originally published in 1779. Bentham was a utilitarian philosopher who wrote of animals, "The question is not, can they reason? Nor can they talk? But, can they suffer?" This statement became the battle cry of both the Victorian and the modern animal protection movement. Bentham maintained that because they can suffer, animals have a right to life, liberty, and the pursuit of happiness.

Best, Steven, and Nocella II, Anthony J. *Terrorists or Freedom Fighters?* Herndon, VA: Lantern Books, 2004.

This book contains a series of essays dealing with the Animal Liberation Front, one of the more radical animal rights organizations. It discusses the history, ethics, politics, and tactics of this organization, which engages in civil disobedience, sabotage, and threats against people who use animals, especially those involved with biomedical or testing issues.

Brown, Anthony. *Who Cares for Animals?* London: Heinemann, 1974.

This book was written for the 150th anniversary of the Royal Society for the Prevention of Cruelty to Animals. It presents a living portrait of the people who work for the Society and the work that they do.

Darwin, Charles. *On the Origin of Species: The Illustrated Edition.* New York: Sterling, 2008.

This book celebrates the 150th anniversary of Darwin's book, in which he discusses his belief that species evolve because of competition for resources and that natural selection provides the fittest organism to occupy a given ecological niche.

Darwin, Charles. *The Descent of Man and Selection in Relation to Sex.* New York: Quill Pen Classics, 2008.

This is a reprint of Darwin's book, originally published in 1902, in which he argues that animals and humans form a biological and psychological continuum. Further, he claims that there is no fundamental difference between man and higher mammals.

Dodds, Jean W., and Orlans, Barbara F. (Eds.). *Scientific Perspectives on Animal Welfare.* New York: Academic Press, 1982.

This book highlights the four basic stages by which scientists are held accountable for the proper use of animals in experimentation. In the first stage, the individual experimenter develops an idea for an experiment and formalizes the idea as an experimental protocol. In the next stage, the research institution, via its institutional animal care and use committee, determines that the protocol is in compliance with local, state, national, and federal standards of animal welfare. In the next stage, the funding agency determines if the protocol has scientific merit and its experimental procedures are humane. In the fourth stage, the experimenter is expected to publish the results of his experiment in a refereed scientific journal, where it is reviewed to determine whether it contains an adequate description of the experimental procedures and results and whether it has scientific merit. The principles of refinement, replacement, and reduction are also discussed, as are the feasibility of reducing the invasiveness of the experimental procedures and the economic and ethical costs of animals used in experimental research.

Favre, David. *Animal Law: Welfare, Interest, and Rights.* New York: Aspen, 2008.

Favre provides an overview of topics including animal ownership, veterinarian malpractice, harm to pets, state regulation of ownership, anticruelty laws, agricultural animals, the Animal Welfare Act, and the jurisprudence and social movements dealing with animal rights. He also discusses access to the courts, focusing of standing and legal injury. Each major section of the book provides an overview of a broad topic and then reviews relevant case law. For example, the section dealing with animal ownership covers what constitutes ownership; how one obtains, transfers, and loses ownership status; bailments (temporary control over or possession of personal property); interference with owners' rights and expectations; the obligations of ownership; and new issues. The section on the Animal Welfare Act provides a discussion of the background of the Act, discusses how the federal law changed over time, and includes the statement of the policy of Congress, as well as reviewing selected committee reports dealing with the Act and how the Act is administered. Each section provides questions and notes.

The section dealing with the animal rights movement begins with a discussion of the background of the movement, including the first national conference at which lawyers considered animal rights issues, which occurred at the Brooklyn Law School in 1981, and the founding of the peer-reviewed *Journal of Animal Law*, at the Michigan State University College of Law.

Fox, Michael Allan. *The Case for Animal Experimentation: An Evolutionary and Ethical Perspective.* Berkeley: University of California Press, 1988.

Fox suggests that modern antivivisectionists are presenting a one-sided, distorted view of animal welfare issues, often focusing on animal suffering during research. He suggests that the antivivisectionists fail to mention the efforts to maintain and improve animal care and/or the benefits gained from the research. Fox holds that animals are not the moral equals of human beings and that there is no compelling reason for treating them as such. In both common and scientific discourse, "animal" is defined as any living thing that is not a plant and thus includes creatures as simple as sea cucumbers or as complex as humans. Fox asks which of these creatures, if any, should be treated as the moral equivalent of humans. He suggests that much of the attention and energy used to improve the lot of animals would be better directed at ameliorating human need and suffering, a goal that he thinks deserves more of our dedication because humans are more important than animals. Fox maintains that there are three factors that led to the controversy about animals: (1) the speed at which new information is acquired and processed; (2) the rise of ecology as a major scientific field; and (3) the general broadening of moral concern that is the legacy of the counterculture and the civil rights and antiwar movements. Further, because of fairy tales and cartoons, as well as bestsellers such as *Jonathan Livingston Seagull* and *Watership Down,* many people have developed a false sense of animals and their abilities and natures and paint a picture of nature as peaceful and idyllic. Fox also contends that existing evidence suggests that humans and their ancestors are natural omnivores.

Fox, Michael D., and Nibert, David, *Animal Rights/Human Rights.* New York: Rowman & Littlefield, 2002.

The authors argue that the treatment of both humans and animals is entangled with the structure of our social arrangements. They argue that human use of animals is unnatural and has done little to improve the human condition.

Fox, Michael W. *Between Animal and Man.* New York: Coward, McCann & Geoghegan, 1976.

Fox, a veterinarian, suggests that veterinary school taught him a good deal about diseases and the healing arts but did not teach him anything about normal behavior or animal psychology. When Fox began to study wild canids (wolves, coyotes, and foxes), his basic view of research began to change. At the beginning, he was a scientist studying animals to gain knowledge for knowledge's sake. But, he gradually changed his view toward conservation and human values. This book highlights his views.

Fox has also written extensively about dogs and cats and the use of companion animals in human therapy.

Francione, Gary L. *Animals, Property, and the Law.* Philadelphia: Temple University Press, 1995 (reprinted with corrections, 2005).

Francione discusses the reasons that animals are considered property and what impact this status has on their treatment. He provides a detailed analysis of the concept of standing, which prevents consideration of the legal rights of animals. He also provides a detailed analysis of the purpose and function of anticruelty statutes and how these laws have allowed the exploitation of animals. In his discussion of the Animal Welfare Act, which focuses on the administrative regulations promulgated for the enforcement of the Act, he discusses the difference between "symbolic" and "functional" legislation and maintains that the Act is symbolic, because Congress failed to address the administrative and political constraints that can block implementation of the Act. Functional legislation, in contrast, instructs agencies, such as the Department of Agriculture, how to balance competing interests when setting standards.

Francione, Gary L. *Rain without Thunder: The Ideology of the Animal Rights Movement.* Philadelphia: Temple University Press, 1996 (reprinted with corrections, 2005).

Francione argues that until the late 1970s, activists' concerns about animals were limited to concerns about humane treatment. In the late 1970s and 1980s, the modern animal rights movement emerged. Animal welfare activists sought to regulate the exploitation of animals, while animal rights advocates sought the abolition of exploitation of animals. Henry Spira, a New York high school teacher and labor organizer, is sometimes called the inspiration for the rights movement. When he found that the American Museum of Natural History in New York was conducting experiments on the sexual behavior of cats, he and his colleagues picketed the museum. Museum officials refused to meet with Spira, so he published a detailed account of the experiments in a New York weekly newspaper. His campaign elicited thousands of letters and phone calls to the newspaper. Spira's activities caught the attention of Congressman Ed Koch, and many members of Congress became interested in the project. The National Institutes of Health withdrew funding, and the laboratory closed. Spira, with the help of other activists, brought about the repeal of the Metcalf-Hatch Act in New York, which permitted research institutions to use unclaimed animals for research.

Hauser, Marc D., Fiery Cushman, and Matthew Kamen (Eds.). *People, Property, or Pets?* West Lafayette, IN: Purdue University Press, 2006.

This book consists of a series of essays dealing with the philosophical and legal issues associated with the views that animals are property and that animals are entities that have rights. It provides a detailed evaluation of "personhood" and discusses the impact of fixing the boundaries that determine whether an entity is a person. Individual essays describe the role of cognitive science in evaluating the status of animals and review the moral and practical issues linked to animal experimentation and the need to develop alternatives to using animals for biomedical research. The authors observe that veterinarians are committed to promoting the health and welfare of animals, as well as reducing potential suffering of animals. Current state and federal laws establish both negative obligations with respect to animals (e.g., state and local anticruelty statutes) and positive obligations, such as providing the great apes with opportunities to engage in species specific behaviors.

Magel, Charles R. *Keyguide to Information Sources in Animal Rights.* London: Mansell Publishing Ltd., 1989.

Magel presents an overview of the animal rights literature, including an annotated bibliography arranged in chronological order and a list of animal rights organizations.

Newkirk, Ingrid. *Free the Animals!: The Untold Story of the U.S. Animal Liberation Front and Its Founder, "Valerie."* Chicago: Noble Press, 1992.

Newkirk, the National Director of People for the Ethical Treatment of Animals, sometimes acts as a spokesman for the Animal Liberation Front. Newkirk discusses the formation of the Animal Liberation Front in the United States and provides insight into the values and beliefs of its leader, known simply as Valerie. The Animal Liberation Front, which focuses on organizations that perform biomedical experiments, uses many different techniques to achieve its goal of liberating animals.

Newkirk, I. *Save The Animals: 101 Easy Things You Can Do.* New York: Warner Books, 1990.

Newkirk, one of the founders of People for the Ethical Treatment of Animals (PETA), maintains that we should question not how animals should be treated within the context of their usefulness or perceived usefulness to us but whether we have a right to use them at all. She provides 101 ways that ordinary individuals can stop using animals. Each chapter is headed by quotes from celebrities and contains specific suggestions, from becoming a vegetarian to avoiding the products of companies that use animals in their product testing.

Nussbaum, Martha C. *Frontiers of Justice: Disability, Nationality, Species Membership.* Cambridge, MA: Belknap Press of Harvard University Press, 2006.

In a chapter titled "Beyond Compassion and Humanity," Nussbaum discusses the ideas of the Greco-Romans, the Stoics, and world religions, as well as of the philosopher Immanuel Kant, concerning the differences between animals and humans. She provides a detailed discussion of utilitarianism, focusing on consequentialism (the belief that the right act promotes the best overall outcome) and sum-ranking (i.e., how to aggregate consequences across lives) and discusses the views of Bentham and Singer. Finally, she suggests how humans should evaluate the capabilities of animals and the effect this should have on our interactions with them.

Regan, Tom. *Animal Sacrifices: Religious Perspectives on the Use of Animals in Science.* Philadelphia: Temple University Press, 1987.

Regan presents an overview of historical and modern Christian, Jewish, Moslem, and Hindu thought on the use of animals in science.

Regan, Tom. *The Case for Animal Rights.* Berkeley: University of California Press, 2004 (originally published, 1994).

The preface of the current book responds to the critics of the 1994 edition. Regan develops a cumulative argument for animal consciousness and the complexity of awareness in animals. He critiques rational egoism, contractarianism, the belief that humanity is an end in itself, and hedonistic and preference utilitarianism. Regan uses the principles of justice and equality to develop a theory of moral rights for humans and animals, which he bases on the inherent value of individuals that are subjects of life. Regan believes that vegetarianism is morally obligatory.

Regan, Tom, and Singer, Peter (Eds.). *Animal Rights and Human Obligations.* Englewood Cliffs, NJ: Prentice Hall, 1976.

This book contains a set of readings on animal rights and is intended for use in college-level courses in ethics and humanities. The authors of the readings range from Aristotle to Henry S. Salt to Peter Singer and Richard Ryder.

Rood, Ronald. *Animals Nobody Loves.* Brattleboro, VT: Stephen Greene Press, 1971.

Rood describes 12 animals or groups of animals that many people do not like. They include the wolf, rat, flea, mosquito, octopus, bat, snake, spider, vulture, pig, eel, and coyote. He suggests that this attitude is based on the way the animal looks or acts.

Ryder, Richard D. *Animal Revolution: Changing Attitudes towards Speciesism.* Cambridge, MA: Basil Blackwell, 1989.

Ryder, who coined the term "speciesism," presents a historical analysis (focusing on Britain) of the changing relationship between humans and nonhumans (sentients). He believes that when we place humans in opposition to animals, it is an expression of prejudice, since humans are animals. Modern animal rights ideology seeks to conquer suffering and to protect nonhuman life universally. He believes that the conclusion that it is illogical and unjust to discriminate on the basis of species arose spontaneously in many people in the 1960s and 1970s. He argues that our primitive ancestors depended on other sentients for food, clothing, and tools but that, because modern people have alternate sources of food, clothing, and power, they no longer need to depend on other sentients for these items.

The central tenet of the book is that species alone is not a valid criterion for cruel discrimination, any more than race or sex is.

Like race or sex, the term "species" denotes physical and other differences that do not nullify the basic similarity of species, their capacity to suffer. This capacity exists because all vertebrate classes possess biochemical substances (e.g., endorphins) that are known to mediate pain. We use emotive words, such as "pest" and "vermin," to stifle compassion toward other species. Modern techniques of molecular biology allow the introduction of human genes into nonhuman species, such as the cancer-prone mouse that was recently patented. Ryder seems to be asking how many human genes are required to make a creature human in the eyes of the law.

Salt, Henry S. *Animals' Rights: Considered in Relation to Social Progress.* Clarks Summit, PA: Society for Animal Rights, 1980.

This is a reprint of a book that was originally published in 1892. Salt wrote more than 40 books dealing with abuses in schools, prisons, and other sites. Although not well known himself, he influenced friends, such as George Bernard Shaw and Gandhi. Salt believed that animals have a fundamental right to live a natural life, which permits individual development. He asserts that the idea that animals are radically different from humans or that animals have no soul or emotional life is wrong and argues that avoidable infliction of pain or suffering is morally wrong.

Sebeck, Thomas A., and Rosenthal, Robert (Eds.). *The Clever Hans Phenomenon: Communication with Horses, Whales, Apes, and People.* New York: New York Academy of Science, 1981.

Clever Hans was a horse that lived in Berlin, Germany, in the early part of the 20th century. He belonged to a retired schoolteacher, Wilhelm von Osten, who believed that animals could be taught to think, talk, and calculate if instructed by the right method. The method, invented by von Osten, was to assign a number to each letter of the alphabet. The association between the number and the letter was learned by the trainer writing the number on a blackboard. The horse used its front hoof to tap out numbers. Eventually, the horse learned to combine letters into words and words into sentences and could also add, subtract, multiply, divide, and solve problems of musical harmony. But, careful experiments by Oskar Pfungst, of the Psychological Institute of the University of Berlin, strongly suggest that Clever Hans could not add, subtract, or do any of the other feats credited to him. Pfungst suggested that

Clever Hans was a careful observer and responded to very small, subtle, and probably unconscious movements by von Osten when the correct number of knocks had been reached.

Sebeck and Rosenthal suggest that the story of Clever Hans should provide a major lesson about the subtlety of communication, witting or unwitting, between members of different species. Further, they and the other authors whose work appears in this book suggest that many modern *thinking* animals, such as dolphins and chimpanzees, may be very subtle examples of the Clever Hans phenomena.

Singer, Peter. *Animal Liberation: A New Ethics for Our Treatment of Animals*. New York: Harper Collins, 2001.

This is a revised edition of the original edition, which was published in 1975. *Animal Liberation* has been called the bible of the animal rights movement. Singer's basic moral postulate is that equal consideration of interests should not be arbitrarily limited to relations with members of our own species. He maintains that humans have ruthlessly and cruelly exploited animals and inflicted needless suffering on them and that this must be stopped. Singer proposes to think through the question of how we ought to treat nonhuman animals and to expose the prejudices that lie behind our present attitudes and behavior. Liberation movements have demanded an end to prejudice and discrimination based on arbitrary characteristics, such as race or sex; Singer argues that liberation movements have also forced us to expand our moral horizons and to view practices that were previously regarded as natural and inevitable as the result of unjustifiable prejudice. Further, he argues that since animals cannot speak for themselves, it is our duty to speak for them. He reasons that the very use of the word "animal" to mean "animals other than human beings" sets humans apart from other animals and implies that humans are not animals.

Singer, Peter (Ed.). *In Defense of Animals.* New York: Wiley, 2006.

This book includes a series of essays that attempt to define the animal liberation movement by activists in Europe, the United States, and Australia. The animal liberation movement is relatively new, a product of the 1970s. It is distinct from more traditional animal welfare movements, most of which were started in the 19th century and which sought to protect animals only when no serious human interest was at stake. In the event of conflict, the animals' interests were to be sacrificed to our own. Modern animal liberationists challenge this notion. They argue that membership in the human species is not morally relevant and that when humans override animals' interests to further their own, it is an example of species-selfishness, or speciesism.

Singer argues that modern Western views of animals arise from ancient Greece, where Aristotle, for example, believed that there is a hierarchy in nature in which those with less reasoning ability exist for the sake of those with greater reasoning ability. In other words, plants exist for animals, animals exist for humans, and so on. The other wellspring of modern thought is the Judeo-Christian view of animals as expressed in the first few chapters of Genesis, where humans are made in the image of God and man is given dominion over animals. Again, the animal liberationists condemn these ideas as examples of speciesism. Further, they argue that when animals and humans have similar interests, such as avoiding physical pain, those interests must be given equal respect.

Young, Thomas. *An Essay on Humanity to Animals.* New York: Continuum International Publishing Group, 2003.

Originally published in 1798, Young's book argues that animals are capable of pleasure and pain and that cruelty is against God's will. Young opposes animal experimentation "only to gratify curiosity" and argues that a morally sensitive person should not walk on worms or snails and should help flies in distress.

Cetacea: The Whales and Dolphins

Lilly, John Cunningham. *Man and Dolphin.* Pyramid Books, 1965.

Dolphins produce a wide variety of complex sounds. Lilly describes a series of experiments in which he and his colleagues attempted to develop meaningful communication between a human and a nonhuman intelligence, the bottlenose dolphin (*Torsions truncates*). Lilly chose the dolphin because it is approximately the same size as a human and because its brain weighs approximately 1,700 grams (the average human brain is approximately 1,450 grams). In many ways this work is far more daunting than attempts to communicate with chimpanzees (see, for example, the Kellogg and Linden citations in the section on primates). This is because we have a good deal of common life experience with large primates. But, a dolphin's life experience is very different!

Lilly, John Cunningham. *The Mind of the Dolphin: A Nonhuman Intelligence.* New York: Avon, 1973.

Lilly describes additional experiments in his attempt to establish meaningful communication between humans and dolphins. On the basis of his work with dolphins, Lilly believes that creatures with a brain above a certain size (e.g., whales, dolphins) should be considered "equal" to humans.

Domestication

The process of animal domestication (that is, the adapting or taming of an animal to live and breed in intimate association with and to the advantage of humans) began about 18,000 years ago, during the Stone Age. Neolithic people were undoubtedly interested in a general-utility animal, one that could serve equally well for carrying loads, for hunting, and, if the need arose, for food. Therefore, they chose hoofed vertebrates, because they were strong and durable and provided a large amount of meat. This included various species and breeds of cattle, sheep, and pigs, supplemented in some localities by goats, reindeer, and rabbits. Birds, such as chickens, ducks, and geese, as well as fish, such as carp or catfish, also supply substantial amounts of meat. Mammals also provide wool (sheep, goats) and hides (cattle) to make clothing and shelter for humans.

It is estimated that of the more than 700,000 species of insects, only the honeybee, the silkworm, and two species of scale insects (used to produce lac, which is used to make shellac, and cochineal, a dye) have been quasi-domesticated. Although the honey and beeswax that bees produce are important products, the bee's most important contribution to humans' wellbeing is as a pollinator. Indeed, some species of food and decorative plants could not exist without bees.

Clutton-Brock, Juliet. *A Natural History of Domesticated Mammals.* Austin: University of Texas Press, 1989.

Clutton-Brock describes the way humans have manipulated and changed mammals, from about 10,000 years ago until the

Roman Empire, when the common domestic mammals were well established as discrete breeding populations that were isolated from their wild parent species.

Humans, unlike other living primates, evolved as carnivorous predators. Therefore, early humans had to depend on their mental and physical prowess to hunt and kill other animals. Later, they learned to domesticate animals, which began to change as a result of artificial selection by humans, rather than as in response to environmental, climatic, or other conditions and reproductive isolation. Humans began keeping wolves during the last Ice Age, more than 125,000 years ago. Most mammals can be tamed if they are taken from their mothers early in life and reared by a human. An animal's relative tameness as an adult depends on the species' innate social patterns, that is, is it solitary (cats, except for the African lion) or social (wolf) in its way of life?

Clutton-Brock divides domestic animals into four major categories: (1) man-made animals (animals that have been inbred and modified), which include dogs, sheep, goats, cattle, pigs, as well as horses, asses, and mules; (2) exploited captives, which include cats, elephants, camels and llamas, reindeer, and Asiatic cattle; (3) small mammals, which include rabbits and ferrets, as well as rodents and carnivores that are exploited for their fur; and (4) animals that are used in game ranching, such as deer and bovids. She discusses the process of domestication for each group and describes the ungulates that were exploited by pre-Neolithic humans.

Clutton-Brock, Juliet (Ed.). *The Walking Larder: Patterns of Domestication, Pastoralism, and Predation.* London: Unwin Hyman, 1989.

Various authors describe the manifold relationships between humans and animals, both in the past and in the present, and how these relationships affect the process of domestication. Early humans were constantly on the move, trying to expand their territory and find new resources. These early humans, like modern humans, needed a source of protein. They found it in the wild animals that they followed and hunted, as well as in domestic animals that they drove along in their travels and which they used as a store of meat on the hoof, that is, as livestock. The book also describes the development of pastoralism (how humans became shepherds and herdsmen) in Europe, Asia, and Africa and discusses the effects of human predation on shellfish, fish, and birds and the impact of predators on humans, who are both competitors and potential prey.

Zeder, Melinda A., Daniel G. Bradley, Eve Emshwiller, and Bruce D. Smith (Eds.). *Documenting Domestication: New Genetic and Archaeological Paradigms.* University of California Press, 2006.

Our primitive ancestors shifted from hunting and gathering to farming. In the process, they domesticated a number of plants, such as maize (corn), and animals such as sheep, goats, and pigs. In the past, our knowledge of the relationship between humans and these domesticated species depended on the archeological record (e.g., seeds or animal bones found around human habitations). Modern DNA techniques, such as analysis of mitochondrial DNA, have allowed researchers to document changes that have occurred to plants and animals over time.

Entertainment

The first time an animal was used to amuse and entertain a human being predates written history. The number of species of animals used by the various components of the entertainment industry varies. The rodeo industry typically uses just two species: horses and cattle. The circus typically uses horses, elephants, large wild cats, domestic dogs, and, more rarely, bears, primates (especially chimpanzees), seals and sea lions, and birds (especially parrots and macaws). The motion picture and television industries use a wide variety of species of domestic and wild animals. Public and private zoos and aquaria generally have the largest number of species of wild animals.

Circus

The one-ring circus has been in existence for at least 2,500 years. The Romans called them *circulators.* They consisted of troupes of jugglers and mountebanks (a con artist, who sells by deception, often quack medicines) who made their living by performing feats of acrobatics and magic and by exhibiting trained animals. The modern circus was born in the 1770s in Great Britain; acrobats, clowns, and trained animals did not appear until the end of the 18th century. Animals have been a popular part of the circus tradition for centuries, and it is likely that as long as the circus exists, animals will be a part of it.

Bouissae, Paul. *Circus and Culture: A Semiotic Approach.* Bloomington: Indiana University Press, 1976.

In this classic, Bouissae provides a brief history of the circus and then describes the culture of the circus. He devotes several chapters to the interrelationship between animals and their trainers. He describes how trainers train a horse to perform in a standard horse act. The process is similar to that of training any performing animal. The first step is to establish rapport with the animal. This is done by presenting the animal with pleasurable rewards such as food (carrots, candy) and scratching or patting the animal while speaking in a pleasant voice. Incorrect behavior is punished with light blows and a disapproving voice. Gradually, the animal learns to recognize the trainer and treats him with attachment and respect, in much the same manner that he would treat a higher-ranking member of his own species. The animal gradually learns to respond to the trainer's hand and body signals. The balancing of rewards and punishment is a delicate task. The goal is not to break the animal's spirit but to teach him to remain near the trainer and follow his movements. For example, horses can be trained to begin and stop pawing the ground when cued by very subtle movements on the part of the trainer. These movements, which should be subtle enough that an observer is unaware of them, are what circus trainers call the *keys* to training.

Films and Television
Animals have been part of the motion picture industry since its beginnings. The first commercial movie was David Wark Griffith's *The Great Train Robbery* (1903), which was a western, or cowboy movie, that used horses. Some animals were stars in their own right, far more famous than their trainers or, in some cases, even their human costars. Many human costars complained about being upstaged by their animal costars. Lassie (reportedly several generations of male collies) and Rin Tin Tin were well-known dog stars. Trigger and Champion, both horses, had almost as much name recognition as their human owners, Roy Rogers and Gene Autry.

In the early days, some trainers used fear and violence to control an animal's behavior. These have been replaced by more rationale training methods based on the method of successive approximations and positive reinforcement.

Helfer, Ralph. *The Beauty and the Beast: Tales of Hollywood's Wild Animal Stars*. New York: Harper Paperbacks, 2007.

Helfer is an animal trainer who provides insight into the training methods he uses. He uses positive reinforcement rather than fear to train his animals

Rodeos

Rodeo is a popular sport in the United States and Canada. The Professional Rodeo Cowboys Association and the International Rodeo Association together sanction more than 1,000 annual rodeos that are attended by more than 14 million paying spectators. Many communities and organizations, such as the 4-H, Little Britches, and Girls Rodeo Association, also sponsor rodeos throughout the spring, summer, and fall.

Rodeo traces its origin back to two diverse sources. The first is the sports and contests of the early working cowboys that they pursued for their own amusement. The second is the uniquely American outdoor entertainment, the Wild West Show, which was started by William Frederick ("Buffalo Bill") Cody in the summer of 1882 in North Platte, Nebraska. This show included performances called "Cowboy Fun," which included attempts to ride wild broncos and mules, steer wrestling, and other skills of the range. In contrast to their modern counterparts, these early cowboys were paid performers. Modern rodeo cowboys get paid only if they win.

Lawrence, Elizabeth A. Rodeo: *An Anthropologist Looks at the Wild and the Tame*. Chicago: University of Chicago Press, 1982.

Modern professional rodeo is almost totally a man's world. Women are typically not allowed to participate as contestants or officials. The typical rodeo is divided into rough-stock (bronco riding, bareback bronco, riding and bull riding) and timed events (calf roping, steer wrestling, team roping, and steer roping). The only event in the standard rodeo that women are allowed to enter is the barrel race. As the name implies, this is a timed event, where the horse races around a clover-leaf pattern around a series of barrels and then races out of the arena in the shortest amount of time possible.

Farm Animals

Prior to World War II, there were about 6 million farms in the United States covering approximately 1,061 million areas of farmland. The amount of farmland has remained relatively constant, but the number of farms has dropped steadily. As the costs of farm labor increased, there was an increased dependence on mechanization, including the adoption of intensive industrialized husbandry methods and techniques for raising cattle, pigs, and poultry.

Coats, C. Davis, and Michael W. Fox. *Old MacDonald's Factory Farm: The Myth of the Traditional Farm and the Shocking Truth about Animal Suffering in Today's Agribusiness.* New York: Continuum International, 1989.

In modern times, Old MacDonald's farm, with a few animals frolicking in a field, does not really exist. Coats and Fox discuss how modern, business-oriented farms use mass-production techniques to produce high volumes of standardized products, whether beef, milk, or pork.

Harrison, Ruth. *Animal Machines: The New Factory Farming Industry.* New York: Ballantine Books, 1966.

In this classic book, Harrison describes modern mechanized factory farming as it is applied to broiler chickens, laying chickens, and veal calves, as well as to rabbits and pigs, in Great Britain. She argues that "more does not always mean better." Farmers add small amounts of antibiotics, such as penicillin, aureomycin, or terramycin, and/or synthetic estrogens to the feed of animals to improve growth rate. But the use of antibiotics will ultimately lead to the development of strains of bacteria that are resistant to these antibiotics, and the synthetic estrogens are contaminating the meat of these animals.

Rollin, Bernard E. *Farm Animal Welfare: Social, Bioethical, and Research Issues.* New York: Wiley-Blackwell, 2003.

Rollin discusses common practices in the beef, swine, dairy, veal, and poultry industries. For example, branding of cattle with a hot branding iron goes back more than 4,000 years. It creates a third-degree burn, which is painful. Alternate procedures of marking animals include freeze branding, which is apparently not painful; ear tags; and implantation of microchips.

Westendorf, Michael L. *Food Waste to Animal Feed.* New York: Wiley-Blackwell, 2000.

Animals grown in concentrated animal feeding operations are often fed grains and other foodstuffs that could be utilized by humans. Westendorf suggests that human waste (garbage) that is high in nutrient value and fat content could be used as animal feed, rather than ending in a land fill.

Zayan, Rene (Ed.). *Social Space for Domestic Animals.* New York: Springer, 1985.

This book presents the proceedings of a seminar that focused on the spatial needs of laying hens in battery cages, as well as the spatial needs of pigs, dairy cattle, and sheep. This book focuses on the relationship between spatial measures (group size and floor space/animal) and social behavior.

Zayan, Rene, and Robert Dantzer (Eds.). *Social Stress in Domestic Animals.* New York: Springer. 1990.

The essays in this volume deal with density and its impact on aggression, productivity, and health.

Fur Farming and Trapping

Fur farmers maintain that natural fur is a green alternative because it is an infinitely renewable, biodegradable natural fiber, whereas synthetic fibers are made from nonrenewable resources. More than 4.5 million mink per year are raised on more than 2,000 family-owned fur farms. In addition to using the fur for clothing, modern industry uses the fat between the skin and the carcass to make mink oil, which in turn is used to make hypoallergenic cosmetics and conditioners for fine leather. The mink carcass is sold to feed companies, which combine it with other meat, fish, and poultry products to make feed for pets and livestock.

Harding, A. R. *Fur Farming.* Columbus, OH: Fur Fish Game, 1979.

Harding provides details about fur farming, including what type of animals are farmed and how they are housed and fed.

Spencer, Jim. *Guide to Trapping.* Mechanicsburg, PA: Stackpole Books, 2007.

Spencer provides a species-by-species review of trapping techniques for animals such as raccoon, muskrat, mink, otter, beaver, coyote, gray fox, red fox, bobcat, skunk, and opossum.

Horse Racing

Horse racing is undoubtedly one of the oldest diversions of humans, probably starting soon after the domestication of horses. Kikkuli, an expert in the employ of a Hittite king, may have written the first treatise dealing with the breeding and training of horses in about 1500 B.C.E. The 23rd Olympiad (about 624 B.C.E.) probably included races involving mounted horses. The Jockey Club, which exercises control over racing and breeding in England, was formed around 1750. The stallions and mares that provided the foundation for American thoroughbred breeding were imported during the 1700s.

Horse racing actually consists of three rather distinct sports. In thoroughbred racing, the jockey is mounted on the horse's back, and the horse races around an oval track. The track is dirt and usually about a mile in length. In steeplechasing, a jockey is mounted on the horse's back and the horse must run a complex course that contains a variety of obstacles that the horse must jump over. The steeplechase race course can contain as many as 30 jumps and tends to be longer than the thoroughbred race course. In harness racing, the driver sits in a sulky, which is a two-wheeled vehicle of the lightest possible construction, with two pneumatic tires. Most harness racetracks are about one-half mile long. The horses are trained to trot or pace.

Mooney, Bill, and George Ennor. *Complete Encyclopedia of Horse Racing: Illustrated Guide to the World of the Thoroughbred.* London: Carlton, 2006.

This book provides an insightful look at horse racing from its beginnings to the present and provides a behind-the-scenes look at the horses and the people who work with them.

Hunting and Fishing

Our primitive ancestors, as early as the Cro-Magnon period, were hunters, and they apparently held the animals they hunted in almost mystical regard. The earliest paintings, such as those in the caves of Lascaux in the Dordogne region of France, which were made in late Paleolithic times, depicted animals such as bulls, horses, and deer. The earliest engravings, reliefs, and sculptures were also of animal subjects. Archaeologists believe that these paintings and other objects were used in magico-religious rites bound up in the hunting culture. In many parts of the world today, people still hunt and fish in order to survive.

In the industrialized countries, hunting and fishing are not typically required for survival but are pursued as sports. Many modern sportsmen claim to have the same regard for the animals they hunt that our primitive ancestors did. They argue that no species of animal has become extinct because of sport hunting or fishing. Game species and their habitats are often better protected than nongame species because of the work of sportsmen. They also point out that, with or without the presence of sportsmen, the fate of most wild animals is death by starvation, disease, or predation.

It was Theodore Roosevelt, an ardent sportsman, who made conservation a household word. Conservation, for Roosevelt and others of his generation, was a reform movement that used political and legal methods to ensure the wise use of limited resources. The Boone and Crockett Club, started by Roosevelt and other prominent sportsmen in 1887, was the first private organization to deal with conservation issues on a national scale. The Sierra Club, started by John Muir, represents the opposite viewpoint. Countless books and magazine articles have been written about hunting and fishing.

McIntyre, Thomas. *The Way of the Hunter: The Art and the Spirit of Modern Hunting*. New York: E. P. Dutton, 1988.

Humans in the developed (industrialized) world do not have to hunt to survive or to put food on their table. But, for some, the pursuit of animals in the wild in order to kill them and consume their flesh provides a connection to our primitive ancestors.

Reiger, John F. *American Sportsmen and the Origins of Conservation*. Corvallis: Oregon State University Press, 2000.

Reiger presents a historical review of the conservation movement and its early leaders, such as Theodore Roosevelt. These hunters held a waste-not want-not ethic that was shaped by organizations like the Boone and Crockett Club and publications like *Field and Stream* and *American Sportsman*. These conservationists helped fund our system of national parks.

Pets

Dogs were domesticated by Neolithic man about 18,000 years ago and were used to help humans hunt, as draft animals, to help control herds of hoofed stock, and, when necessary, for food. They also provided early and modern humans with companionship. More recently, in the 19th and 20th centuries, a variety of species of small mammals, birds, reptiles, amphibians, and fish have been quasi-domesticated and kept as pets.

Anchel, Marjorie (Ed.). *Overpopulation of Cats and Dogs: Causes, Effects, and Prevention.* New York: Fordham University Press, 1990.

This book presents the proceedings of a conference sponsored by the New York Humane Association. It provides an overview of the problems associated with surplus animals, especially unwanted cats and dogs, and possible solutions to help resolve them, such as neutering (castration or spaying) and euthanasia. It also discusses who is responsible for pet overpopulation, how animals are controlled in rural, urban, and metropolitan areas, and the role of animal shelters and pounds. It also stresses the importance of education and appropriate legislation in preventing pet overpopulation.

Anderson, P. Elizabeth. *The Powerful Bond between People and Pets: Our Boundless Connections to Companion Animals.* Westport, CT: Praeger, 2008.

Anderson provides an insightful analysis of the relationship between humans and companion animals. She discusses studies that demonstrate that people who have a companion, human or animal, generally feel better and live longer. Because of the unconditional, nonjudgmental love displayed by these animals, they often have a therapeutic effect on their human owners.

Beck, Alan M. *The Ecology of Stray Dogs: A Study of Free-Ranging Urban Animals.* West Lafayette, IN: Purdue University Press. 2002.

Unwanted dogs are often just abandoned at the curb to fend for themselves. These dogs often form small packs and tend to be active at night and are cautious of humans.

Primates

Carl von Linne (better known by the Latinized version of his name, Linnaeus), the great classifier, placed the human species, which he named Homo sapiens (*Man, wise*), in the same order as the monkeys and apes. He named this order Primates; the order consists of 11 families, 60 genera, and approximately 191 species.

Recent research suggests that the African apes (that is, the gorillas and chimpanzees) and humans split off from a common ancestor about 4 million years ago. Modern geneticists tell us that humans and chimpanzees share in common 99 percent of their genes.

Recently, reports of remarkably human-like behaviors such as fashioning and using simple tools, learning and even inventing new signs in the American Sign Language, and learning to manipulate tokens in a totally synthetic language suggest that we might have to re-evaluate our ethical and moral stand with regard to chimpanzees and the other great apes.

The Food Security Act of 1985, Subtitle F, Animal Welfare (Public Law 99–198, 99 Stat. 1645) amends the Animal Welfare Act of 1966 and extends the minimum standard of care to provide a physical environment that is adequate to promote the psychological wellbeing of primates.

Fossey, Dian. *Gorillas in the Mist.* Boston: Mariner Books, 2000.

Fossey founded the Karisoke Research Center, in Rwanda, to study mountain gorillas in 1967. In this book, she describes her studies at the Center. Fossey, who was murdered on December 26, 1985, strongly opposed the poaching and capturing of gorillas for zoos or scientific exploitation.

Goodall, Jane. *Through a Window: My Thirty Years with the Chimpanzees of Gombe.* Boston: Houghton Mifflin, 1990.

Goodall has had a unique life experience. She has spent most of her adult life studying and living with chimpanzees in their natural habitat, treated as almost one of their number. She eloquently makes the point that chimpanzees are more like us than any other living creature. This book reads like a novel describing the daily life of the chimpanzees at the Gombe Research Station.

Goodall, Jane, and Hugo Von Lawick (photographer). *In the Shadow of Man.* Boston: Mariner Books, 2000.

Goodall was one of the first humans to spend a significant amount of time observing chimpanzees in their natural habitat. She provides one of the first descriptions, if not the first, of tool making and use by chimpanzees. She describes how a chimpanzee strips the leaves off a small branch and inserts the stick into a termite mound to extract termites. Tool making and language (see Liden, this section) are two hallmarks of *humanness,* the characteristics that separate humans from the rest of the animals.

Kellogg, W. N., and L. A. Kellogg. *The Ape and the Child.* New York: McGraw-Hill, 1933.

In one of the first attempts to establish meaningful communication between a chimpanzee and a human, the Kelloggs took a seven-and-one-half-month old female chimpanzee, Gua, from its mother and raised it alongside their own nine-month-old son, Donald. They compare and contrast the growth and development of the two infants.

Kirkwood, James K., and Katherine Stathatos. *Biology, Rearing, and Care of Young Primates.* Oxford: Oxford University Press, 1992.

In the past, nonhuman primates used in research, for display in zoos, or for pets were captured from their natural habitats. This is no longer possible because many nonhuman primates, including all of the great apes, are considered endangered species. Therefore, it is vital that we develop the methods and procedures needed to breed and maintain primates in captivity. This is especially true since it is likely that populations of many species of primates, especially the great apes, will continue to decrease in their natural habitat because of poaching and habitat destruction. It is vital that we maintain sufficient numbers of selected primates to maintain genetic diversity for the future.

Kirkwood and Stathatos provide basic information about the appropriate sex ratio, gestation period, breeding season, and longevity of 18 species of primates, including representatives of 9 of the 11 primate families. It also describes details on infant management, accommodation, and how to reintegrate artificially reared infants into peer or family groups. It also provides important information about energy intake throughout the period of growth and development.

Linden, Eugene. *Apes, Men, and Language.* New York: Penguin, 1981.

Although chimpanzees are relatively close relatives of human beings, their vocal tract is relatively short and poorly controlled. Therefore, it is unlikely that they can produce speech.

Linden provides a popular overview of the work of Drs. R. Allen and Beatrice Gardner, who attempted to teach a chimpanzee, named Washoe, American Sign Language, or Ameslan. Ameslan is a language developed to help deaf people communicate. It is based on a series of hand and arm gestures that signify words or concepts. Ameslan gestures can be supplemented with finger spelling to convey ideas for which there are no gestures. While their claim is still controversial, the Gardners and their associate, Dr. Roger Fouts, assert that Washoe used Ameslan in a very human-like manner.

Linden also provides an overview of the work of Dr. David Premack and the chimpanzee Sarah. The language that Sarah is learning is very different from Ameslan. It consists of a series of arbitrarily shaped and colored plastic tokens. The tokens represent specific concepts, and Premack and Sarah communicate by arranging these tokens into messages written from top to bottom.

Novak, Melinda A., and Andrew J. Petto (Eds.). *Through the Looking Class: Issues of Psychological Well-Being in Captive Nonhuman Primates.* Washington, DC: American Psychological Association, 1991.

The only rational reason for using nonhuman primates as surrogates for humans in biomedical or psychological research is that they resemble humans so closely. Chimpanzees, for example, and humans share 99 percent of their genetic material.

Clearly, an unhealthy primate, whether physically or psychologically unhealthy, is not an accurate model of humans. Therefore, scientists and clinicians have sought methods and procedures to maintain the physical and psychological health of the primates in their charge long before the mandates outlined in the 1985 amendments to the Animal Welfare Act of 1966 (Food Security Act of 1985, Subtitle F, Animal Welfare (Public Law 99–198, 99 Stat. 1645, see also chapter 3).

This book describes how to evaluate psychological wellbeing in nonhuman primates and describes some of the methods and procedures that can be used to promote their psychological health. It also provides a brief overview of public (nonscientist) perceptions of primate research.

Reynolds, Vernon. *The Apes: The Gorilla, Chimpanzee, Orangutan, and Gibbon: Their History and Their World*. Boston: E. P. Dutton, 1967.

In this classic, Reynolds provides an excellent introduction to the behavior and natural life of the great apes, that is, chimpanzees, gorillas, gibbons, and orangutans. He describes the circumstances under which humans first encountered these species. The natural environment of each species and their adaptations to their natural environment are described. All of the great apes are considered endangered species in their natural habitats. Hunting or trapping these species has been illegal for several decades, but poaching is still a problem, as is the loss of habitat because of human development.

Because of their similarity to humans, great apes have been used as surrogates for humans in medical and psychological experiments. The great apes, and particularly the chimpanzee, have made invaluable contributions to the study of the causes of various diseases, including malaria, poliomyelitis, diphtheria, syphilis, whooping cough, heart disease, and cancer, and to the development of methods to prevent or cure these ills. In the early 1960s, two chimpanzees, Ham and Enos, made important space flights that demonstrated that launching, acceleration, weightlessness, and reentry were safe for human beings. These early chimpanzee flights allowed manned space flight to develop, allowed humans to set foot on the moon, and will (it is hoped) allow us to visit the other planets in our solar system and ultimately to reach the stars.

Schaller, George B. *The Year of the Gorilla*. Chicago: University of Chicago Press, 1997.

Schaller provides an overview of the scientific literature dealing with the ecology and behavior of the mountain gorilla and supplements this information with his own observations of mountain gorillas in their native habitat.

Yerkes, Robert M. *Chimpanzees: A Laboratory Colony*. New Haven: Yale University Press, 1943.

Yerkes was one of the pioneers in the study of the behavior of nonhuman primates. Most of his work focused on the study of the abilities of the chimpanzee. This book provides an overview of his work and describes the methods he and his colleagues used to set up one of the first laboratory colonies, if not the first, for the breeding and study of nonhuman primates.

Vegetarianism

Many animal rights activists argue that animals have an equal natural right to life and that vegetarianism is therefore morally obligatory.

Davis, Brenda, and Melina Vesanto. *Becoming Vegan: The Complete Guide to Adopting a Plant Based Diet.* Summertown, TN: Book Publishing, 2000.

This book provides a historical overview of the beginnings of the vegan lifestyle and discusses how to achieve that lifestyle by avoiding animal products in the diet.

Greeley, Alexandra. *The Everything Guide to Being Vegetarian: The Advice, Nutrition information, and Recipes You Need to Enjoy a Healthy Lifestyle.* Cincinnati, OH: Adams Media, 2009.

Greeley, a former editor of *Vegetarian Times*, provides an overview of the vegetarian lifestyle, including how to obtain complete proteins and iron. She also discusses preparation of soy based foods. She discusses the difference between vegetarians and vegans.

Hur, Robin. *Food Reform: Our Desperate Need.* Austin, TX: Heidelberg Press, 1975.

Hur maintains that the vegan diet, which avoids animal fat and protein, sugar, salt, and processed foods, leads to a decrease in degenerative diseases.

Inglis, Jane. *Some People Don't Eat Meat.* n.p.: Oakroyd Press, 1987.

This book is designed to describe the vegetarian lifestyle to primary and elementary school children.

Marcus, Erik. *Vegan: The New Ethics of Eating.* Ithaca, NY: McBooks Press, 2000.

Marcus provides an overview of the vegan lifestyle, which eliminates all animal products from both the diet and daily life.

Perry, Cheryl L., Leslie A. Lytle, and Teresa Jacobs. *The Vegetarian Manifesto.* Philadelphia, PA: Running Press, 2004.

This is a handbook designed for teenagers and young adults who want to eliminate meat and fish from their diet. It provides background on what vegetarian is, describes living in a nonvegetarian world, and explains how to maintain good health with adequate whole protein and maintain a safe and healthy weight.

Robbins, John. The Food Revolution: *How Your Diet Can Help Save Your Life and Our World*. Newburyport, MA: Conari Press, 2001.

Robbins argues becoming a vegetarian helps feed the hungry, prevents cruelty to animals, and enables people to avoid genetically modified foods and live longer.

Salt, Henry S. *The Logic of Vegetarianism: Essays and Dialogues*. n.p.: BiblioLife, 2008.

In this classic originally published in 1906, Salt provides arguments for vegetarianism and refutes common arguments against it.

Tryon, Thomas. *The Way to Health, Long Life and Happiness*. London: Andrew Sowle, 1683.

Tryon was born in 1634; in 1657, he decided to avoid eating any kind of flesh, confining himself to bread and fruit, to which at a later point he added butter and cheese. This is the first book in the English language to use the term "rights" in regard to animals. Tryon was widely read in both England and America, and Benjamin Franklin was greatly impressed after reading these books and reportedly became a Tryonist for a time.

Zoos and Aquaria

Menageries have existed since ancient times in Egypt, Rome, and China. Modern zoo keeping dates from the founding of the Imperial Menagerie at the Schonbrunn Palace in Vienna in 1752. It opened to the public in 1765 and is still in operation. The Zoological Society of London established its collection in Regents Park in 1828. This zoo was one of the first to replace its traditional cages with more natural habitats. The first zoological garden was established in the United States in Philadelphia in 1874.

Today, virtually every major city in the United States has a zoological garden, and several cities, such as Chicago and New

York, have several. In the past, zoological gardens housed one or two members of each species in small cages with iron bars across the front. Today, these cages are being replaced by larger, more natural habitat areas. Recently, drive-through nature parks have become popular. In these parks, the humans remain in their car and the animals are allowed to roam free. In the United States, these parks generally contain exotic hoofed stock and large birds (ostrich, emu).

Many zoological gardens are attempting to set up breeding populations of specific species. Young produced by these breeding populations can help replenish the zoo's own collection and provide animals to other zoos. This breeding program is especially important for species that are endangered in their natural habitat, such as the great apes and the large carnivores.

Zimmerman, Alexandra, Mathew Hatchwell, Lesley A. Dickey, and Chris West (Eds.). *Zoos in the 21st Century: Catalysts for Conservation?* Cambridge: Cambridge University Press, 2007.

This comprehensive book, which focuses on science-based techniques, provides an insightful discussion of the way zoos and aquaria can help maintain threatened and endangered species.

Government Publications

Animal Welfare Information Center Bulletin

The Bulletin is distributed free by the National Agricultural Library. It is designed to provide current information on all aspects of animal welfare to scientists, technicians, administrators, and the public. It is available online at http://www.nal.usda.gov/awic/pubs/bulletin.shtml.

Guide for the Care and Use of Laboratory Animals

The Institute of Laboratory Animal Resources (ILAR) of the National Research Council was founded in 1952 to act as a national and international clearing resource for compiling and disseminating information on laboratory animal resources and promoting high-quality and humane care of laboratory animals in the United States. The ILAR published the first edition of the *Guide for Laboratory Animal Facilities and Care* in 1963. The publication was revised in 1965 and 1968. In 1972, it was revised again and given its current title; yet another revision was published under that title in 1978. The 1996 edition is the most recent version and is widely accepted by scientific institutions as the primary reference on animal care and use.

The *Guide* puts the requirements and recommendations of Public Law 89–544 (Animal Welfare Act) and its amendments, as well as other federal, state, and local laws, regulations, and policies, into a practical format that can be used to make day-to-day decisions about the care and use of laboratory animals. It is important to note that "Nothing in the *Guide* is intended to limit an investigator's freedom—indeed obligation—to plan and conduct animal experiments in accord with scientific and humane principles."

The *Guide*'s longest chapter deals with laboratory animal husbandry. It discusses space recommendations for laboratory animals and covers issues such as opportunities for social interactions, temperature, humidity, ventilation, illumination, noise levels, food, bedding, water, sanitation and waste disposal, and vermin control (for pests such as cockroaches, flies, wild rodents). A standard for veterinary care, such as daily observation of all animals to assess their health and welfare and using appropriate methods to prevent, control, diagnose, and treat diseases and injuries, is presented. Veterinarians are also expected to monitor surgical programs and postsurgical care and to guide scientists and other animal users on handling, restraint, anesthesia, analgesia, and euthanasia.

The requirements of the physical plant, such as appropriate building materials for floors, walls, and ceilings; the placement of drains; the size and placement of doors and windows; and how an aseptic surgery should be set up and run are discussed, as are methods for controlling hazardous agents, such as chemical carcinogens. Each chapter has a detailed bibliography. Three appendices are provided: a detailed bibliography of books and journal articles dealing with laboratory animal care and use; a description of the professional organizations that deal with laboratory animals and the organizations that certify personnel who work with animals; and a summary of the laws that deal with laboratory animals. The *Guide* is available online at http://www.nap.edu/openbook.php?record_id=5140.

Public Health Service Policy on Humane Care and Use of Laboratory Animals

This is a policy statement of the Public Health Service, National Institutes of Health, Office of Protection from Research Risks (OPRR), whose goal is to help scientists and other individuals who have grants from or contracts with one of the National Institutes of Health or another branch of the Public Health Service to implement the regulations and recommendations contained in the Animal Welfare Act (Public Law 89–544) and its amendments, other federal statutes, and the "U.S. Government Principles for the Utilization and Care of Vertebrate Animals Used in Testing, Research, and Training," which was developed by the Interagency Research Animal Committee.

This policy statement deals primarily with the Institutional Animal Care and Use Committee (IACUC), focusing on its constituency and its responsibilities. When a grant proposal or contract is submitted to the Public Health Service, it must be accompanied by a verification letter from the IACUC stating that it has reviewed the proposal and found that it is in compliance with all of the requirements of PL 89-544 and its amendments, as well as with other federal statutes dealing with animals and animal use. A sample verification letter is provided.

The policy can be found online at http://grants.nih.gov/grants/olaw/references/phspol.htm.

Law Compilations and Legal Sources

U.S. Code Congressional and Administrative News

This is an unofficial, chronological (arranged by congressional session) compilation of federal statutes. The text of each statute is presented, as well as its legislative history. The legislative history includes an opening statement, a statement of the purpose of the statute, a summary of the outcome of congressional hearings, and a list of the committees that worked on the statute and their reports. A chronological record of the actions of the House and the Senate with regard to each bill and the passage of each statute is included.

U.S. Code.

The U.S. Code is the official compilation of law, arranged by topic. The sections dealing with animal welfare are found in Title 7, Agriculture, Chapter 54, Transportation, Sale, and Handling of Certain

Animals, Sections 2131–2159. The most recent version is for 2007 and is available online at http://www.law.cornell.edu/uscode/html/uscode07/usc_sup_01_7_10_54.html.

U.S. Code Annotated (U.S.C.A.). St. Paul, MN: West.

This is a multivolume, unofficial compilation of federal statutes and their amendments, arranged by topic. In addition to the text of the statute, *U.S.C.A.* presents historical footnotes, annotations to law review articles, and cases construing various statutory provisions. It is updated annually by pocket pieces and paperbound advance sheets.

Code of Federal Regulations

This official, multivolume compilation of federal regulations and their amendments as issued by federal agencies is arranged so that regulations covering the same topic are printed in the same section of the book. Federal regulations are published chronologically in the Federal Register and then codified in the *Code of Federal Regulations.* Federal regulations dealing with animal welfare are found in Title 9, Chapter 1, Animal and Plant Health Inspection Service, Department of Agriculture, Subchapter A, Animal Welfare. The 2009 revision is available online at http://ecfr.gpoaccess.gov/cgi/t/text/text-(idx?sid=81664c32190028ab4383ef9078a40369&c=ecfr&tpl=/ecfr browse/Title09/9tab_02.tpl.

Corpus Juris Secundum

CJS is a multivolume treatise or commentary on the law. It provides an analysis of federal, state, and local statutes and regulations, as well as case law (court decisions, both federal and state) dealing with a wide variety of issues, including animals and cruelty to animals (vol. 3A).

Favre, David S., and Murray Loring. *Animal Law.* Westport, CT: Quorum Books, 1983.

Favre and Loring provide a detailed analysis of the humane, anticruelty, and duty-to-provide-care laws, including a comparison of individual state statutes. They also discuss the powers and duties of Societies for the Prevention of Cruelty to Animals. Ownership, limitations of ownership, bailment, sale, medical care, and recovery for injury by animals are treated in individual chapters with detailed bibliographies.

Moretti, Daniel S. *Animal Rights and the Law.* New York: Oceana, 1984.

This book introduces the reader, in nontechnical language, to the subject of people's legal rights and responsibilities with respect to animals. Moretti presents a state-by-state overview of anticruelty laws, laws on animal fighting, humane slaughter, and transportation regulations, including the citations needed to find the official text of the law. State and federal wildlife protection laws, with appropriate citations, are also discussed, as are animal trapping laws. Moretti also discusses the case of *Edward Taub v. State of Maryland* (1983) (Silver Springs Monkey Case), which is the first example of a scientist being convicted of violating a state's anticruelty statute (Code 1957, 1976 Repl. Vol. 27 § 59); he also discusses how Taub's conviction was overturned on appeal.

Congressional Hearings

Congress, both the House of Representatives and the Senate, have a large number of committees and subcommittees that deal with a wide variety of issues. These committees periodically hold hearings about topics pertinent to the committee at which witnesses with expertise in the issues under consideration are called to testify. These experts may be members of the Executive branch, especially employees of the various Cabinet departments, such as the Department of Agriculture and its agencies. Experts who are not employed by the government may be academics, attorneys, and businesspeople, and others with special knowledge. Much of the work of Congress takes place in these committees, including drafting of new acts, some of which will become laws.

Hearing before the Committee on the Judiciary, U.S. Senate, 108th Congress, Serial Number J-108–76, May 24, 2004, Animal Rights Activism vs. Criminality (Y 4.J 89/2:S HRG.108–764). This report is available online at http://purl.access.gpo.gov/GPO/LPS59196.

   Senator Orrin Hatch of Utah was the chairman of this committee. The witnesses called to testify included Jonathan Blum, Yum! Brands; William Green, Chiron Corporation; John Lewis, Deputy Assistant Director, Counterterrorism Division, Federal Bureau of Investigation; Scott McGregor, U.S. Attorney, Eastern District of

California; and Stuart M. Zola, Director, Yerkes National Primate Laboratory.

The Committee was investigating fringe animal activists, extremists who have resorted to criminal activity to further their goals of eliminating all human use of animals. These include groups like the Animal Liberation Front (ALF), the Earth Liberation Front (ELF), and Stop Huntingdon Animal Cruelty (SHAC). As its name implies, SHAC focuses its efforts on Huntingdon Life Sciences, which tests drugs using animals, and any companies that do business with it. SHAC, which is active primarily in Great Britain, uses a pattern of vandalism, arsons, animal releases, and harassing telephone calls directed at the staff of Huntingdon, as well as the staffs of companies that do business with Huntingdon.

These organizations target individuals and companies that use animals in research and use a variety of tactics, including vandalizing and pipe-bombing research facilities, threatening employees and the families of employees, and posting the names and telephone numbers of employees on the Internet. These acts are not carried out by individual activists but appear to be carefully planned and executed efforts to threaten and ultimately shut down lawful enterprises.

Hearing before the Subcommittee on Crime, Terrorism, and Homeland Security of the Committee on the Judiciary of the House of Representatives, 109th Congress, May 23, 2006. H.R. 4239, Animal Enterprise Terrorism Act (Y 4.J 89/1:109–125). This report is available online at http://purl.access.gpo.gov/GPO/LPS74929.

The chairman of the Subcommittee was Congressman Howard Coble of North Carolina. The witnesses included Brent McIntosh, Deputy Assistant Attorney General of the United States; Dr. Michele Basso, Department of Physiology, University of Wisconsin; William Trundley, Vice President GlaxoSmithKline; and William Potter, journalist.

This hearing was held to determine whether the existing animal enterprise terrorism statute, 18 U.S. Code 43, should be expanded to prohibit the use of force, violence, or threats against entities that do business with animal enterprise organizations.

Hearing before the Committee on Environmental and Public Works, U.S. Senate, 109th Congress, May 18, 2005, Eco-Terrorism Specifically Examining the Earth Liberation Front and the Animal

Liberation Front (Y 4.P 96/10:S.HRG. 109–947). This report is available online at http://purl.access.gpo.gov/GPO/LPS86049.

The chairman of the Committee was James M. Inhofe, of Oklahoma. The witnesses included Bradley Campbell, Commissioner, New Jersey Department of Environmental Protection; Carson Carroll, Deputy Assistant Director, Bureau of Firearms and Explosives; John Lewis, Assistant Director, Federal Bureau of Investigation; David Martosko, Director of Research, Center for Consumer Freedom; Monty McIntyre, Garden Communities; and David Skorton, President, University of Iowa.

As the name of the hearing implies, it focused on the domestic activities of the Earth Liberation Front and the Animal Liberation Front. These organizations may have common personnel and are designated as terrorists because they use intimidation threats, acts of violence, and property damage in an attempt to force their views on others. They use arson, sabotage, and harassment to cause fear as a means to obtain their goals. It is estimated that they have caused more than $110 million in damage in more than 1,100 acts of terrorism in the decade that preceded this hearing. In November 2004, the University of Iowa laboratory suffered $450,000 in damages, and the names and addresses of the professors associated with the laboratory were published on the ALF Web site, inviting further acts of terror against these individuals. ALF reportedly caused damages of more the $20 million to Garden Communities by burning down the condominium complex, reportedly leaving a banner that read, "If you build it, we will burn it, the ELFs are mad."

Hearing before the Committee on Environment and Public Works, U.S. Senate, 109th Congress, October 26, 2005, Eco-Terrorism Specifically Examining Stop Huntingdon Animal Cruelty ("SHAC") (Y 4.P 96/10:S.HRG. 109–1005). Available online at http://purl.access.gpo.gov/GPO/LPS92610.

The chairman of the Committee was James M. Inhofe, of Oklahoma. The witnesses included Richard P. Bernard, Executive Vice President, New York Stock Exchange; Mark L. Bibi, general counsel, Huntingdon Life Science; Skip Boruchin, Legacy Trading Company; John E. Lewis, Deputy Assistant Director, Counterterrorism Division, Federal Bureau of Investigation; Barry M. Sabin, Chief, Counterterrorism Division, Federal Bureau of Investigation; and Dr. Jerry Vlassak, press officer, North American Animal Liberation Press.

This hearing focused on the activities of the Stop Huntingdon Animal Cruelty (SHAC) against the Huntingdon Life Science, a drug-testing company that uses animals as part of its testing protocol.

Nonprint Resources

Databases

AGRICOLA

AGRICOLA is an online searchable database of the National Agriculture Library that contains more than 2 million records. It provides information about agricultural books and articles and is available online at http://agricola.nal.usda.gov.

PubMed

PubMed is the most comprehensive searchable database of articles dealing with the life sciences and biomedical research. It contains more than 11 million records from more than 7, 300 journals worldwide. It provides bibliographic information, an abstract, and a list of articles of related interest. It provides hyperlinks to the full text of most articles, some free and some that are available for a fee. Searches begin online at http://www.ncbi.nlm.nih.gov/PubMed.

Computer Simulations

SimEarth is a life simulation game that allows the player to vary a planet's atmosphere, temperature, and land masses and introduce various forms of life to watch them evolve. The challenge is to develop sentient life, which develops an advanced civilization, while avoiding natural disasters such as hurricanes, wildfires, and volcanic eruptions. This game can be downloaded at http://www.abandonia.com/en/games/185.

Video/DVD

There are hundreds of videos dealing with animal rights and animal welfare at YouTube (http://www.youtube.com/).

Meet Your Meat is a video narrated by Alec Baldwin that shows factory farming footage from birth to slaughter. This is a very graphic video. It can be viewed at http://www.goveg.com/factoryFarming.asp.

People for the Ethical Treatment of Animals provide several hundred videos, including celebrity interviews, dealing with a variety of issues such as animal abuses in laboratories and farms. These videos are available on the PETA Channel on YouTube at http://www.petatv.com/tvpopup/archive.asp. Many of these videos are very graphic.

The Test of a Civilization, narrated by James Cromwell, describes medical and product testing on animals from mice to nonhuman primates. *The Case for Animal Bill of Rights* is narrated by Dr. Tom Regan. These videos, as well as the other videos at this site, are quite graphic. They, as well as other videos, can be viewed at http://animalrights.change.org/blog/view/10_recommended_animal_rights_videos.

Glossary

Animal Rights   Believers in animal rights argue that because humans are animals, at least some animals (e.g., great apes) or all animals should have the same rights as humans.

Animal Welfare   Animal welfare activists believe that animals should be treated humanely and not subjected to unnecessary pain.

Anthropomorphism   Anthropomorphism is the practice of attributing to animals or inanimate objects human-like characteristics.

Autonomy Value   Some believers in animal rights assign an arbitrary number to an organism that determines the level of rights that that organism should have. Humans are assigned a 1.0, making them legal persons with full rights, whereas the great apes and whales and dolphins have a value of 0.8, granting them the right to bodily integrity and bodily freedom.

Battery Cage   A cage about the size of a file drawer (e.g. 18 × 20 inches) that houses as many as 11 chickens is known as a battery cage.

Broiler   Broilers are a type of chicken or turkey that is raised for its meat, generally in large houses containing hundreds of thousands of birds.

Buller   In a feedyard, bullers are steers that are ridden by other steers.

Cetacean   The order "cetacean" contains whales, dolphins, and porpoises.

Companion Animals   "Companion animal" is another term for pets, especially dogs and cats

Concentrated Animal Feeding Operation   (CAFO) CAFOs are operations that house large numbers of animals for part or all of their lives. For example, cattle feedlots are CAFOs.

Consequentialism   A moral theory, consequentialism holds that a morally right action is one that produces a good outcome.

Consciousness   The ability to remember the past and to plan for the future is called "consciousness."

Cull An animal that is discarded because of some undesirable characteristic (e.g., day-old male chickens because adult male chickens have a gamey taste) is referred to as a cull.

Equality Equality is the belief that things that are alike should be treated the same way.

Free Range Some chickens and other farm animals, called free-range animals, are not caged but allowed to roam freely in a barnyard.

Frontal Cerebral Cortex The part of the cortex involved with memory, planning, creativity, and other complex activities is called the "frontal cerebral cortex."

Gate Control Theory Two sets of fibers are found in the spinal cord that are theorized to control the perception of pain.

Gene The fundamental unit of heredity found on the chromosomes is the gene.

Genetically Modified Food A plant that has had a specific gene inserted in it that originally occurred in an unrelated plant is considered to be genetically modified.

Hybrid The result of breeding two pure stains of an organism, such as corn, to produce a stronger plant with higher yields is called a "hybrid."

Hypothalamus The hypothalamus is a switching center located near the center of the brain that controls eating, drinking, and sexual behavior.

Invertebrates Animals without backbones, such as mollusks (e.g., snails, clams, or squids) and crustaceans (e.g., lobsters, shrimps, crabs, wood lice, water fleas, and barnacles) are invertebrates.

Lacto-ovo Vegetarian A vegetarian who does not eat meat, fish, or birds, but does eat dairy products and eggs is called a "lacto-ovo vegetarian."

Lacto Vegetarian A vegetarian who does not eat meat, fish, or birds but does eat dairy products is called a "lacto vegetarian."

Layer A chicken that is raised to produce eggs is known as a layer.

Limbic System The limbic system is a group of structures in the brain that are involved in the sense of smell and the display of emotions.

Nociceptor A nociceptor is a relatively unspecialized nerve ending that senses noxious stimuli.

Ovo Vegetarian A vegetarian is a person who does not eat meat, fish, birds, or dairy products but does eat eggs.

Pain A sensory event that is unpleasant and that is avoided if possible is called "pain."

Pâté de Foie Gras Pâté de foie gras is a dish made from the fatty liver of a duck or goose that has been force-fed grain.

Pattern Theory Pattern theory proposes that pain is the result of a specific pattern of stimulation that reaches a threshold.

Pesticides Chemicals that help control insects, weeds, and other undesirable organisms are called "pesticides."

Rider In a feedyard, a "rider" is a term for a steer that rides another steer.

Right A theoretical advantage of one person over another is called a "right."

Sapience Sapience is the state of having a memory of the past and the ability to plan for the future.

Sentience The readiness to receive sensations is called "sentience."

Service Animals Animals, generally dogs, that help people (e.g., seeing-eye dogs, guard dogs) are called "service animals."

Speciesism Some humans deny that they are part of a larger group that includes other living organisms, including animals.

Specificity Theory The theory that stimulating specific pain receptors transmits information directly into the pain centers of the brain is known as specificity theory.

Suffering Suffering is an unpleasant and disagreeable experience that virtually everyone would attempt to avoid.

Thalamus The thalamus is a switching center located near the center of the brain that is involved with all of the senses except smell and that controls the muscles.

Utilitarianism Utilitarianism is a school of philosophy that holds that each action is judged by its utility or usefulness and that strives for the greatest good for the greatest number.

Vegan Vegans do not eat meat, fish, birds, eggs, dairy products or honey and do not use animal products, such as leather, wool, or silk.

Vivisection The cutting of animals, as while performing experiments, is called "vivisection."

Index

About the Author

CLIFFORD J. SHERRY received a Ph.D. in psychology from the Illinois Institute of Technology and a paralegal certificate from the University of Texas at San Antonio. Dr. Sherry has more than 60 professional publications in refereed scientific journals. He has taught human physiology, psychopharmacology, introductory psychology, and sensation and perception. He has written *Opportunities in Medical Imaging Careers: Revised Edition; Medical Imaging Careers; Contemporary World Issues: Endangered Species; Contemporary World Issues: Animal Rights; The New Science of Technical Analysis: Using the Statistical Techniques of Neuroscience to Uncover Order and Chaos in the Markets; Inhalants; Opportunities in Medical Imaging; Drugs and Eating Disorders;* and *Mathematics of Technical Analysis: Applying Statistics to Trading Stocks, Options, and Futures.*

ML   5/10